REDEFINING TERTIARY EDUCATION

ORGANISATION FOR ECONOMIC CO-OPERATION AND DEVELOPMENT

ORGANISATION FOR ECONOMIC CO-OPERATION AND DEVELOPMENT

Pursuant to Article 1 of the Convention signed in Paris on 14th December 1960, and which came into force on 30th September 1961, the Organisation for Economic Co-operation and Development (OECD) shall promote policies designed:

- to achieve the highest sustainable economic growth and employment and a rising standard of living in Member countries, while maintaining financial stability, and thus to contribute to the development of the world economy;
- to contribute to sound economic expansion in Member as well as non-member countries in the process of economic development; and
- to contribute to the expansion of world trade on a multilateral, non-discriminatory basis in accordance with international obligations.

The original Member countries of the OECD are Austria, Belgium, Canada, Denmark, France, Germany, Greece, Iceland, Ireland, Italy, Luxembourg, the Netherlands, Norway, Portugal, Spain, Sweden, Switzerland, Turkey, the United Kingdom and the United States. The following countries became Members subsequently through accession at the dates indicated hereafter: Japan (28th April 1964), Finland (28th January 1969), Australia (7th June 1971), New Zealand (29th May 1973), Mexico (18th May 1994), the Czech Republic (21st December 1995), Hungary (7th May 1996), Poland (22nd November 1996) and Korea (12th December 1996). The Commission of the European Communities takes part in the work of the OECD (Article 13 of the OECD Convention).

Publié en français sous le titre :
REDÉFINIR L'ENSEIGNEMENT TERTIAIRE

FOREWORD

Large volume participation in tertiary education is a common feature in the OECD area. To acknowledge this is not to say that there are settled views on policy directions to meet the new challenges raised for quality, relevance, effectiveness and cost in programmes, teaching and learning at this level of education.

Policy interest and action are everywhere evident. Committees of inquiry or high level policy reviews of tertiary education have been undertaken recently in Australia, France, Germany, Japan, New Zealand and the United Kingdom (in Australia, New Zealand and the United Kingdom, to re-visit comprehensive reforms implemented from the late 1980s). In Belgium (Flemish Community), Denmark, Norway, Portugal, Sweden and the United States, reforms of tertiary education structures and programmes, governance and finance represent often dramatic new directions in these policy fields. These twelve countries are, in this respect, representative of the OECD Membership. All have participated in the OECD Education Committee's "thematic review" of the first years of tertiary education, the findings and conclusions of which are presented in this report.

The timeliness and relevance of the issues and conclusions of this work were attested by a lively one-day debate when officials from the participating countries, colleagues from other OECD Member countries and observers reviewed findings and suggested directions for policy. The views presented and discussed revealed the depth of concern, scope of policy action and general agreement that the nature and extent of the national policy debates now underway throughout the OECD area may signal nothing less than a fundamental shift in thinking about the context for tertiary education and its aims. In this respect, the comparative report usefully sets out a vision for debate and reflection, perhaps marking a turning point as did the seminal OECD reports Towards Mass Higher Education (1974) and Universities Under Scrutiny (1985). The changes are set in a new context, one in which much greater value is being placed on the skills and flexibility of individuals as a key to reducing unemployment and improving economic performance as described in the OECD Jobs Study (1994) and education and training are seen within a lifelong approach to learning as agreed by OECD Education Ministers in Lifelong Learning for All (1996). While all might not agree with the details of the vision, the forces at play suggest a sweeping shift in orientation toward even higher levels of participation at the tertiary level, driven strongly by demands reflecting the diverse interests of clients rather than the supply-led, institution-directed expansion witnessed previously.

This shift in orientation raises numerous questions and challenges, analysed in this report and evident in the Education Committee debate, for governments, students, institutions, teaching and research staff, employers and enterprises, regions and communities. Among the challenges are:

How should tertiary education better respond to the interests and choices of "clients", students foremost among them? While countries differ in the levels, sectors and settings in which the demands for post-schooling education are met, all are now endeavouring to meet them. In all countries, participation rates have increased, drawing in ever wider segments of the population, notably mature-age students and women. There is growing competition and choice; "drop-out" in this respect may be less an indication of student performance than of student choice to leave, because they find that the programmes and teaching are poorly suited to their particular needs, interests and backgrounds. It will be important to better understand the implications of demand and choice in tertiary education, and useful to monitor country experiences with policies which are seeking to promote greater responsiveness to meet those demands.

How should the needs and interests of those not now being served in the first years of tertiary education be addressed? With the emergence of high and rising rates of participation in tertiary education, a tension exists between the politics of inclusion and the policies of institutions based on selection. Thus far, much of the policy debate on quality and costs has reflected a perspective of limitation and selection. On the other hand, both individual aspirations (fuelled in part by government policies aimed at improving student success through secondary education) and employer and enterprise interests are giving rise to pressures for continuing expansion of participation, inevitably from previously under-served groups. Changes are occurring, and more are required to meet the educational needs of these new waves of students.

How should costs be shared? On this, there are different views among countries and systems, and not only on the issue of tuition fees or charges. Differences in levels of public funding for tertiary education for different providers might well be re-examined in the light of the emergence of demand-led, large volume provision. More relevant is whether and how public funding might vary according to cultural and geographic factors, and national goals.

How should government drive large, diverse tertiary education systems comprised of varied and increasingly autonomous providers? Considerable sensitivity is needed in the face of long-established academic values, yet the importance of tertiary education in contemporary social and economic life inevitably raises issues of public policy. Governments cannot stand aside, but neither can they attempt detailed direction. A common approach for governments now is to set the overall framework, permitting greater or lesser variation within the framework and aligning incentives and steering in support of it. Countries now use a variety of means, often a combination of means, among them demand and the "market", "steering", public funding and specific policy instruments. But, should "the market" play a greater role? Should governments participate in different ways and to a different degree than in the past, "re-centralising" through, for example, closer monitoring and dissemination of information, more frequent and in-depth accreditation, new criteria for the allocation of staff and finances, a more transparent and coherent framework of qualifications or more fully developed assessments of learning outcomes?

Experiences with new approaches in these areas are still limited, and they bear watching.

These questions and challenges point to several of the wide range of issues discussed in this report. It is clear that countries will continue to benefit from further exchange of policy experience in this very dynamic field. The analysis of country experiences undertaken in the "thematic review" of the first years of tertiary education is at once impressive in its breadth and depth and provocative in its vision. It will serve well as a basis for debate, reflection and exchange as all parties seek to maintain and extend the contribution of tertiary education to the improvement of the economic and social well-being.

This publication marks the culmination of three years of work in which the Education Committee broadly applied its well-established policy review procedures in undertaking a comparative review of a more focused set of issues and developments. The Education Committee welcomed and supported this innovative approach, which could be implemented only with active contributions from participating countries and numerous individuals including members of the review teams, the Advisory Group of country representatives and experts; their names appear in Annexes 3 and 4 of this report. The Secretariat has played a leading role, through the preparation of this report. In addition to its authors, Malcolm Skilbeck, Alan Wagner and Eric Esnault, assistance was provided by Christy Kim, Kerry O'Brien, Keisuke Isogai, Laura Tardino and Pierre Laderriere, and by the production team of Ginette Meriot, Bernadette de Maillardoz, Carola Miras, Sophie Urrutibehety, Jill Gaston and Léa Duboscq. The thematic review is continuing in a second stage, to include follow-up and focused analyses of specific issues for tertiary education policies, dissemination of a set of country-specific reports which provide an overview and analysis of the developments, issues and policies in each participating country (available through the OECD's Internet site) and review visits to countries which were not able to participate in the first stage.

This report is published on the responsibility of the Secretary-General of the OECD.

This monograph is dedicated to the memory of Dorotea Furth, pioneer and leader of higher education studies for many years in the OECD.

TABLE OF CONTENTS

EXECUTIVE SUMMARY

In initiating a comparative review of the first years of tertiary education in a wide range of Member countries, the Education Committee had several purposes in mind.

- to provide an account of significant trends and issues in a sector that is experiencing remarkable growth in many Member countries and, in others, is developing further in response to large volume participation;
- to develop new perspectives and concepts to inform and strengthen policy analyses;
- to determine key aspects of change and problem areas in which a co-operative international review could facilitate policy development;
- to explore new methods of undertaking OECD education policy reviews by defining a theme of common concern and adopting innovative procedures in review design and management;

Ten countries have participated fully in the review and the experience of many countries, the research literature, and other sources, have been drawn upon in collecting and analysing data. The ten countries, in order of visits by review teams are Australia, New Zealand, Norway, Japan, Sweden, Belgium (Flemish Community), Denmark, Germany, United Kingdom and United States.

The terms "tertiary education" and "first years" indicate the scope of the review. "Tertiary" refers to a stage or level, beyond secondary and including both university and non-university types of institutions and programmes. The "first years" are those leading to an initial qualification recognised as of value on the labour market.

Although tertiary education is considerably wider in scope and purpose than the educational process leading to an initial qualification, it is here that the pressures of growth and high volume demand for access, and the expansion in numbers and diversity of the student population, are most directly and acutely felt. These pressures are the source of considerable difficulty and challenge:

in accommodating students, addressing their varied needs, mobilising the energies and expertise of staff and institutions, providing adequate resources, devising appropriate curricula, adapting teaching procedures, and meeting rising costs within heavily constrained budgets.

Demand, both individual and social, is seen as the driving force. Individuals seek access to a form of education which meets their personal and professional needs and society needs a highly-educated citizenry and workforce. The expression of these demands challenges all governments, whether systems are predominantly public, private or mixed. It is on the institutions that prime responsibility rests to find appropriate openings and pathways of study. Educational policy needs to take account of several key perspectives: those of the clients – the students – and those of the stakeholders who include employers, social partners, and various economic and social actors with a vital interest in the outcomes of tertiary education. The task of governments becomes increasingly complex and new roles and relationships are developing as public authorities adopt more strategic stances, orchestrating, co-ordinating, steering and – to a large extent – resourcing but not controlling.

The trend in the countries participating in the review is towards ever higher levels of participation by students of all ages. Many countries are experiencing or envisage the phenomenon of mass participation from which universal participation may be projected. Whereas two decades ago "universal" was taken to mean 50 per cent of the age cohort, now it may be 80 per cent or more. Hence a new paradigm is emerging whereby participation in some form of tertiary education may be expected to become the norm in our societies. Tertiary education is already or will eventually become "the place to be" – an experience for all, not the selected few.

It is inevitable that questions of the quality and relevance of provision will become more acute. Regardless of the structure and the organisation of tertiary systems – unitary, binary or multi-sectoral, private or public – provision needs to be diverse and responsive if it is to be of value to a highly varied clientele of students and meet societal and economic requirements. Provision needs to become more attuned to changing occupational structures and employment realities, not by merely "fitting" students to the job market but through industry-education partnerships in curriculum design and delivery, work experience for students and a greater emphasis on competences and skills across the curriculum.

In a system where provision is diversified, in a situation where students are increasingly mobile, and wish and are able to pick courses, change direction, and combine study programmes, there is need for more and better information and guidance through various means, not least well-informed teachers at both secondary and tertiary levels. Also needed are improved arrangements for cross-crediting and the articulation of programmes and courses of study, as well as recognition of varied forms of learning, formal and non-formal. The issue is not simply co-ordination across sectors, institutions and programmes and greater recognition of the value of different forms of learning, but unified and coherent policies which treat the first years of tertiary education as one element in a much longer cycle, stretching back to schooling and forward to advanced study and continuing education over the life cycle. As yet, policy development has not proceeded as far as it needs to in these directions.

Three traditions and sets of educational values have a long history and are strongly represented in institutional policy and practice: unfettered, curiosity-driven intellectual inquiry; high-level professional studies and service; and meeting industrial and commercial requirements through specific vocational programmes. Cutting across these three are two kinds of policy discourse: utility in the market place and the independent or unconstrained advancement of knowledge. Although the traditions and the policy discourses have generated divergent views about the purposes to be served by tertiary education, there is widespread agreement on such needs as an informed electorate, cultural tolerance, social justice, a high quality of education and preparation for the workforce. These generalities have to be transformed into curricula and ways of teaching and learning. There is a tension between the requirements of a more general or holistic education and the highly specific requirement of individuals and professions. This can be either a source of dis-

cord or generative of new patterns of teaching and learning.

Tertiary education is changing to address client and stakeholder expectations, to respond more actively to social and economic change, to provide for more flexible forms of teaching and learning, to focus more strongly on competences and skills across the curriculum. Decision-makers, managers and educational leaders have major responsibilities in fostering such developments and in taking actions to overcome dichotomies, status differences and other barriers that stand in the way of intelligent decision-making by individual students and strategic resource allocations.

As devolution and decentralisation of decision-making proceed across all sectors of public administration, new responsibilities fall upon local and regional bodies. Tertiary institutions are no exception and stronger and better institutional governance and management are required. These need to be fostered and cultivated and there are roles for public policy, government and national agencies, regional and local bodies as well as the institutions. Greater autonomy entails greater responsibility and accountability. Hence the strengthening of accountability measures and the introduction of more rigorous procedures of quality control. These all require a rethinking of educational concepts of quality and standards for an era of mass or approaching universal participation.

New curriculum designs and strategies for teaching and learning are emerging. Many issues arise: the interplay between teaching and research and between the institution and industry; the need for well defined and organised learning pathways and curriculum structures; better uses of information and communication technologies; and ways of reducing the inefficiencies of high drop-out and failure rates. While there are many initiatives in institutions across the participating countries, many challenges remain. Are countries getting the expertise they need? What do students need and wish to know and be able to do? New subject matter, new combinations of courses and more varied forms of learning are part of the answer but few would claim that ways have been found to provide a high quality of education for all or that the educational function of the institutions is sufficiently well recognised and resourced. There are, indeed, some who doubt the value of further growth and would perhaps challenge the view that institutions, the universities especially, need more innovative teaching and more student-centred curricula. Governments have to set overall goals and tasks; it is clear from this review that the way ahead is more growth and greater responsiveness.

The challenges are diverse and complex, hence the elevated expectations for institutional management and leadership and for policy-making of a far-sighted, strategic kind. As expansion continues, ever greater demands for resources can be expected. The two targets are to improve efficiency, thereby lowering costs without sacrificing quality, and mobilising resources on a community-wide basis. Although arguments are heard for shifting more of the cost burden to the immediate beneficiaries – the students – there is a very strong case for treating universal tertiary education as primarily a charge on public finance with shared contributions by the students and the stakeholders. The ultimate objective in recognition of the value of tertiary education to individuals and society is to find all means possible to encourage and support participation in the expectation that everyone will share the benefits of a high-quality education for all.

INTRODUCTION

1. WHY A REVIEW OF THE "FIRST YEARS": PURPOSE AND DIRECTIONS

Tertiary education is now of high and vital public interest in all Member countries. Major shifts in policy and structural reforms have occurred in several of them; but many issues of long standing remain unresolved and new ones emerge as countries experience considerable adjustment difficulties. The developments giving rise to new expectations and demands falling on the first years of tertiary education are common to most OECD Member countries. The principal ones are:

- extensive student participation at the tertiary level which continues to expand;
- much greater diversity in those seeking access to tertiary education;
- expanding needs and expectations of students, families, employers and the community;
- growing concerns over quality and purposes;
- questioning about the contribution of tertiary education to the economy and the well-being of the society as a whole;
- the emerging scenarios of lifelong learning;
- competing demands for scarce public resources;
- challenges and opportunities presented by information and communication technologies.

These developments at the tertiary level are occurring in an increasingly globalised world where education is expected to promote social, economic and cultural development, extend democratisation and contribute to the well-being of all individuals.

Policies are required on the appropriate scale of participation in some form or other of tertiary education – university or non-university, part-time or full-time, for those leaving school or adult entrants. Demand is the driving force of expansion and government itself must find new roles, relationships and policy approaches. The policy debate embraces issues of the fundamental purposes of tertiary education as it progresses from its elite origins through mass participation towards universality. In its evolving state, tertiary education is the most dynamic and complex sector of educational policy and practice with ramifications throughout the society and economy.

Policy development is a continual process but one of changing character. For tertiary education policies can be neither forged nor implemented without the close engagement of the tertiary institutions. There are major stakeholder interests: first, government, which provides fundamental policy directions, resources and a legislative and regulatory framework, then community interest groups and the extensive networks of which they are part, and professional bodies, cultural organisations and others. Moreover, there are the clients, the students themselves, whose education is the prime purpose of the whole enterprise.

The challenges are formidable and it is of vital importance to the future of our societies that they be mastered. It is the principal objective of this report of the multi-country review of the first years of tertiary education to draw out the dimensions of the challenges as they relate to the first or initial years of tertiary level study, those that culminate in the first award leading to entry to the labour market and the assumption of various civic roles. To these challenges must be added the responses by the sector itself, those that are occurring or might seem necessary. But the starting point for the inquiry and the main perspective throughout is neither that of government *per se* and the various stakeholders nor that of the main providers, the educational institutions. Rather, it is that of the clients, the students. Thus in this report the purview is that of demand and access, of participation, of opportunity, of the experiences designed to support and foster learning and progression and of the means needed to make this possible.

Not so long ago, tertiary education was a distant goal for a small minority; now participation in some form of education at the tertiary level is moving towards the norm. In his State of the Union Address in February 1997 US President Clinton boldly declared that at least two years of college would be "as universal in America by the 21st century as high school education is today." The government of Finland has declared that at least 60 per cent of the age cohort will participate in tertiary education by the early 21st century. The Council for Industry and Higher Education in the United Kingdom estimates that six out of ten 18 year-olds will participate in higher education at some stage in their lives. By 1995, 63 per cent of the 18-year-old cohort in Japan was enrolled in some kind of tertiary institution; the comparable figure in 1965 was 17 per cent. Belgium (Flemish Community) is one of several countries where all students who qualify at the end of secondary schooling can have access to tertiary education, which is heavily subsidised; more than 90 per cent of the age cohort qualified in 1993. These are remarkable changes whose significance has yet to be fully grasped.

This review is focused on developments and trends in the representative Member countries of the OECD which hosted visits by OECD review teams. Drawing on those visits and other data sources, the review is designed not only to highlight the issues arising but to provoke a dialogue about future directions, among clients, providers and all those with an interest or stake in the role of tertiary education in our societies.

2. THE MEANING OF TERTIARY

But what, precisely, is tertiary education and what if anything distinguishes it from higher or post-secondary education? In the fluid environment which is being addressed in this inquiry, precise, prescriptive definitions are likely to be misleading and will themselves be part of the analysis. "Tertiary" has been chosen in preference to "higher", partly because "higher" so often connotes university whereas much of the development now taking place is in the so-called "alternatives to universities" (see OECD, 1991). Several such institutions have been established, for example the *Fachhochschulen* of the German-speaking countries, or Norway's recently reconstructed colleges, to provide another form of advanced education. Their programmes are usually of shorter duration than universities, more closely linked to the labour market than many university programmes, and they often have limited or more practice-oriented research roles. "Tertiary" also has value in that in the sequential logic of primary then secondary education, it refers to the next phase or stage. Instead of being a separate, self-enclosed domain, "tertiary" has become more integrally related with what goes before in a situation where participation has shifted from a highly selective and narrow base to one of broad inclusiveness.

As for "post-secondary", it is widely used with reference to a level of provision which, while beyond secondary, is regarded as below higher education (and is reflected thus in the ISCED classification of levels). The position taken in this review, however, is that more radical thinking is needed in acknowledgement of the trend towards universal participation beyond secondary school and the need to develop new, more subtle forms of differentiation responding to the multiple, diverse needs of students and of society more generally. Thus "tertiary" embraces the many different kinds of institutions and programmes which represent a progression beyond secondary level programmes. This progression is not defined only in academic terms since experience and maturity may also be conferred an equivalent value for example in admissions procedures.

The new approach of tertiary education acknowledges both part-time and full-time modes irrespective of the duration of study; it includes students of all ages; it covers a very wide spectrum of interests and aptitudes; it can incorporate different interpretations by countries of what constitutes "the first years"; and it acknowledges a wide range of institutional types – from research universities to two-year vocational colleges – together with a diversity of functions and status of awards and qualifications. Inevitably, therefore, in international comparisons considerable care is needed to specify contexts, structures and processes. Thus a key theme in the report is diversity: the existence and value of a variety of forms and structures together with the need for recognition of the different kinds of performance that those forms and structures entail. While difficulties arise in efforts to compare outputs and standards they do not stand in the way of a comparative overview of country trends and experiences; on the contrary, they illuminate the cross-country debate and mutual learning, which should be among the fruits of this inquiry.

All stages of education, at any point in the life cycle, have the potential and need to contribute to the well-being of individuals and society. The distinctiveness of the tertiary stage is that, as it follows primary and secondary education, it is more than ever before the gateway into employment and citizenship roles for very large numbers of young people. Not only them, however; for adults of all ages, tertiary education is a point of re-entry to formal, structured learning and a means of reorienting careers and life interests and expectations. Participation in tertiary education reflects current cultural aspirations of and for youth, the growing interest of adults in systematic learning to advanced levels and the emergence of a knowledge-based society in which prolonged education becomes a social norm.

As the transformation of "elite" to "universal" proceeds, questions naturally arise about what has often seemed to be a self-contained, exclusive and esoteric sector with its own highly specialised and frequently self-determined or narrowly focused missions, structures and traditions. Can, or should, the distinctive and prized socio-cultural formations of the universities, the high-level professional institutions and the colleges in the elite academic and specialised training traditions continue as they are or will they reconstruct themselves to form part of a continuum of lifelong learning? To Lord Melbourne, a British Prime Minister towards the middle of the 19th century, this question would sound rhetorical. In setting up reform commissions for Oxford and Cambridge universities, he remarked "universities never reform themselves". Modern governments usually take the view that some encouragement is needed if directions are to change. In New Zealand, the term "seamlessness" has been adopted as a signal of the direction government wishes to take in creating a more coherent education system. But no country can be sure of the shape of the garment that is being crafted and the pieces of cloth often fit uneasily together.

In practically all OECD countries, given the vastly increased pressures on the first years of tertiary education and when competition has never been sharper for shares of public budgets, institutions and country authorities must make searching appraisals of existing programmes, courses, teaching and learning and must consider new possibilities. There is need for innovation and reform, sometimes on a large scale. In several countries comprehensive initiatives have been undertaken or are under way: the amalgamation of institutions; the dissolution of binary lines; the establishment of new kinds of institutions; the introduction of new funding formulae and financing regimes; new kinds of national steering and institutional management; new degree programmes; and new partnerships between education and industry. It is not too much to say that it is an era of searching, questioning, and at times of profound uncertainty, of numerous reforms and

essays in the renewal of tertiary education across the OECD and far beyond its membership.

3. THE ACTORS: CLIENTS, STAKEHOLDERS AND PROVIDERS

From which quarters or from whom is action to be expected? Tertiary education is the responsibility and concern not only of government or the institutions; there is the active engagement of the professions, of industry, of families and communities and, pre-eminently, of students. It is largely under the direct control of educational institutions which incorporate in their staffs a formidable array of intellectual, cultural and other talents. Thus, in many societies, research universities play major roles in carrying forward the revolution in knowledge which underpins the most advanced technologies and industrial development, providing a large part of the dynamism of modern economies. Where the tertiary institutions are not directly involved at the frontiers of knowledge, their graduates increasingly are foremost among those who are in the creation and diffusion of ideas and techniques, the invention of new machines and processes, and the resolving of complex social and economic problems. It is the general education and vocational programmes, both initial and continuing, of colleges and universities that prepare the generations for increasingly demanding jobs and provide opportunities for continued learning and career development.

The fundamental importance of the institutions is not in doubt. However, since the orientation of this report is towards meeting student needs and those of the society and economy, the institutions are approached, not so much from the standpoint of their own self formations, their traditions, culture and inner workings but insofar as they address and meet the needs of clients. The term "client" which we have chosen as a dominant motif of this inquiry, is frowned upon in some quarters, as a perverse concession to the consumer society and a failure to acknowledge the independence of knowledge and critical inquiry. Certainly a balance is needed: the culture of institutions of which students are a part but not the whole remains a central consideration; if students are seen as clients, then other stakeholders and interests, too, have their place. But the client perspective, in challenging many of the orthodoxies and pre-suppositions of institutional life is on the one hand consistent with demand-driven policies and structures in our societies and, on the other, emphatic that there are new needs to meet as we move towards universal tertiary education.

The thematic review has thus gone beyond institutional concerns as such to draw out broad policy issues and particular aspects from the perspectives of students and graduates and views of business, the professions and communities. In its comparative approach, the review presents and analyses the range of experience with regard to a number of questions. How has demand evolved and grown and what are its specific features now? Are the new societal challenges, the advancement of knowledge, the globalisation of economic affairs, the impact and opportunities of the new technologies and the shifting demographic patterns being picked up? What is the nature, quality and relevance of the provision made to meet needs? What problems and difficulties arise for students and providers, and how are they being addressed? What promising trends, innovations and ideas give leads for possible future policies? Is there a continuing quest for quality and relevance in provision? Are procedures adequate and effective for decision-making, leadership, governance, financing and policy formation and implementation? Questions such as these are at the heart of the current debate.

On any definition, *tertiary education* thus refers to a large and expanding range of activities and interests, across institutions and beyond them. It commands substantial resources, private as well as public, and has an increasing part to play indirectly if not directly in all spheres of public policy. From an institutional perspective, tertiary education means structures, programmes, personnel, resources and services from the first undergraduate years up to and including post-graduate courses, and relates closely to the research and community service roles of institutions. The point of the definition is to emphasise types of education, their levels or standards, and a sequence of studies rather than to specify particular institutional settings or delivery mechanisms. Nevertheless, "tertiary education" usually, but not inevitably, invokes certain kinds of institutions, universities, colleges and the like. In the visits to countries the reviewers encountered a wide variety of such institutions. A historic shift seems to be taking place under the pressure of the external environment. While some institutions will retain a quite distinct identity with long-established forms of internal definition and control, others have become much more open to influences from the wider society, with elaborate mechanisms for interpreting and interacting with the environment.

4. THE "FIRST YEARS"

This review has addressed not all of tertiary education but the "first years", those leading to an initial award or qualification. Attention is directed to "first years" in "formal" tertiary education ("regular" diploma and degree courses), which account for the large proportion of the flow, although reference is also made to other forms of study and learning at this level. The institutions, programmes and study patterns differ widely among countries. What is reviewed is drawn from the full range of provision (or perception of needed provision) in each country, which leads to the first qualification at this level recognised on the labour market and having wider social currency.

Although a full review of tertiary education could not be restricted to the first years – the first major qualification – but would have to take into account also the dramatic increase in post-graduate enrolments, the vast enterprise of research, of technology transfer, consultancy and sale of services, there are good reasons to take the first years and the initial qualifications as a focus.

In most if not all Member countries, increases in participation rates in upper secondary education have, as a natural consequence, put acute pressure on access and entry to tertiary education. Where these rates are already very high – in Belgium (Flemish Community) and the United States for example – efforts continue to reduce drop-out and school failure or weak performance (see Table 1). The pressures and demands which as a consequence fall upon tertiary institutions are of such a

Table 1. **Ratio of upper secondary graduates to population at typical age of graduation by type of programme, 1995**

First educational programmes

	Total	General	Vocational and apprenticeship
Australia	–	65	–
Belgium (Flemish Community)	110	33	76
Denmark	81	46	36
Germany	88	24	64
Japan	94	69	25
New Zealand	95	65	30
Norway	106	44	62
Sweden	64	25	38
United Kingdom	–	–	–
United States	76	76	–

– Data not available.
Source: Education at a Glance (OECD, 1997), Table G1.1.

complex and weighty kind as to call into question many of the long-established structures and procedures for the education and the support of students. The review demonstrates a mixture of successful responses and problems to be addressed.

The above considerations help to explain why public policy is being challenged to mobilise new resources and to introduce new procedures for setting directions, monitoring and adjusting the levers of influence, guidance and control. Tertiary education has emerged from the wings it has long occupied and moved to centre stage in national educational policy. This review has, therefore, as one of its objectives the illumination of key policy concerns and has been undertaken in order to assist Member countries to take the next steps in policy formation. If it achieves nothing more, it should enable countries to benefit from a comparative analysis and to orient their own viewpoints and procedures to a dynamic, cross-national setting.

5. METHODS OF WORK

In establishing this multi-country review, the OECD Education Committee has aimed *i)* to set in motion a thoroughgoing inquiry into the extent to which programmes, teaching and learning in the first years of tertiary education in Member countries are evolving to meet the expectations and capabilities of students and the needs of the economy and society; and *ii)* to analyse how future policies might best promote needed change. The Committee and Secretariat have been impressed by the readiness of so many Member governments to embark upon the review and to devote the necessary resources to it. Originally we envisaged that three or possibly five countries would join a pilot project and that perhaps two or three others would join a second stage. In the end ten participated fully in a single, continuous exercise, two others contributed to that exercise, and more have declared interest in a further stage. Several wish to host follow-up seminars and some have already done so. All have requested individual country notes on the findings of the review teams, which the Secretariat has provided. Some of these are being separately published by the respective governments. An international conference to diffuse the findings and broaden the debate is to be held. These are all indicators – and there are others – of the relevance of the inquiry to educational policy. The Education Committee, having already discussed an earlier draft of this report, set aside a day in its April 1997 meeting for a full-scale debate. Gratifying

as all this is, the success of the review will be judged by the clarity it brings to the issues, and the insights and stimulus it provides to future policy and action.

In the long-established context of OECD reviews of national educational policy, the thematic review has developed several innovative procedures. First, it interrelates countries' experiences around a common set of prepared questions and issues. Second, it presents a synthesis of the perceptions, judgements and analyses of teams of reviewers, developed by the Secretariat through continuous and close co-operation and exchange of information and views: with public authorities, responsible organisations, concerned interest groups and individuals in each participating country. Third, it draws upon a wide variety of data, from official sources, the research and policy literature and the perceptions of many highly experienced experts and interlocutors. Fourth, the Education Committee and an advisory group, representing all the participating countries and including independent experts, have been actively involved throughout. Fifth, unlike the single country policy reviews, the thematic review does all this on a consistently cross-national basis.

The review has been grounded in a sequence of country visits by Secretariat-led teams of reviewers of wide and varied experience (two of the four members of each team came from the Secretariat – see Annex 3), over the period June 1995-October 1996.

The first step was the preparation by the Secretariat of an issues paper and questionnaire, revised following review by the Education Committee and advisory group (see Annex 4). Each review team started its inquiry by examining an often substantial background report and other materials submitted by the country authorities in response to a common list of questions. Information obtained and observations in the course of interviews and meetings during an eight-to ten- day intensive study visit in each participating country provide the basis for critical analysis of what is happening on the ground. In their responses to questions, country authorities exercised some flexibility. While decreasing the level of strict comparability, the variety of responses has provided a benefit: qualitative information in depth on the full range and variety of settings, structures, approaches and policies. Comparability was subsequently reinforced in the course of the study visits, follow-up exchanges with country authorities and the work of the Secretariat in preparing notes and reports.

Relatively short visits to countries, snapshots of institutions and single, compressed meetings with representative organisations have many limitations. Their purpose, however, is not to provide carefully controlled data for in-depth research studies or fully representative samples of activities and ideas but to yield illustrative material and insights into issues and trends identified in the country reports and other sources. They have enabled reviewers to clarify issues, check perceptions and exchange viewpoints. The teams' country notes, subsequently prepared as reports by the Secretariat and submitted to the national authorities, led to further exchanges and adjustments to texts. These individual country reports are both the basis for and complementary to the present document; it is for country authorities to make such further use of them, including possible publication, as they see fit.

The findings and conclusions of the review teams for each of the participating countries have been deepened through numerous other sources. In addition to data from and discussions with authorities in the two countries, viz. France and Portugal, which were visited by review teams in 1997, these sources include: single-country reviews dealing with higher education policy (California, Austria, the former Czech and Slovak Federal Republic, Finland, Mexico); contributions of countries to the Education Committee's activity on individual demand and access to tertiary education and the seminar on financing mass higher education (constituent parts of the thematic review); the OECD Education Indicators; findings and conclusions of the meeting of the Education Committee at Ministerial level (January 1996) and of the OECD *Jobs Study* and its follow-up. Key findings of other work underway or recently completed in the Centre for Educational Research and Innovation (CERI), the programme on Institutional Management in Higher Education (IMHE) and the decentralised Programme on Educational Building (PEB) are also drawn upon; a literature review was completed; and extensive commentary and advice have been provided by the advisory group of national representatives. These and other sources including the work of other international agencies have given greater depth and comparability to the thematic review than would otherwise have been possible. They are, nevertheless, background; the foreground is the findings from work in the participating countries and the unparalleled opportunity

their participation has provided for an analysis of current and emerging trends and issues. The Education Committee and the Secretariat wish to pay warm tribute to the co-operation and the most generous support given by the very many people, institutions, agencies and government departments and ministries at all stages in the review.

6. A BRIEF ROAD MAP OF THE REPORT

The report aims to provide the kind of overview and constructive critique of "the first years" that will assist countries in the continuing development of tertiary education. It is descriptive, analytic and normative. Starting with an appraisal of increasing demand, it puts to the forefront the needs and expectations of the actual and potential users of tertiary education. But these needs and expectations are not unproblematic and they must be counterpointed with existing policy trends and structures of provision. To assess how far and in what ways the sector is responding to the challenge set by client needs and by changes in society and the economy, it is necessary to go into the institutions. Hence the focus on the design and delivery of the curriculum, teaching and learning. But there are problems: many students fail or drop out prematurely, others queue for entry and prolong studies. There are consequences for success in studies and prospects in the labour force. The causes are multiple but issues of quality and relevance of curriculum and teaching inevitably arise. To strengthen the responsiveness, effectiveness and efficiency of the system, new forms of evaluation and accountability are being introduced. They have a major role to play in the self-regulation of tertiary education and in increasing its responsiveness to multiple clients. New balances are required between system-wide direction or steering and the self-regulation of the institutions, with consistent recognition of the centrality of demand and of client needs. Leadership and strengthened management at both system and institution levels are necessary if the challenges discussed throughout the report are to be adequately met. Finally, the report addresses the difficult questions of costs and financing. There are acute pressures and only if countries can move towards new ways of mobilising resources and sharing costs can a vision approaching universal tertiary education be realised.

2

DEMAND, ACCESS AND GROWTH IN PARTICIPATION

The starting point for the enquiry is demand. This is individual and highly variable; it is also collective or social; and it is potential as well as overt. Demand is for opportunity, achievement, competence, expertise and levels of performance not just for entry. Demand for access has far exceeded projections and plans based on historical trends, demographic calculations, the regulated supply of resources, the provision of facilities and the surfacing of learning opportunities. From demand, the client orientation naturally emerges even if it is not always clearly seen in the density of existing provision and presuppositions about institutional organisation and teaching. There is a constant interplay between client and stakeholder perspectives – those of students, employers and other social agents – and the perspectives on knowledge and inquiry which find their place in colleges and universities. Sometimes these are hypostatized, as if the structures and procedures of disciplined knowledge and inquiry had their own dynamic or imperative. It is necessary at any rate to take a step beyond the expressed aspirations and needs of the aforementioned clients. The mastery and advancement of structured knowledge, whether in the form of the more theoretical or the more applied disciplines, depend upon highly organised and specialised effort. There are standards to be met, and a knowledge culture to be understood. Although not Platonic guardians of this culture, teachers and researchers in colleges and universities have a responsibility to set forth its requirements and demands. Thus a distinctive feature of tertiary education is the conjunction of these two: demand as expressed by individuals and society and the structured domains or ways of knowledge and experience. Creative reconstructions are needed to achieve it.

1. DEMAND AND RESPONSE

Like our cities, tertiary education systems and the majority of institutions were designed for less "traffic". The most striking phenomenon of recent decades and the one which gives rise to urgent and wide-ranging challenges to policy – from the national system to the individual institutions, to students and staff – is not just the increased scale but the wider diversity of demand. This relentless process reflects both the rapid and profound changes in economic life, to which tertiary education is peculiarly if not always immediately sensitive, and the perceptible increase in all societies of individual, family, and group aspirations. The demand is not just for individual access, personal development and acquisition of marketable qualifications. It is also for the advancement of knowledge, the development of competence, and the renewal of culture. Societies and their individual members share an ambition to advance, to develop, to achieve.

Growth has been a key word in all societies in the second half of this century and a feature of Europe and the European diaspora since the Renaissance. In the present century, in all sectors of economic and social activity, continuing expansion and the ambition to make progress have been not only an objective but in most cases a reality, although chequered as in the years following the 1970s oil crises. Thanks to unprecedented increases in prosperity, more people have had access to, and wished to emulate, ways of life that were previously the preserve of an elite, or at least of privileged groups in society. The historian Eric Hobsbawm, in documenting these changes globally, treats the thirty years since the 1950s as a period of unprecedented expansion of aspirations and material advancement (Hobsbawm, 1994). Participation in education is no exception. Increasing numbers of families have wanted their children to reach more advanced education and training levels than they were able to reach themselves, in part because they have seen the value of education or competence in cultural and social terms, but also because education, including recognised qualifications, is perceived as the way to social mobility or to more secure and rewarding positions in employment. Increasingly, workers seeking to adapt to new technologies, prepare for new posts in their enterprises or avoid the risk of becoming unemployed, have felt the need to acquire higher levels of competence and qualification and public policies have reinforced these attitudes. If progress is a delusion and education its handmaiden, the OECD countries have nevertheless embraced them, conferring upon tertiary education unprecedented expectations and demands.

Two related aspects of educational growth call for special attention. The first is increased participation in courses and programmes in the upper secondary stage, which in a number of OECD countries now tends to become, or already is, universal and is driving demand for more advanced education. The second is substantially increased access to and participation in tertiary education, not only by school-leavers but by adults of all ages. Of course, there are differences across countries: expansion in the 1990s has generally been faster or greater at stages or in countries where participation rates were relatively low; Australia, Portugal, Sweden and the United Kingdom are examples. Also striking is the difference in growth rates between tertiary and secondary education. At the upper secondary stage, in most cases increases in participation rates have been slow and progressive, whereas at the tertiary stage, starting sometimes from rather low rates, growth at times in recent decades reached astronomic levels. A historic shift is occurring in the second half of the 20th century: tertiary education is replacing secondary education as the focal point of access, selection and entry to rewarding careers for the majority of young people. That entry is still socially-biased, however, and it remains true that in many countries public policy, notably towards students entering tertiary education from school, contains a net subsidy to the middle class and economically better-off families.

At the tertiary stage, issues, problems and reforms have been at the top of the political agenda, whereas growth in upper secondary education has seldom been questioned. With the rise of youth unemployment, a number of governments have wished to prolong the period of schooling, developed "youth" or "qualification" policies to ensure that all young people have access to further education and training or a job, and accepted the resource implications of full secondary schooling for all youth. Some countries, Japan for example, have explicitly recognised a popular desire for further broad education alongside an increased demand for more specific training.

It is inevitable that youth education policies have, as a pipeline effect, increased pressure for access to tertiary education. Thus far, this pressure has more than compensated for demographic downturn which until recently in several countries led to predictions of stable or declining demand from school-leavers in Australia, France and Japan for example. In some countries, there are now signs of a levelling-off in school-leaver demand, but the overall trend remains upward.

"Democratisation" was a strong political argument in the 1960s. It explicitly referred to access to higher education and more specifically the universities or their equivalents; the barriers of social class bias and restricted entry were to be pulled down and equity goals vigorously pursued. This argument had its effect on the political agenda, producing changes among which widening the entrance gateway to existing institutions has proved enduring. With huge enrolment increases and mass participation, the policy compass needle has now shifted somewhat, to the quality of provision, its economic relevance and ways of meeting costs. One key issue is the possibly devastating effects of a large increase in enrolments on the role, identity, ethos and day-to-day work of institutions, especially the universities in the older European tradition. In several of the countries reviewed, the universities have borne the brunt of expansion, especially those in favoured large city locations. Many German universities, for example, have trebled or quadrupled in size in a matter of decades; in Denmark, the attractions of the capital city produce disproportionate increases in size as between Copenhagen and provincial city institutions. Similar pressures may be observed in France.

Another central concern is rising costs. Policies to contain public expenditure are in place everywhere and the resilience of private sector funding is in doubt. Cross-nationally, there are very significant variations. Students in the large private sectors in Japan, Portugal and the United States, often have to meet a high proportion of tuition as well as living costs whereas most students in Continental Europe are heavily subsidised. Australia has experimented with a deferred contribution scheme contingent on subsequent earnings. New Zealand permits institutions to charge fees whereas in the United Kingdom the government has proposed means-tested tuition fees alongside means-tested income-contingent loans for student maintenance. No definite relationship could be established in the course of the review between charges levied and participation (although behaviours of both students and providers might be affected in other ways). Thus far, overall demand appears to be very flexible in relation to price. We deal further with these matters below when discussing costs and finance.

There has been a variety of responses at the tertiary level to the rapid increases in participation and student demand. Among the responses – more open entry and admission requirements, diversification of institutions and of programmes – some were dictated by a concern for economic needs, or for reasons of equity and social relevance; others were clearly dictated by a wish to protect the traditional university. Yet the democratisation issue has not disappeared. Inequality of opportunity, socio-economic distortions of access, and imbalance between the sexes and ethnic groups in demand for specific fields of study are of continuing concern. Democratisation and mass participation have changed the face of institutions (if not always their inner workings), reoriented policy, and fostered a new language. But, for all its changes, some parts of tertiary education have been stubbornly resistant or unable to accept that basic structures and mechanisms continue to favour "him that hath".

The changes are striking, though, in other ways. At an OECD conference on the future structures of post-secondary education (Paris, June 1973), Martin Trow (see OECD, 1974) defined mass participation as participation rates exceeding 15 per cent, and universal participation when they went above 50 per cent. Despite large differences across countries, nowadays such figures seem very low (Table 2).

However, at that time the main idea was that the existing set of institutions, in particular the universities, would be unable to meet the increase in demand without losing most of their identity, roles and functions: a number of structural reforms were needed. To their credit, systems and institutions across the OECD have risen to these challenges and there have been many quite spectacular successes. Present concerns and difficulties need to be set against the immense achievements of the past twenty-five years. Yet the urge to set limits, for example to continuing expansion of the universities, as in Germany and Belgium (Flemish Community), expresses not only concern for the higher overall cost of university compared with non-university provision, but also a continuing belief in the value of a distinctive mission for the university. This remains a cultural credo reflecting the power of academic tradition in this age of massification. A key issue is research and research funding: how far and in what ways should these be spread across tertiary education? Does increased demand suggest a need for new structures, new kinds of differentiation?

Today, with much higher levels of participation and new waves in the pressure of demand, the central issues and concerns still include the question of identity and uncertainty over roles and functions. Students and families have often wished for a university education even when this means overcrowding and diminished chances of acquiring a qualification. Limited or non-existent personal attention, protracted periods of study and delayed earnings also contrast with conditions often found in

Table 2. **Net enrolment in public and private tertiary education by age group, 1985-95**

Based on headcounts

	Ages 18-21			Ages 22-25			Ages 26-29		
	1985	1990	1995	1985	1990	1995	1985	1990	1995
Australia	–	–	29.8	–	–	14.1	–	–	8.9
Belgium[1]	24.5	–	40.7	7.2	–	16.5	1.5	–	3.6
Denmark	7.4	7.4	8.9	16.3	17.9	22.6	8.2	9.3	11.2
Germany	8.8	8.5	10.6	15.5	15.9	17.0	8.9	10.4	11.4
Japan	–	–	–	–	–	–	–	–	–
New Zealand	14.9	20.8	28.6	9.6	13.8	13.3	–	–	7.2
Norway	8.8	14.4	17.5	13.2	18.9	23.6	5.7	8.2	10.0
Sweden	7.9	8.7	13.0	11.3	11.4	16.6	6.5	6.1	7.5
United Kingdom	–	16.1	25.8	–	4.7	9.3	–	–	4.8
United States	33.0	36.2	34.7	14.5	17.1	20.7	8.2	8.5	10.5

Note: Data refer to all enrolment, not just first years.
– Data not available.
1. For the Flemish Community (1994), Ages 18-21: 36.5; Ages 22-25: 11.4; Ages 26-29: 3.2 (data supplied by the Ministry of Education of the Flemish Community)
Source: Education at a Glance (OECD, 1997), Table C5.2b.

the non-university sector. Very much to the point is whether education and training systems are able to adapt to the pace of change in individual and social demand and whether current patterns of provision are attractive, relevant and of a standard suited to the needs, aspirations and interests of individuals and of society as a whole. The evidence of this review is that, if parts of education and training systems have maintained or redefined clear profiles, high standards of quality and relevance, there are also serious gaps and many challenges to address.

The Finnish authorities maintain that the target of participation by 60-65 per cent of the age cohort in tertiary education will be achieved by the early 2000s with no diminution of quality. This and similar target setting in other countries raises the question of whether new definitions and concepts of quality are needed; comparisons based on traditional measures of excellence, single measures of attainment with predefined cut-off points, will scarcely suffice. The transition to mass participation has been implemented in Member countries in quantitative terms, but its implications have not always been perceived or mastered. To put the matter in a sharper perspective, expansion in response to demand has brought its own problems which, in many cases, have compounded long-standing difficulties or weaknesses. There is, for instance, nothing new in the under-representation of minority and underprivileged groups, the lack of equal treatment of mature-age students, biased sex participation in some professional programmes and occupations, the dearth of information facilitating intelligent student choices, the inadequacy of guidance and tutoring in study skills, and complacency over high attrition rates. The need for progress in such matters is all the greater when participation rates climb steeply. In a new context the old problems need to be seen in different ways; but this is all the more difficult to achieve when unit costs are sharply decreased.

While the new contexts are often disturbing and perplexing, they are also rich in opportunities, providing scope for innovation and creativity. Those countries, systems and institutions that accept the challenges and seize the opportunities in a quest for new solutions seem likely to do best. Not all seem well placed to do so, or to be able to make the changes perceived to be needed. There are many impediments – habits, attitudes and structures among them. Help, in the form of untied government funding, will not be at hand. There is now a high premium on leadership, good management and creativity in solving problems.

2. SOME EFFECTS OF GROWTH

Successive if variable waves of growth in enrolments have put education systems under severe pressure over several decades. This is likely to continue, notwithstanding some easing. In the United States, an increase in the size of the youth cohort is expected further to raise demand. Between 1996/97 and 2005/2006 a 17 per cent increase in the number of high school graduates is anticipated, with some states experiencing a 30 per cent increase. Overall college enrolment is projected to rise by 14 per cent and a larger percentage of the future students will be minority, female, at-risk and first-generation college students. The demand for access by adult students is also expected to increase although by a rate which cannot be predicted. According to some commentators, drop-out rates may also increase since the highly flexible, expanding community college system is likely to absorb the bulk of the increase, and drop-out rates from these institutions are, for a variety of reasons, high. Since the relationship between education and employment, in that society at least, turns not only on access but on success, there are questions about economic benefit and there is need for other forms of verifiable learning and outcome measures than traditional forms of certification. Yet it is these forms that enjoy recognition and currency. Since tertiary education has a growing role to play in socialisation and civic formation the access-success equation is crucial. What is especially interesting in the United States case is that participation rates are already very high, provision is highly diverse and there is a wide range of recognised qualifications. Still more is sought.

Growth across the OECD membership has been accommodated through an expansion of education and training opportunities and places, including in smaller cities. Indeed, the establishment or enlargement of institutions in regional centres has been an explicit policy objective in many countries, Finland, France, Germany, Japan, Norway, Sweden, the United Kingdom and the United States among them. "Network Norway", a scheme to improve co-operation and a division of labour among institutions throughout the country, acknowledges the need for a balance between regional and localistic tendencies and a system-wide distribution of facilities. In France, a number of national policies seek to foster the development of links between tertiary education institutions and regional or local authorities and among tertiary education institutions in a region (e.g. the establishment of regionally-based *pôles universitaires*). Regional development, with tertiary education a full partner in many new industries, is an encouraging trend in Sweden in the university colleges. For some countries, Germany and Norway included, the introduction or strengthening of alternatives to the universities has been a significant asset in handling growth of demand. Japan and Portugal are good examples of growth being accommodated through the rapid expansion of largely private institutions. This growth, however, has given rise to quality concerns and, in Japan, the public authorities aim to increase subsidies to the private sector and, for both public and private sectors, to encourage institutional self-evaluation to ensure that standards are being maintained. A similar approach is being implemented in Portugal.

Concern over the capability or preparedness of entering students is widespread, and was explicitly raised in Australia, Belgium (Flemish Community), the United Kingdom, the United States (Virginia) but is an issue in all countries. The existence of "queues at the door" in Norway and of restricted or directed entry to certain programmes both result from quantitative growth, although other factors are also at work. The reasons are understandable but a much wider issue arises: to what extent government can or should even attempt to impose restraints. Increasing overall costs are a major consideration but so also are specific costs. Expensive public

medical services in Belgium (Flemish Community) and Germany were given as a reason for restricting entry to medical courses, *i.e.* the follow-on as well as the direct costs of medical education. Both countries recognise right of entry – guaranteed by the Constitution in Germany – but not necessarily to a chosen subject or professional field. There is thus a tension between regulatory, restrictive practices and the exercise of student choice or client preference, which cannot be the sole determinant. It is also argued by some economists that there are "too many" graduates for the labour market (Keep and Mayhew, 1996). The inference is that through restrictions, price mechanisms or incentives, would-be students can and should be "steered" into programmes leading to qualifications more in demand on the labour market. Such steering, however, is fraught with difficulty and evidence from several countries is that it has been of limited effectiveness.

Growth has resulted in structural reforms as well as alternatives to the existing pathways. Many efforts are in hand in all the countries reviewed, aimed at ensuring the quality of teaching and learning as well as the relevance of provision to economic, social or individual needs as the number of students has increased. Pipeline effects have to be taken into account, for example that from undergraduate to subsequent post-graduate study (see Table 3). Planning must extend over five- to ten-year cycles, a perplexing problem in public systems subject to much shorter budget cycles and to private institutions under financial strain. Overall, more attention is needed to the "knock on" effects of the

Table 3. **Ratio of tertiary graduates to population at typical age of graduation (times 100), by type of programme, 1995**

	Type of programme				
	Non-university tertiary	Short first university degree	Long first university degree	Second university degree	Ph.D. or equivalent
Australia	–	34	x	12.1	0.8
Belgium (Flemish Community)	28	n.a.	26	5.2	0.7
Denmark	8	21	8	2.1	0.6
Germany	12	n.a	16	n.a	1.6
Japan	29	23	x	1.9	0.4
New Zealand	17	21	5	9.8	0.5
Norway	48	17	5	8.4	0.9
Sweden	9	8	8	2.8	1.7
United Kingdom	17	31	x	11.2	0.9
United States	22	32	x	12.0	1.2

n.a. Data not applicable.
– Data not available.
x Data included in another category.
Source: *Education at a Glance* (OECD,1997), Table G2.1.

expansion of initial provision, as is the case in New Zealand, with regard to budget obligations.

At both upper secondary and tertiary levels a key issue is whether growth can be accommodated within the existing set of institutions, or whether new forms of provision and new pathways have to be offered, or the whole system restructured. It is particularly difficult to maintain quality and purpose when cultural backgrounds and expectations in the student population are changing substantially. It is not surprising then that some institutions, or sectors of the system, suffer more than others. Growth is not only quantitative expansion; it is qualitative too, creating many different and new challenges to government as well as institutions. One result of the depth of these challenges is the emergence of powerful new forms of surveillance. Expanding educational demand and opportunities at the upper end of secondary and the first years of tertiary education leads to increased spending by the state, hence in steering and accountability measures. Rising costs are a concern for families as well as governments. In Japan, for example, it has been estimated that on average families with students are spending one-quarter to one-third of their income on education. In the United States a major cause of public disquiet over college education is that tuition fees in recent years have risen much faster than inflation rates. Student organisations in several countries reported concern over increasing levels of indebtedness even under favourable loan regimes; Sweden, in response, is moving to reduce the loan component of financial support provided to students. Increased overall costs are an obvious consequence of increased participation rates. Questions of relative priority in public policy – health, welfare, crime control, education; the balance between teaching and research – all are directly affected by growth on the scale witnessed during the past two or three decades. The implications for academic standards and quality is seen in some countries – the United Kingdom for example – as requiring a new, standard-setting definition of "the graduate". But are all graduates equal? Should they be measured against a single standard or does diversification suggest the need for multiple standards?

3. PARTICIPATION AT THE UPPER SECONDARY LEVEL

Statistical evidence on upper secondary schooling – allowing for differences in levels and patterns of participation across OECD countries – shows a definite tendency towards universal participation, if it is not already a social norm or a government guarantee (see Table 1). However, there are also significant differences between countries with disturbing weaknesses in performance and attendance by particular groups in most countries. Participation levels mask disparities in the quality of the experience and the effectiveness of secondary education in the progression towards tertiary education. A common complaint in all of the countries is lack of preparedness of many secondary school graduates, even some of those with high scores in tests and examinations. Cramming for examinations, condemned in the highest educational and political circles in Japan, nevertheless continues. The problem is different in other countries where – in Belgium (Flemish Community) for instance – we were informed of weak relationships and inadequate pedagogical as distinct from bureaucratic contact between the secondary and tertiary education sectors. Responsibility for improvement is acknowledged to rest with both.

One particular problem is the attitude of young people towards education, culture (academic, artistic or vocational), work and their role in society. These attitudes appear to be changing across the OECD membership, nowhere more so than in Japan, which has long been admired as a highly stable society on a sharp trajectory of wealth-creating development. Commentators in Japan, the United Kingdom and in the United States are deeply concerned about what they see as the decay of fundamental mores, traditional values and personal conduct. Similar concerns are also expressed in other nations. Thus, there seems to be a growing gap between the goals and values of education and youth culture; it will not be possible to force old values on new situations and realisation of this is leading to much social criticism and soul searching.

These are among the reasons for growing hierarchies in schooling. Hierarchies have always existed informally, both in the academic or general and vocational sectors, but may become such that some institutions will be even more careful in selecting their students, whereas others have to accept the less gifted or less motivated. At first glance this might suggest functional differentiation but it is at odds with equity purposes, and behind its apparent functionality are serious distortions and inefficiencies. If the objective is, while increasing participation and widening access, to strengthen quality and broaden the avenues of successful learning of an acceptable standard for all students, hierarchies among schools and their implications of social status often stand in the way. Conditions in highly favoured schools in wealthy neighbourhoods and highly selective academic institutions may be highly commendable but they compare most unfavourably in many countries with schools in poor neighbourhoods. Success rates in the former are counterbalanced by high failure rates and low performance on average in the latter. Such inequities and inefficiencies, deeply embedded in our societies, affect access and success at the tertiary level. Policies spanning both sectors are needed with a wider frame of reference than average levels of performance, progression rates and selection procedures. The review teams were unable to gain precise data but were made aware of several significant problems and inefficiencies at the secondary stage: variable information and guidance, resitting of exams to improve one's place in the queue, inadequate training in study skills and weak intersectoral relations. It is often said that the goal of secondary education is not merely preparation for higher education. This is fair comment: there are many goals and many pathways. However, as tertiary education becomes the norm, the secondary-tertiary sequence grows in importance.

Another set of issues relates more specifically to the position and role of the vocational programmes, tracks and institutions at upper secondary level. In many countries, increased participation at this level has meant a shift in demand from the vocational sector towards the more general or academic programmes. Sweden is an exception probably because of the major reform of upper secondary education some years ago, whereby the old vocational/general education distinctions have been removed; Norway, too, has instituted reforms aimed at avoiding such a shift in demand. Many graduates of vocational programmes apply at tertiary level, which means that at least some vocational programmes are considered or used as another route to the tertiary level. Increasingly, students in Japanese secondary vocational education aspire to pursue tertiary-level studies.

The content of some vocational programmes once leading directly into jobs is now tending to resemble a foundation course for further studies at tertiary level. A question arises about the suitability of sharply drawn lines. The impact on general secondary education of tertiary, especially university-wide and programme-specific entry requirements, has often been remarked; of growing importance is the effect on vocation-specific courses at secondary and post-secondary levels of the phenomenon of student progression to the tertiary level. Some vocational programmes are not first in the pecking order. These are likely to recruit among the less gifted. This suggests that these programmes may become remedial, rather than vocational, and the final certificate may eventually have a negative, rather than positive image. The future of the vocational sector at upper secondary level is becoming an open question. How at this level is an appropriate variety of programmes to meet the diversity of needs and interests to be maintained? On the one hand, there is an actual or potential loss of identity of many vocational programmes. But, on the other hand, the growing convergence between general, academic and vocational programmes or orientations, in Australia, Sweden, the United Kingdom and the United States offer many benefits as preparation for employment is increasingly postponed until the tertiary level. Japan, too, has sought to move in this direction with the introduction on an experimental basis of a more flexible integrated course at the secondary level. But some systems, Germany, Belgium (Flemish Community) and France for example, seek to maintain strong, well differentiated vocational sectors.

There is great difficulty in achieving coherent policies and systemic reform where there are sharply divided responsibility, different funding bases, different mechanisms for steering and monitoring and weak bridging procedures. These issues were considered in the November 1994 OECD Conference on Vocational Education and Training for the 21st Century; they are being addressed again in the current OECD thematic review of the transition from initial education to working life.

4. PARTICIPATION AND RESPONSES AT THE TERTIARY LEVEL

Country reactions or responses have been very different to the growth of demand at tertiary level, including the more recent wave. They reflect a range of values underlying the institutional frameworks, the specific rules and procedures for access to tertiary education and local circumstances. Some countries have shown more flexibility than others in meeting the increased pressure of demand. Access in principle is open to all qualified candidates in most if not all countries, but as we have seen, queues have emerged, signalling unmet demand and *numerus clausus* is applied in some subjects. Relatively little is known about the effects of these procedures on the quality of students' learning or their motivation. The Commonwealth of Virginia (United States) has such a diversified array of provision that there is a place somewhere for everyone but this does not mean a place of first choice. In Australia, there is a place for (nearly) everyone but the institutions and programmes are markedly homogeneous within the two sectors, *i.e.* universities and technical and further education colleges. There is choice but status differences exist as in New Zealand and the United Kingdom. Germany maintains a policy of equality among institutions across the country, but there are "magnet" cities, institutions and programmes. Similar geographic differences in the attractiveness of institutions to potential students may be found in Denmark and France. In the European countries, places are still at relatively low cost to students, whereas in Japan and the United States students may have to pay heavily for a place in a programme or institution of their choice. Demand is met because of the diversity of funding sources and provision. In Japan, the demographic downturn is increasing competition among institutions and causing many to wonder about their future. To all outward appearance, then, demand for access is acknowledged and met but in many different ways. From a client standpoint, there can appear to be a variable mix of free choice, opportunity, inequity and inefficiency. Part-time students of limited means may pay fees while full-time students from well-off families do not; quotas in subjects or programmes may be socially or economically desirable but can result in students taking possibly inappropriate courses; non-existent or inadequate articulation, credit-transfer arrangements or recognition of prior learning add time and costs unnecessarily to study programmes; they also inhibit mobility. If none of these is a direct consequence of volume increase in demand, they certainly are compounded by it.

The most visible and immediate issue arising from growth in demand is thus the capacity of systems to provide access to appropriate programmes and to maintain adequate conditions of study. Some have declared a limit. As a *pro tem* measure the United Kingdom in 1996 capped growth of full-time undergraduate numbers in the wake of rapid growth following the government's 1991 White Paper. In Belgium (Flemish Community), the official position is that there is "freedom of education" regardless of type of programme or philosophical or religious orientation of the institution (private or public); nevertheless, there is a view that a natural "limit" has

been reached to the expansion of university places. Inevitably in many countries, increasing competition for public funding is forcing a rethinking of guarantees and rights of access. That is not always feasible in practice. The German Constitution provides a right of access and where this is denied, albeit for very practical reasons, students may – and do – institute legal proceedings.

Complaints about overcrowding are not new: they were already being heard in many countries in the 1960s. Overcrowding remains a specific institutional issue in several countries prompting much publicity and sharp political debates, for example in France and Germany. The reviewers were conscious of certain institutional and legal rigidities to say nothing of attitudes and conditions of employment in some countries which seem to inhibit the kind of day-and-night, year-long use of space and the flexible use of personnel that are marked features of the more dynamic institutions in the United States Whatever the exact cause, in all countries taking part in this review, there is greatly increased pressure on resources, whether human or financial. Creativity and flexibility in policy and institutional management are more than ever needed. Staff/student ratios, although by no means uniform across countries or institutions, have tightened, albeit with exceptions here and there, *e.g.* Sweden. Formerly well-resourced tutorial systems, in Australia, New Zealand and the United Kingdom, for example, have been abandoned or diminished. Space pressures and inadequacies continue and there is a continuing need for new or remodelled teaching and learning spaces and for staff development and training to ensure that full advantage is taken of the potential of new spaces and facilities. Equipment, especially in technical subjects, is often inadequate or outdated, more so in several countries in the universities than in the "alternatives", and is expensive to maintain and replace. These may be regarded as normal problems of expansion, but they are exacerbated in an era of stable or reducing budgets. The quality of student learning and the conditions under which many tertiary teachers and administrators work must be of concern to policymakers, institutions and individuals. The question is not, however, whether or not expansion should continue: the pressures in countries are such that it is virtually certain to proceed, despite fluctuations.

The overcrowding debate is relevant. In Germany, for example, the review team questioned whether the overcrowding issue has actually been addressed, whether other avenues have really been explored, in terms of the efficient use of resources and facilities and especially of more innovative teaching methods and practices, extended hours of opening and greater use of distance education. If many large-city universities are oversubscribed, small *Fachhochschulen* offer another outlet and more are being established. Methods and practices, designed in times past for much lower levels of participation and very specific styles of teaching, are still uncritically used. In several countries, it seems that no solution other than major political initiatives relating to conditions of employment and legally-defined rights could be found to what is in effect a complex set of organisational, legal or constitutional problems. The emphasis has often been placed on the development of alternatives to the universities, to which admission could be controlled in one way or another. However, the problem of the universities remains. The introduction or increase of fees – for admission and tuition – has also occurred where not already in place, but in many European countries this is against the law or prevailing values. Yet supporters of fees argue that they could augment resources for institutions, improve facilities, staff/student ratios and so on, and strengthen institutional decision-making. Substantially increased demand results in heavier cost burdens; costs should not, however, become a barrier to access where policies aim to foster growth in participation. The heavy subsidies most evident in Europe are coming under question in several countries as demand increases. Ideally, supply should not be rationed nor demand deflected where well-qualified applicants seek entry, but, as we have seen, pressure on public budgets means that both are occurring. As discussed in the meeting of the Education Committee at Ministerial level in January 1996, new sources of finance are needed. We return to these issues in further detail below.

In some countries, institutions or the government, or sometimes local authorities, have managed to mobilise enough resources – perhaps with industry support, *e.g.* in tertiary-level vocational programmes – to maintain the same or comparable conditions of teaching and learning as hitherto. Often, however, we observed that these are for particular groups. While it is gratifying that the necessary resources have somehow been found to sustain tertiary education expansion, this provision may not best serve the needs and purposes of high-quality education for all. Should countries, under the pressure of particular groups or ideologies, continue to provide "more of the same"? Conversely, it may be

asked whether tertiary education conceived as a "market" is the most appropriate instrument to ensure the responsiveness of provision to the new demand. The idea is often seen to be based on a cost/benefit calculation which assumes the benefit as certain, an assumption which may be more and more questionable in the present context of varied and high unemployment, causing concern and sometimes unrest among students as they see their investment not rewarded by recruitment or career prospects.

The reviewers concluded that more inventive solutions, offering all students access to some kind of attractive and worthwhile educational experience are needed. This can mean, as in Germany, expanding places in the *Fachhochschulen* or, as in France, new approaches to the structure of first-years' curricula in the universities and new programmes and services aimed at improving student life, or, as in the United States, a greater diversity of institutions, wider provision of good facilities for part-time study, including distance education and more experimentation with innovative methods of teaching, tutoring and advising large student intakes. Examples of the latter are to be found in many countries but need to be generalised. Simply opening the doors without changing teaching and learning is not a solution. Queues and forced allocations are expedients, substitutes for educationally sound policies of distribution. The answer does not lie, Canute-like, in seeking to set back the tide of demand but in ensuring that it finds appropriate channels.

5. OPEN AND REVOLVING DOORS

Countries have all recognised that growing levels of demand will result in further widening access, regardless of particular problems arising. But, as has been remarked of the open door policy of the British Open University, unless there are considerable changes in induction arrangements, curricula, teaching, guidance, assessment and transition routes through upper secondary into tertiary education, the open door can become a revolving door. Attrition rates are high in most countries and time taken to complete study programmes and gain qualifications has on average lengthened. There are many explanations including the great increase in some countries in part-time student numbers. But it is inescapable that the quality of the provision and of the educational experience is one of them.

Dropping out is a troublesome issue, particularly when in some institutions or disciplines it may be as high as one-third to one-half of the enrolling students, or even more. In most cases, such as in France, dropping out occurs early in the course, sometimes in the first semester, most often in the first two years. "Year" in this case refers to the year of the course, which may not correspond to the lapse of time since first enrolment (see Table 4). In practice, many students who fail to obtain the required credits have already repeated the year or semester, so that the second year of the course could actually be their third or fourth year of study. In some countries, such as Germany, drop-outs occur later, possibly because when students are already 26 or 27, have a job, a family and children, they give up; but also because the tradition in the universities is not to impose any examination or other obligation until the third or fourth year of

study. Students in this situation are often left with little guidance in terms of career choices or on how to organise their work, and have limited personal contacts with their teachers. Dropping out commonly – but not only – takes place in countries, or institutions where admission is not restricted and where assessment at the end of the first (or second) year of the course is the true basis of selection, as noted in a recent European study (Council of Europe, 1996). In the United Kingdom and some other countries, attrition is relatively low on average. Averages, however, can disguise significant variations across subjects and institutions, and even in the United Kingdom, the phenomenon appears to be increasing.

Relatively few people met in the course of the review visits expressed concern over drop-outs or the magnitude of the queues for access. No specific administration is responsible for this heterogeneous

Table 4. **Age distribution of tertiary-level graduates, 1995**

	Age at 25th percentile	Median age	Age at 75th percentile
Short first university degree programmes (e.g. U.S. bachelor's)			
United Kingdom	21.0	22.0	24.9
Australia	20.9	22.4	26.9
New Zealand	21.3	22.5	25.9
Norway	23.4	25.3	29.5
Sweden	24.0	26.2	30.1
Denmark	24.8	26.7	29.9
Long first university degree programmes (e.g. German Diplom)			
New Zealand	21.7	22.7	24.7
Norway	23.8	25.2	27.5
Sweden	25.3	26.9	29.4
Belgium (Flemish Community)	20.5	27.3	29.6
Denmark	26.5	28.2	30.5
Second university degree programmes (e.g. US Master's)			
Belgium (Flemish Community)	22.9	24.0	27.7
Norway	25.4	27.1	30.0
New Zealand	23.4	28.4	37.7
United Kingdom	24.2	28.6	36.6
Denmark	26.8	29.4	33.5
Sweden	26.2	30.5	38.1
Australia	26.4	32.8	> 40
Non-university tertiary programmes			
Belgium (Flemish Community)	21.2	22.4	26.6
Norway	21.4	23.1	26.3
United Kingdom	20.7	24.2	33.4
New Zealand	21.1	24.5	34.6
Sweden	22.4	25.2	33.2
Denmark	23.8	25.8	29.1

Note: Countries are ranked in descending order of median age of graduation for each type of programme.
Source: Education at a Glance (OECD,1997), Table G2.3.

group. In too many institutions, little concern is shown about the causes of dropping out or the relevance and value to learners of the provision itself; sometimes indeed the proportion of drop-outs is considered an indicator of quality. Some university and college teachers are proud to warn their first-year students that most of them will not have access to the second year of the course. It is difficult to find an intelligent rationale for this attitude other than survival tactics for teachers who often do have to work under trying conditions. A financial tactic in some cases is to have high drop-out rates in large first-year courses in order to subsidise small later year classes. This is like robbing Peter and paying Paul. There is also the argument that selection is delayed until the end of first year and that all should have a chance. But a chance to fail with all the entailed losses does not seem to be a sound policy either educationally or financially. Steps are being taken in some countries and some institutions to address the problem, but we are not persuaded that there has been sufficient attention to understanding what the problem is.

In some countries we were informed that because students who drop out come back later or start another course of study, on the whole the number of real losses is at acceptable levels. "Stop-out" in Norway, for example, refers to those who are pausing, for shorter or longer periods. Studying for one or two years may well be a positive experience even if no formal qualification follows. Changing orientation can have positive as well as negative aspects: positive, if students can better choose a career in line with their aspirations and capacities; negative if the number of changes represents a high level of wastage and suggests high levels of frustration and a sense of failure among students. In most countries, there is a striking and regrettable lack of data on these problems to support a deeper analysis and debate. Means for acquiring these data are not easily put in place anywhere; in Germany and the United States privacy rights and legal requirements, let alone the volume and mobility of those following other than prescribed study timetables, would make detailed monitoring of progression and flows exceedingly difficult, perhaps impossible. Nevertheless, there is scope and need for improved statistics and for research studies to analyse efficiency and effectiveness issues. Further consideration is given to these issues, as they relate to the curriculum, teaching, learning and educational quality, later in this report.

Account must be taken of the specific national or institutional context in which queuing, dropping out, repeating, or changing orientation take place. As we have noted, in many countries, open and restricted admission sectors coexist, especially within the universities. Usually medicine or engineering are more restricted than the humanities, sciences and social sciences. Some of the "alternatives" to the universities, however, have stricter admission requirements than the universities, in Denmark, France and Germany for example. But this is not so in Australia, Belgium (Flemish Community), New Zealand, the United Kingdom and the United States. Within the same country there may be programmes with high numbers of drop-outs, repeaters, etc. and others where there are very few, to the extent that, if an equivalence or credit transfer system exists, it may be a sound strategy for students to enter the course where the risk is lower and to transfer to the other after two or three years of study. This kind of "pathway" may be a growing option but reliable data are not available across countries. Whatever the scale of such movements may be, admission considerations contribute to another quantitative consequence of massification: excess/additional demand is being channelled towards the more open, more vulnerable parts of the system, for example the humanities, social sciences and business studies.

Indeed these courses or disciplines, because they are less costly or less controlled by the professions or government planning units, are the usual destination of the bulk of demand. This may have reflected positive reactions to changes in employment prospects, for example when, in the early 1980s, demand shifted from teacher training programmes towards business and law, precisely at the time when commercial and financial services were the main job-creating sectors. However, in many cases, there is no such rationality and the floating demand can shift or be shifted from humanities to business or from psychology to sport, from one year to the other, in unpredictable ways. Educationally, it can be questionable practice just to enrol students in currently popular, low-cost, high-volume courses, but institutions often have no choice: students' legally well protected rights, or institutions' cost structures, or governmental pressure may lead to admission practices that are more expedient than educationally valid. High levels of enrolment in relatively low-cost subjects are also a phenomenon of the shift in balance towards part-time and female students, for example in Australia and the United States.

Although it is not suggested that efforts to lower costs are targeted on these groups or on certain kinds of institutions while others are protected, the quest for lower costs often in practice results in the growth of particular kinds of programmes and institutions not always well matched to client needs. The issues are quite complex since in demand-driven systems large volume courses are just that – an expression of demand – and it is this, not the low cost of providing the courses which is the determining factor. But as indicated, institutional management can take advantage of these circumstances.

The issue of costs is intertwined with that of progression rates and attrition. But educational considerations need to be foremost since it is an education that students seek and society needs. Ways to provide a satisfactory education at a reasonable cost is a universal objective in tertiary education policy; the image of the "revolving door" is a reminder that for significant numbers of enrolled students that objective is not being achieved.

6. NEW COURSES, PROGRAMMES AND INSTITUTIONS

Our emphasis thus far has been on the effects of increased enrolments within the existing set of institutions; these aspects are usually at the centre of the debate, because they affect well-established and known institutions. But new courses, programmes and institutions are being created throughout Member countries; they accord with defined student needs and central planning decisions or principles; or they are on the basis of local initiatives, responding to the needs of enterprises and the professions, or to the judgements of for-profit institutions. Expansion of supply may take the form of new university campuses, of private institutions, of vocational and technical programmes and of study programmes whether theoretical or applied which take account of new fields and disciplines of knowledge. Sponsors may be central or local government, the institutions themselves, individual academic departments, private bodies, industries and professions, individual firms and particular administrations within or outside the education sector. In every country visited there are many examples of varied supply side responses, including efforts to improve access and increase learning opportunities through the adoption of new forms of delivery.

Distance education is a notable example of innovative structure and practice although it is still often seen as peripheral. That relationship is, however, beginning to change as the lines between "distance" and "on campus" blur. The needs of the large number of part-time students who find campus attendance very difficult or impossible are being recognised. Designated open universities and colleges have been established for example in Australia, Germany, Japan, New Zealand, the United Kingdom and the United States. Some date back to the earlier years of this century but the big wave has come since the 1960s. Increasingly through the growth of information technology, conventional or face-to-face institutions have developed distance education facilities, thereby becoming dual mode. These developments, directed especially at undergraduate students, have been more conspicuous where there are traditions of part-time study for first degrees or their equivalent. Effectiveness in the distance mode requires a high degree of planning and organisation: curricula have to be redesigned or newly created, communication systems established to ensure reliable exchange of course materials, assignments, assessment exercises and so on. Despite the lure of the new technologies and the facility they provide for interactive and group learning and for self-directed study, for reasons of cost and accessibility by very large numbers of students great use is still made of print materials and the postal service. The key is flexibility – students can study in their own time and pace, at home or in the workplace. A major objective has been to widen access including for mature-age people who could not or chose not to embark upon tertiary education in their youth. It has also been possible to achieve significant cost savings, at least to the public budget. Gradually, prejudice has been overcome and misconceptions cleared. Even so, relatively few examples of institutions making substantial use of distance education were drawn to the reviewers' attention notwithstanding its presence in countries and institutions visited. Distance education, despite its enormous potential, has yet to enter the mainstream.

Varying degrees of flexibility and readiness to address different client groups were encountered. Many of the new programmes or institutions have been created to meet social as much as economic demands. The needs of women and of minorities have already been mentioned as significant factors, likewise those of mature-age students. There are perceived gaps in existing provision to fill; and there are responses to make to commercial or electoral interests. The cost of courses in the social sciences, law, humanities are low relative to the costs of technical courses; moreover, student demand for technical courses has often been weak in relation to the existing capacity. There is considerable scope for private providers and much more activity, for example in the fields of business, commerce and consumer services, than commonly appears in official statistics.

On the whole, government policies or expressions of concern aimed at shifting demand – for example to sciences and engineering in Australia and Denmark – have had very little impact as indicated by trend data over three decades. There are exceptions: some of the new initiatives have been highly successful in terms of access to employment. Computer studies have been fostered in most countries through active government policies, but their success probably reflects the general spread of a technological culture as much as specific interventionist policies.

Qualitative consequences of a substantially increased participation are discussed below in relation to curriculum, teaching and learning issues. Here, the point is whether at the system level (including private and local initiative) provision is structured to meet the needs and interests of the new clientele. When mass participation was first discussed in the OECD (see OECD, 1974), the emphasis was on the different school and cultural backgrounds of the "new" students and how to adapt teaching and learning of the existing courses and programmes to their specific demands. Although still relevant, the scope here is broader.

There are needs to be recognised and systematically addressed as tertiary education expands and diversifies. They are a mix of the highly specific and the general, the transient and the enduring. The conclusion from the review is that what is needed includes:

- more individualised courses of study which facilitate career prospects and are motivating for continuing learning;
- challenging and well-defined learning targets that all or practically all students nevertheless can succeed in meeting, with commitment, effort and persistence;
- programmes and courses of study that clearly respond to society's needs for well-educated, competent workers and citizens;

- increased institutional flexibility and creativity, grounded in appraisals of the needs of all students.

These are highly generalised requisites; they have implications for curriculum, teaching, learning and institutional leadership and management which we take up later. When combined with the kind of environment and changes all countries are experiencing, they lead to large structural and organisational changes in both secondary and tertiary education.

As pointed out in the discussion of trends at upper secondary level, young people are tending to prolong the duration of general education, postponing to a later stage direct preparation for employment and a career. What does this mean for tertiary education? Improving the cultural level of young people through a longer duration of general education is a generous and worthwhile objective. It has already been implemented in some countries, including Japan, and has been formulated in various ways in all Member countries. France, for example, wishes to bring 80 per cent of each cohort to the level of the *baccalauréat*; in Sweden the objective is to bring the country to parity with its partners and competitors; in the United Kingdom, where historical levels of upper secondary participation have been low, there is a national training target of 60 per cent of young people attaining level 3 (A-level General Certificate or equivalent of the National Vocational Qualification).

If the trend in demand is clear (allowing for significant differences among countries), if the processes are varied and flexible, this does not mean that the outcomes are clear. Many of the vocational programmes, for example, are firmly anchored at upper secondary level, or designed for a given age group, often through a rich body of legislation. It may prove difficult to transform them or to transfer their functions increasingly to the tertiary level, although this has been done in Japan and the United States, and, to a limited extent, in Finland and the Czech Republic. There may also be resistance or reluctance at that level. Existing institutions may be more concerned with the difficulties of adapting to the interests of their own students than with the need to set up or integrate new institutions at tertiary level, in particular when the prospect of demographic decline may represent a threat to their future intake, hence to their resources. In that sense, there is a contradiction between the trend towards mass participation, which means meeting a much broader range of interests and abilities, and demographic decline, which may enable existing institutions to improve quality, but encourage them to focus on their more traditional functions. This is an issue on which countries have very different views. Should existing institutions assume roles and functions to include the upgrading of vocational programmes – at the possible expense of their quality and identity? There was an impression in some of the countries visited that the existing "higher" education institutions (the universities in particular) are not prepared to respond to a change of this scale; others, however, have embraced vocational programmes which previously were of a lower level or conducted by non-university institutions. There is no unanimity on this point across countries, some adopting an inclusive model of the university, others aiming to maintain a clear distinction between "university" and "non-university" or "tertiary" and "non-tertiary".

In future, however, participation in a very broadly defined tertiary education will be in all probability "natural". This is a cultural change which may be encouraged by the current unpredictability of employment prospects, but it is evident too in countries of relatively low unemployment, notably Japan and the United States. However, should participation be organised around the traditional disciplines? Should the duration of studies continue to increase? There is no clear consensus around these questions. Many, on the contrary, emphasise the need to facilitate transition into employment, particularly through providing the new clients of tertiary education with usable qualifications and competences.

7. ACCESS AND EQUITY

As we have seen in all participating countries there are various approaches towards the management of demand, with a view to responding better to individual aspirations and employment outlets. Strengthening the vocational sector, including at upper secondary level; developing respectable alternatives or more varied pathways at tertiary level; strengthening selection and guidance mechanisms; and reviewing cost regimes are among the approaches. But they are not uniformly successful. For example, although advanced in some quarters as means to help pay for expansion and therefore promote social equity, fees and other charges fall unequally on students. And proposals for fees have provoked strong reactions in France, Germany and the United Kingdom; review teams in Scandinavia

were told that fees were neither wanted nor needed since public revenue sources and expenditure plans would suffice; increased and differentiated contribution levels, recently introduced by the Australian government, are controversial changes to the scheme of deferred contribution to tuition; in New Zealand, the reviewers met many complaints from students. In all of these instances, equity issues figure in one way or another.

Strong and growing demand raises issues of access and equity. These are not new. Most of the arguments developed over several decades remain relevant but, in the context of mass participation, may have to be formulated differently. Consider the articulation between general secondary education and the universities. In several countries, particularly in Japan, competition for entry to universities, which might have been expected to decrease in line with broadened access, has in fact been exacerbated. Certain universities in Japan (as in other countries) are still visibly at the top of the tree and entry to the most prestigious ones has been a guarantee of lifetime employment in leading companies, professions and the public service. From one standpoint, the broadening of opportunities to young Japanese through private universities, special training schools and a very large number of two-year colleges and vocational colleges is an example of greater equity. But when considerable differences of esteem exist and access to particular kinds of institutions is socially and economically structured – as in many countries – equity issues take on a particular character. In the age of mass tertiary education they are no less salient than in the earlier periods when opportunities for tertiary education were fewer and demand was less.

Equity is commonly set as a policy goal. In Sweden for example, the formula guiding education at all levels is equal opportunity for all regardless of location or ethnicity. The nine-year common school is an expression of this ideal. Yet tertiary education still has a socially biased, meritocratic flavour. The opening of new university colleges in areas of low participation in Stockholm and Malmö is a response to this problem.

Despite the best endeavours, research studies indicate that deep-seated equity problems continue: there is disproportionately small participation by lower socio-economic groups in all countries; students from such groups, in Japan and Portugal for example, are less likely to enrol in public universities where studies are better subsidised and qualifications generally are more valued on the labour market and in society; subject and professional cultures that provide few incentives for women to enter persist; some minorities *e.g.* Blacks in the United Kingdom and African-Americans in the United States are under-represented, tend to perform less well and, as a group, have poorer job prospects even when they graduate. Equity issues thus arise not only in relation to access; they are no less relevant to the programmes themselves and their outcomes. On equity grounds there should be as much concern for success in tertiary education and career profiles as for access. If broadened access has improved opportunities for new groups, inequalities are still highly visible in terms of failure or drop-out at the tertiary level and disparities in employment on graduation.

Where concern is expressed, it is perhaps too often about the poor preparation of students or inappropriate orientation or guidance mechanisms. These are of course relevant but many non-university institutions or programmes demonstrate, through smaller student groups, continuing monitoring and close relationships with teachers and instructors, that there are effective ways of helping the transition of students to a more demanding curriculum. The same is true of universities where special efforts are made, for example the "historically black" colleges in the United States or those new universities in the United Kingdom which have very high enrolments of black students. Very interesting efforts are being made to enable students more generally to cope successfully with the demands of study in the first year: substantial investments of resources and expertise are being made in institutions for example in Australia, Belgium (Flemish Community), Denmark, France New Zealand and Virginia (as well as other states) to assist students in improving their study skills and learning performance. New units have been established in faculties, tutoring and counselling strengthened and more emphasis placed on monitoring student progress. Questions were often raised in country visits about the suitability of many students for tertiary-level study. That, however, is scarcely the point once they are enrolled. The reality of growth is that institutions must change to accommodate students. Diversity of institutions and programmes and more sophisticated selection and allocation procedures are doubtless part of the answer but, having enrolled students, all institutions are under a moral obligation to educate them well, regardless of their capabilities. Students, too, have an obligation to make the necessary commitment and to apply themselves wholeheartedly. Equity is not one-sided.

8. GEOGRAPHIC ACCESS AND THE ROLE OF SMALLER INSTITUTIONS

Accessibility has another dimension: the creation and viability of distributed local education and training opportunities to balance the concentration of resources in favoured urban centres. Some argue that institutions have to reach a "critical mass" if they wish to ensure academic respectability, others emphasise the greater accessibility and impact on local cultural and economic life of smaller institutions. Both are right, depending on the nature and comprehensiveness of the institution considered: advanced scientific research usually requires the resources of large and comprehensive universities and academic staff, graduate students and technicians increasingly working in cross-institutional teams, free-standing research institutes and industry. But very small colleges, whether rural or urban, can also sustain research and high standards of teaching and learning and can participate in wider networks. The Norwegian regional colleges, and the Danish and Swedish regional universities are convincing demonstrations of the educational success, the economic and cultural impact of smaller institutions and the equalising of study opportunity regardless of location. New opportunities are brought to people living in these regions and study conditions are often highly favourable. Large institutions tend to have fewer links with the local community, are more concerned about their place in the international or national scientific community and are often bent on becoming centres of power and prestige.

There are other advantages that local institutions, regardless of scale, can offer. In France, when the *Instituts universitaires de technologie* (IUT) were created in the late 1960s, it was planned that the *Sections de techniciens supérieurs* (STS), belonging to the vocational (upper secondary) administration would be gradually suppressed. In practice, enrolment growth in the STS was much faster than in the IUT, a major reason being that opting for the STS (both courses last two years and, although different, are more or less of equivalent level) usually meant staying in the same town or even institution. Despite the onward march of cosmopolitanism and globalisation, localism and regionalism remain potent cultural and economic forces.

There are thus strong arguments in favour of smaller institutions spread over the country in the framework of regionalisation policies aiming to facilitate not only access, but equity of access. In Australia, as in Norway, one of the goals in supporting rurally-based institutions is the improvement of traditionally low participation rates in rural areas. Distance education programmes also have, as one of their targets, access for students whose geographical location makes attendance very difficult if not impossible. The arguments as heard in the country visits include but go beyond education: the social argument – serving families where it is not usual to leave the home and city to study; and the economic argument – serving and strengthening local enterprises, contributing to the development or creation of new activities. There is a third argument sustaining or helping create local and regional cultures: in some countries and regions, cultural and intellectual life seems to have emigrated to a few large urban centres if indeed it ever had strong local roots. A tertiary education institution which requires staff with motivation, scientific culture, methodological rigour and experience of active life, can become the embryo of cultural life. The Nordic countries set an admirable example in positive policies to enhance the vitality of rural areas and provincial towns through well-functioning networks of tertiary (as well as primary and secondary) institutions. Other striking examples are the spread of the two-year community colleges across the State of Virginia and the location of German *Fachhochschulen* in or on the outskirts of provincial towns.

There are some dangers of a demand-led movement, based mainly on expressed community preferences or the wish for a prolongation of studies to avoid the risk of unemployment and acquire a higher level of qualification, rather than specific interest in a discipline or profession. Highly localised socio-economic demand can be parochial and self-serving, resulting in broader and longer-term inefficiencies. Not all rurally or provincially located institutions do well. Local ambitions can override educational standards. Hence the proliferation of course offerings which may be of poor quality and with meagre employment outcomes. Small institutions in regional centres must make special efforts to ensure that a high quality of education is sustained, that good links are maintained with other institutions and that the benefits of academic cosmopolitanism are shared. A balance is being sought between addressing local and regional needs and the wider national and international settings to which all tertiary institutions perforce must relate. This challenges institutional providers and system policy-makers alike. Recent efforts by the Norwegian government to strengthen the nation-wide Network Norway, including a new national authority now under discussion in parliament, in order to rationalise provision, build centres of excellence and encourage wider access to them will be watched with interest. Opportunities for staff to participate in academic and professional events, well-organised libraries and information centres linked with state, regional, or national and international networks, and the development of research and development projects that reach out beyond just a local service function are all needed. In general, the forces at work as the tertiary sector continues to expand and develop favour the larger centres. All countries need to pay close attention to the different ways in which students located outside the major concentrations can have access to much that the big city institutions provide. Technological development can be a means to this end and, again in Norway, distance education is a powerful instrument whose potential is yet to be realised. Australia, New Zealand and the United States, by contrast, have over many decades demonstrated the value of nation-wide education networks which overcome what has been aptly called "the tyranny of distance" and might be subtitled "the penalty of parochialism".

One key element of success for smaller institutions, whether in rural or urban settings, seems to be employment relevance, not conceived in classroom terms (*e.g.* applied rather than theoretical subjects), but in terms of active involvement in local economic activities – with students spending part of their time in enterprises or other services as part of the curriculum and under the control of their teachers, as well as enterprises contributing through their staff to teaching in the institution. Typical of the German *Fachhochschulen*, this is found in Sweden and in both provincial and cosmopolitan centres in all the countries visited.

Another element of success is well-grounded structures and well-functioning procedures for evaluating quality. The idea of institutional networks, which is not new, has revived with the need for rationalisation and an effective use of available resources. It can also be seen as a quality assurance device for smaller institutions whether in rural or urban settings. A very positive aspect is that such networks can give recognition to and stimulate the work of specialised local institutions in their teaching and research, providing national and even international links. On the other hand, a network is not an end in itself; it has to serve specific purposes, such as facilitating exchanges of students and teachers or researchers in a specific field of competence or technology transfer. When smaller local institutions become the subcontractors or colonies of the larger ones, which prefer to concentrate on graduate study and research work, new horizons open and new relations need to be established. One example of this is the franchising movement which undoubtedly extends access and is the basis of new networks. There are quality issues arising to which we return below.

3

TERTIARY EDUCATION FOR ALL

1. A NEW PARADIGM

What conclusions emerge from the trends in demand and access and their impact as developed from the country reports and visits? The overriding impression of quantitative increase and increasing diversity is tempered by two considerations: first, rates of increase are quite variable and some caution is needed in projecting continued growth; second, despite the often heroic efforts made to satisfy demand, many gaps and shortcomings remain. On the first point, although there is considerable unevenness and countries are at different stages or levels in respect of access and participation, we have suggested that there are very good reasons to suppose that the trend will continue upward. Thereby wider and more diverse categories of students will be embarking on "the first years" and their requirements will set new targets and standards for provision. As for the gaps and shortcomings, they should be seen in relation to very complex and varied environments in which progress is subject to varied constraints. This is not to say that as much as possible is being done.

Reflection on the numerous sources and forms of demand points to the need for a new paradigm for tertiary education. Its elements include:

- the continually rising aspirations and expectations among individuals and societies;
- the universalisation of full secondary education, a phenomenon in most countries of only the past three or four decades;
- the directions of public policy in many countries which project eligibility for tertiary education of 60, 80 or 100 per cent of those completing secondary education; and, in the case of one (the United States) of entry into some kind of tertiary education by everyone;
- the realisation by adults of the need to continue or restart formal learning and of the opportunities to do so;
- the constantly reiterated social demand and human capital theses which are a stimulus to individual and social investment in ever higher levels of skills and competences;
- the equity-based attention to previously under-represented groups;
- the relative ease of access to highly flexible and accommodating forms of study whether home-, workplace- or institution-based.

These and other sources and forces are most likely to continue stimulating demand even if there are countervailing factors such as increased costs for clients and labour market changes affecting graduates. Often passing unnoticed is the massive campus building and renovation programmes which, as the reviewers frequently observed, are creating new kinds of living environments for students of all ages. Tertiary education is becoming "the place to be, the experience to have", prized and valued for all, not just a privileged minority. The direction is universal participation: 100 per cent participation with fair and equal opportunities to study; in some form of tertiary education; at some stage in the life cycle and not necessarily end-on to secondary education; in a wide variety of structures, forms and types of delivery; undertaken on equal terms either part-time or full-time; publicly subsidised but with shared client and stakeholder contributions; closely involving partners in the community; serving multiple purposes – educational, social, cultural and economic. Access, therefore, is not merely to an institution but to a way of life, not for the few but for all. The further implications of this shift form the subject of the remainder of this report.

2. RELATIONSHIPS WITH EMPLOYMENT: CHANGING OCCUPATIONS AND THE EXPECTATIONS OF GRADUATES

Students, on their own testimony, want and need jobs or further career development; equally, they want opportunities for personal fulfilment, access to ideas, time to share and reflect on beliefs and the opportunity to assess values. They seek a broadening as well as a deepening and are not content with a narrowly specialised education that might contain them within the bounds of particular disciplines and professions. Society needs capable and responsible citizens performing a multitude of adult roles in a civilised fashion, and it needs many more people with these qualities and interests. The economy continually demands a highly proficient workforce able to rise to the challenges of globalisation and technology and to create new openings for growth. Although, taken to an extreme, any one of these sets of demands can drive out or distort the others in system-wide and institutional policies, balances, more or less harmonious, are being sought.

There are special features of the economic criteria which call for attention at this time. The OECD *Jobs Study* (OECD, 1994) and its follow ups (*e.g.* OECD, 1996a) have demonstrated that, across the OECD, persistently high rates of unemployment and particularly youth unemployment seriously impede growth with many attendant social risks. In several countries graduate unemployment rates have reached significant levels and there are in many cases lengthy periods between graduation and first jobs (OECD, 1997). What is the role of tertiary education in relation to these problems?

In discussions of the trajectory into employment, the most widespread view, encountered in all countries and frequently in the literature, is that tertiary education graduates overall have better prospects of early entry into the jobs market, better jobs and incomes, and less risk of becoming unemployed than school-leavers. Some argue that investment in education provides better returns, in terms of access to qualified jobs; others, that it improves the graduate's position in the queue for good jobs. As a result it is often considered that investment (public or private) in tertiary education would alleviate employment problems and contribute to the required increase in the qualifications of the workforce. However, there are some problems with these appraisals, which must change as ever higher proportions of the population acquire tertiary qualifications and the knowledge that underpins the "knowledge-based economy" is subject to critical scrutiny.

The employment destinations of the various categories of pupils and students vary with the level of their qualifications. In recent times, young people with no, or only elementary, qualifications went to agriculture, public works or manual labour; those with vocational secondary qualifications went to industry or crafts; those with general secondary qualifications, to private services; and tertiary graduates, to public employment and the leading professions. This picture is of course schematic, Platonic even in its hint of a fixed order of roles and relationships in the republic: it is also dated. For example, there have been massive falls in recent decades in industrial employment and in the rural sector; the service sector has continued to expand; private-sector employment provides new openings for graduates. Individuals in these various categories in the past did not compete on the same markets, in terms of occupation or economic activity, and salaries have been discussed and determined according to different rules and within different contexts. The transformations of the public sector in many countries together with the rebirth of the enterprise culture, entailing reduced employment security and more hazards, means that graduates can no longer take traditional graduate jobs for granted. This is yet another cultural fixture that has been prised loose.

The situation varies across countries, particularly in line with recent patterns of educational growth and current specific levels of participation in tertiary education. Historically, the destinations for university graduates have broadened to new sectors and careers: from the professions (including the church, medicine, the law) to public employment (including public research and education) and, more recently in many countries, from the public to the private sector, in commercial or financial services and white-collar jobs in industry. This corresponds to real differences in ethos and mentality, particularly of course in the universities, as was noted in many of the country visits. Obviously, the universities still serve the traditional professions which sometimes include engineering; in some other countries, particularly those in Continental Europe, the main destination for university graduates, besides these professions, remains the public sector, with some variation according to field of study. But here, too, the outlets have broadened, during the 1980s, to the private sector, industry and services. The universities in several countries have also taken in such "new" professions as nursing, accounting, business studies, primary school teaching, computing and various paramedical and science-technical fields. In the non-university institutions the range of occupational fields is very broad and is being restructured, in line with changing occupational and employment boundaries.

Not all occupational structures are equally flexible in their response to increased tertiary or secondary participation. Some sectors recruit people with higher levels of qualifications for the same posts or – seen from another angle – graduates at various levels have to accept, temporarily or not, lower-level occupations than they may have expected. This trend challenges conventions regarding stable relationships between graduates and particular types and levels of jobs. The extent of occupational flexibility varies across countries. Such flexibility depends on a number of socio-cultural factors. For example, well-established hierarchies, forms of communication and authority especially in the older professions and traditional industrial settings make change very difficult. It is sometimes easier to maintain traditional work organisation in existing plants and to introduce changes in occupational structures, technology and organisational method in new locations, with a view to establishing a new enterprise culture. Here the typical worker may have a tertiary, or at least a strong upper secondary qualification. Studies reveal different trends in the extent to which jobs themselves are transformed to take advantage of the skills and competences of more highly qualified post holders; some employers told us of the initiative taken in recruiting tertiary education graduates to effect just such changes. The new professions, especially those based on new information and communication technologies, often display innovative cultural and occupational settings, authority patterns and work styles. These call for different competences, attitudes and behaviour. In discussion with recently employed graduates and employers' bodies, the qualities of adaptability, creativity, initiative and team work were always to the fore.

Another factor is the behaviour of individual graduates. Previous OECD studies have suggested that university graduates tend to prefer a job in the same sector as their predecessors, even at the price of substantial downgrading, various forms of under-employment or even unemployment. One such study reported that one of the highest unemployment rates was among Ph.D.s in physics, who expected to find jobs in research. Public employment is the place where downgrading is more common, particularly as economic downturns affect the private sector and young graduates would accept any job in the public services with the greater security it usually provides. Conversely, in some countries traditional manufacturing industry has little, or is losing, attractiveness for university graduates; in most cases, marketing and retail sales, a developing sector, have more opportunities than candidates.

It does not follow that tertiary institutions should immediately try to change discipline mixes or that students should look only for immediately useful vocational courses. "Responsiveness" is more complex than that. For example, jobs and occupational changes over the lifespan are becoming more frequent, hence the prominence of the generic or transferable skills movement. Graduates may also have to make their own career, run their own business, move from one region or country to another. The forward-looking employers' organisations recognise this and in meetings with them, while institutions were challenged to be more efficient and cost effective, they were also being advised to maintain a breadth of studies and to provide broad theoretical foundations for applicable skills. Similar messages are coming from national and international business/higher education round tables.

Although the debate usually focuses on employment prospects for university graduates, these cannot be discussed in isolation: employment prospects have to be considered in a comprehensive way, for the full range of qualifications and sectors. In particular, outlets for technicians, higher technicians, graduates from non-university tertiary programmes, now much better documented than hitherto, have to be considered. In some cases, such as in the *Fachhochschulen* in Germany, these programmes were reported as giving better access to employment, better incomes and career prospects. In other countries, graduates find difficulties in recruitment, for example engineers prepared at colleges in Norway. In some cases, reasons for the difficulties may be found in the content and relevance of the programmes; in others, in the fact that these graduates find themselves squeezed between skilled workers and technicians and traditional university graduates.

Forecasting future employment prospects for various categories of tertiary graduates becomes increasingly difficult. Many now have difficulties in securing access to stable occupations; short-term contracts are common. Whereas some trends can still be identified, more and more countries, in the context of the global economy, are exposed to drastic changes on markets where they have or had a strong position: New Zealand in the 1980s was a dramatic example. Such risks exist in all countries, not only smaller ones such as Belgium (Flemish Community) or Norway which have a limited number of strong sectors active on international markets. The larger economies, such as Germany and Japan, where an increasing number of plants or units of production are "relocated" to countries where costs are lower or markets more promising, are exposed to ever more intensive competition. In Germany, labour costs are markedly higher than in competing countries, and in Japan, the United Kingdom and the United States, there is an increasing realisation that past practices (and hegemony) are over and a new global balance has to be sought.

The comfortable nexus between graduate status and secure employment can no longer be taken for granted if indeed it ever could, apart from cyclical upturns. Tertiary institutions are having to adopt approaches which include scanning the changing employment market and adjusting programmes and courses accordingly, giving much greater attention than hitherto to the value of work experience, internships and collaborative arrangements with industry. Increased investment in career counselling and job placement are also called for. Where provided, such counselling and the role of institutional careers agencies in linking with industry are not, however, always well understood or incorporated in course planning and teaching. Nor is the growing range of contacts of programmes and their staff and students with enterprises sufficiently drawn upon in the development of counselling and careers advice. In one large university which provides a comprehensive careers service of high quality, we were told that these functions and information flows are often only very loosely coupled. There is a need for better integration of "careers and courses", deriving from system-wide and institutional appraisals of the knowledge and skills students need if they are successfully to negotiate crucial transitions from tutelage to the labour market and in the transitions likely to become more common during their working and adult lives. Some countries are considerably more advanced than others: the United States has highly developed procedures, as increasingly do Australia and the United Kingdom. Where there are close links with industry and commerce, as in the German *Fachhochschulen*, the IUT (*Instituts universitaires de technologie*) in France or the technology-focused university colleges in Sweden, graduates are in a favourable position. New curriculum designs and industry-education partnerships discussed below illustrate the responses.

The question posed by the review team in Belgium (Flemish Community) is pertinent in all countries: Are students being adequately prepared for a rapidly changing world of work whose bearings in the foreseeable future are likely to be global as much as regional or national and for which highly competent, energetic and creative individuals will be needed in increasing number? Many answers are given but perhaps more to the point is whether the

question is regarded as relevant, central even to the mission of the tertiary institutions. For many the answer is in the affirmative: the German *Fachhochschulen*, the professional schools and faculties of universities everywhere, the departments and faculties engaged in partnerships with industry and commerce in the United Kingdom, the universities introducing *stages* and vocationally-oriented study programmes in France, the polytechnics in New Zealand and so on. For others, the answer is qualified or negative: the relationship is questioned for a variety of reasons. It is argued that the high-level functions for which tertiary education prepares its graduates are affected by technological and social change and are variable and unpredictable; that academics, even those in vocational institutions, cannot reflect the whole range of occupational needs and potentiality; and that the initial years of tertiary education can provide a foundation but not a tailor-made graduate for a specific occupation. There is considerable force in these arguments but they tend to widen a breach rather than point towards the accommodation that is sought – by students, by employers and by policy-makers.

That accommodation, on the evidence of this review, seems to be possible if certain conditions are met: first, that there is an open-minded attitude by all concerned to the education-employment relationship, paving the way to dialogue and partnership without preconditions; and second, that tertiary institutions, together with employers, take forward the protracted discussion of generic, transferable skills and learning processes, as templates to lay over the rich array of course and study programmes that, today, are most often formulated as bodies of specialist knowledge. Such positive steps as these will serve not only to demonstrate that action is being taken on the growing concern about graduate unemployment and job placement but also that there is a real mutuality of interests between tertiary education and the changing labour market.

3. DIVERSIFICATION AND DISTINCTIVENESS

There was no need for a thematic review in order to bring to light the variety of education and training provision in Member countries, but, with its focus on the first years of "tertiary" education, this study has disclosed the key role played by the diversity of structures in educational development and the transition to mass participation. Diversity can take different forms, however. In the OECD perspective, it implies that distinct courses or institutions serve distinct objectives, receiving and responding to distinct streams of students. This may mean that they are located in different buildings or belong to different administrations. Or, belonging to the same administration or in the same section (for example in unitary systems), the courses and institutions vary in their offerings and style to meet the needs of different clients. Diversity is not always a matter of deliberate policy. In response to local circumstance, history or opportunity, institutions and programmes vary greatly in size, in the balance between undergraduate and post-graduate, in courses offered, in the provision – or not – for part-time and off-campus students. Many of these differences are summed up by Trow (1996) as follows: "By diversity in higher education I mean the existence of distinct forms of post-secondary education, of institutions and groups of institutions within a state or nation that have different and distinctive missions, educate and train for different lives and careers, have different styles of instruction, are organised and funded differently and operate under different laws and relationships to government." Clearly in this definition there are degrees of diversity. There are also limits to diversity: government policies, for example; the internationalisation of science and culture; concepts such as generic skills and consistent standards; the benchmarks of a liberal education; and not least, the relative homogeneity of background of many tertiary teachers. Diversity is thus not unconditional, but it denotes choice and responsiveness to client demand, it stimulates institutional initiative and it is essential if tertiary education is to become universal. As a strategy, it can be pursued within unitary, binary or multi-sectoral systems and is not to be confused with these macro-structural arrangements. The university of the future, for example, may be comprehensive and differentiated, well able to take in and educate cohorts of students whose attainments and aptitudes vary widely. Such universities exist now, notably in unitary systems in Australia and the United Kingdom and in the multi-sectoral system in Virginia. On the other hand, in Germany, Japan, and other countries in Europe, while there is diversity in the university system, the distinctions in style, structure and approach are much more apparent as between universities and non-university institutions.

The policy debate has, as a result of the equating of diversity with sectoral distinctions, often centred on binary or multi-layered vs. unified systems of tertiary education. With its universities and regional colleges, Norway belongs to the binary cat-

egory – even if the recent emphasis on Network Norway and some mergers have somewhat blurred this image. Provision in France is highly structured, while the Czech Republic seeks to find ways to introduce a new, separate sector not unlike the recent initiatives in Austria and Finland or the experience in Belgium (Flemish Community) and Denmark. Also, Australia now has a "unified" system, with the promotion of the former Colleges of Advanced Education to the status of universities as does the United Kingdom with the translation of the polytechnics into universities. Yet in Australia the Technical and Further Education Sector (TAFE) and in the United Kingdom the Further Education sector provide a number of degree-level programmes. In New Zealand, with the currency given to the concept of "seamlessness" there is a clear intention to interrelate programmes and institutions which have typically been separate and independent of one another. In all systems, irrespective of basic structures, diversification is balanced by, first, rules and procedures setting directions and limits and, second, efforts to establish and strengthen credit transfer and other linkages.

The tertiary scene is now open, broad and mixed; it includes more and more courses and programmes, in line with prolonged education and the postponement of preparation for employment. At the same time, its diversity is structured and regulated and this applies to the private as well the public sector.

The distinctive features of the "non-university institutions" were reviewed in the OECD report *Alternatives to Universities* (OECD, 1991). The image of short-cycle, more practical and vocational programmes is certainly useful, as it exemplifies a contrast between usually longer and more academic or theoretical university courses and those "alternative" programmes. However, it now needs to be qualified. Not all programmes and institutions in the non-university sector are directly vocational in nature: the junior college in Japan, even if it now gives importance to foreign languages and the use of computers, is basically a prolongation of secondary general education. Many "non-university" institutions were designed as two- or three-year programmes, as opposed to university courses lasting four, five or more years. The associate degree programmes of US community colleges are a case in point. However, a broader view of the tertiary landscape reveals other cases. For example, the German *Fachhochschulen* now offer a four-year programme (including practice and final project) as opposed to the theoretical five year programme in the universities; the Portuguese polytechnics may award a specialised diploma which is recognised as equivalent to the *Licenciado* or, under certain conditions, the *Licenciado* itself; the two-cycle *hogeschool* programmes in Belgium (Flemish Community) are of similar duration to the first degree programmes in universities. An important feature of these institutions is the style of teaching. In most cases, groups are smaller than 30 or even 25 and the figure is still lower for workshop or laboratory work. There are a number of specific examinations during a course, rather than a comprehensive or final exam at the end of the year or cycle. As a result, the proportions of failure and drop-outs may be very low. As already pointed out, however, drop-out rates can also be high, as in the US community colleges.

Where, as is usual, these courses or programmes have a strong and explicit vocational orientation, perhaps half of the time is devoted to workshop or laboratory in the institutions and further substantive time is devoted to periods in enterprises – at least in engineering courses. One other feature is the participation of teachers coming from industry and the professions, whether full- or part-time, and the very close links with the local community and enterprise sector. However, since many universities now adopt similar practices, the sharpness of the earlier distinction is being lost. Distinctiveness is often less a function of the type of institution or the sector to which it belongs than of particular study lines and styles of teaching and learning within the institutions. For example, whether programmes in subjects like surveying, landscape design, environmental and waste management, architecture and traffic engineering are in universities or non-university institutions, they commonly include placements in private enterprise or in public agencies, substantial practical work and, increasingly, a mixture of computer simulated and real life projects. Similarly, the distinctions between university and non-university business studies, for example in Belgium (Flemish Community) or Denmark, become more difficult to discern.

There are various policy positions, from diversification by sector or institutional types to a differentiation of purposes and functions within the same type of dominant institution. One key conclusion, however, is that a strong political will is needed at all levels to maintain the required diversity of cultures and forms of education and to strengthen articulation, cross-crediting and so on. The real issue is not so much rigour in distinguishing types of programmes, institutions and sectors but how best to meet the widely ranging needs of students for different levels and kinds of tertiary education. The question is profoundly disturbing given the efforts that continue to be made to sustain distinctive structures which often owe more to history than to present need. To place the student at the centre of the analysis and to ask what is required to meet students' needs and expectations and, by extension, those of the society, is to approach the matters of demand, structure and provision from a rather different standpoint than has frequently been presented hitherto.

Structures, once designed for the search of knowledge and teaching an elite or highly-selected cohorts of students, are now receiving a high proportion of each generation. Are the students having to fit these moulds or can systems, whether unitary, binary or multi-sectoral, comprehensively and differentially meet the diverse needs of the very large waves of students and of our changing societies? There may be many options, but two stand out: to pursue more thoroughgoing policies of institutional diversification or to seek greater differentiation within a reconstructed or new kind of university or college. The move towards unitary systems in some countries might indicate a preference for the latter but there are significant countervailing forces. For example, the research drive and the standardising effects of technology and of internationalisation, all potentially beneficial, can detract from a differentiation of the curriculum and of pedagogy.

Policies of diversification, when resulting in different sectors with different missions, have another kind of problem with students who, in periods of difficult access to what they regard as good jobs, seek to improve their position by transferring to an institution in another sector or simply prolonging their studies. But while some students, whether younger or older, are forced into these choices and moves, others are not. There are those who seek to improve employability by mixing programmes, for example through double qualifications regardless of sector. Their aspirations might be better met if systems were to find ways of facilitating these moves and seeking greater efficiencies.

4

CHANGING EDUCATIONAL VALUES AND NEW DIRECTIONS OF POLICY

There is little argument about the strategic importance of tertiary education in contemporary society. This does not mean that there is agreement over the distribution of resources as between pre-school, primary, secondary, tertiary and continuing education or the balance between teaching and research or between the undergraduate and post-graduate stages. Different administrations, different interests and different revenue sources complicate the efforts needed to bring all this together in a coherent policy of lifelong learning (OECD, 1996b). For the first years, once questions are raised about the kinds of policies and reforms that are needed, important differences of view arise reflecting differences of value, purpose and interest. These differences, evident in the country visits and in the contemporary analytical and policy literature, have a background in the several traditions, philosophies and theories that inform current expectations, thinking and practice. If not a bedrock, these provide a backcloth for policy directions and discourse.

The critical intellectual tradition, highly valued in the older universities in the European tradition, stresses reason, proof, evidence and unfettered inquiry structured by the concepts and methods of knowledge disciplines, with social relevance and application as only secondary considerations. Students are to be inducted into these values and pursuits. Overlaying this is the tradition of high professional standards – of knowledge, competence, ethics and service to society embodied in long and demanding courses, *e.g.* in medicine, law, engineering, theology and preparation for high-level public service jobs. Students are to become responsible professionals performing essential roles in society. The United States land grant and the British civic universities in the late 19th and 20th centuries in extending this ideal have drawn much closer to the everyday working life of society and the economy, broadening the range of courses and widening access. Students are to service the modern society and the economy. Finally, the institutions in the tra-dition of vocation-specific preparation and technical education, treating the needs of industry and commerce as of primary importance, set out to provide a very wide and diverse array of programmes and courses which are usually designed and delivered in close partnership with the employment sector.

I. TWO KINDS OF POLICY DISCOURSE: UTILITY IN THE MARKET PLACE AND THE ADVANCEMENT OF KNOWLEDGE

The above schematisation of traditions of study and value orientations is merely suggestive. In each of the separately identified strands, there are corresponding theories, exponents, critics and rationales. But while there is a broad correspondence of programmes and institutions, in reality these schematisations are intermingled. Reviewers heard the virtues of scholastic theologian Bernard Lonergan extolled in curriculum discussion in a large technological institution in Australia and the value of university students spending time in community-based learning projects praised in prestigious academic institutions in Virginia and Sheffield. Students everywhere are being taught the importance of evidence, of formulating and testing hypotheses about the interrelationships of theory and practice. Does this imply a mushy melange of ideas, values and traditions, or a naive eclecticism in institutional policy-making? Although historically distinct traditions and values are increasingly intermingled in institutional practice and brought together in policy formulations, it is not to be expected that in pluralistic democracies such distinctions will be dissolved and their supporting interest groups merged. All can agree that tertiary education should or is able to provide such common benefits to society as (Taylor, 1996):

- a more informed and responsive electorate
- cultural tolerance and understanding
- progress in social justice
- an improvement in the overall quality of life

– a self-reliant, innovative and competent workforce.

But these can be the products or consequence of different policies, with different orientations.

Diverse, sometimes conflicting, viewpoints about the orientations and directions of policy for the first years of tertiary education emerged in the country visits and feature in the contemporary literature. The basic and very general orientation in all countries is that of public authorities interpreting society's interests in a broad and balanced way, systematically addressing demand and treating tertiary education as an investment in the future. Two other positions were also frequently advanced. The first, held by many academics, is that tertiary education, based on the disciplines of knowledge, ideally requires a measure of distance, a kind of separation even from other mainstreams (sometimes termed "the mainstream") of society. This gives rise to claims about a quite distinctive, sometimes an essentialist mission which distinguishes universities in particular from other kinds of institutions but touches some others as well. The two key concepts are research-based teaching, or teaching in a research environment and institutional autonomy often linked with intellectual freedom. Hence the purpose of the institution is the pursuit, advancement and diffusion of knowledge respecting its disciplinary structures. The second view is that tertiary education needs to become much more responsive to and related with "the market", to introduce modern management practices many of them pioneered in business, to lay greater emphasis on immediately useful or applicable knowledge and to construct its mission, organisation, curriculum and pedagogy accordingly.

The differences are not simply those between older universities and newer ones, between the university and the non-university sectors. Indeed, these two orientations coexist certainly within the university sector and to some extent across all of tertiary education, and within single institutions.

As presented, they are often seen to be mutually exclusive; their proponents tend to use them as weapons of criticism, one against the other, and in relationship to directions of public policy. In Australia and New Zealand, for example, some of our university-based interlocutors were highly critical of "instrumentalism", taken in their view to an extreme in some elements of government policy. There is also, in the United Kingdom, for example, a strong line of student and teaching staff criticism of policies that suggests institutions are behaving too much like commercial enterprises, in their senior staffing arrangements and income earning – the sale of full-cost places to overseas students for instance. By contrast, in the United Kingdom and several other countries, from the viewpoint of representatives of business, the tertiary institutions were, notwithstanding the innumerable changes in recent years, seen as in need of still further market-type rigour, particularly in matters of cost containment, overall institutional management and the sale of services.

It would be a mistake to suppose that there is a neat line separating business critics and academic reactors, with governments in the uneasy and thankless role of mediating these and other interests. The defence of what might be termed classical liberal values of higher education also comes from business groups like the European Round Table of Industrialists, the Japanese Employers Confederation and joint bodies such as the British Council for Industry and Higher Education. Managerial values and responsiveness to market opportunities and demand are advocated and now well established not only in the heart of many university and college administrations, but in the academic boards and programme committees and not only those responsible for directly vocational courses. In the arenas of debate and policy-making, fundamental ideas about direction, purpose and value are, in one of the favourite New Zealand words, "contestable".

The dichotomy is arguably a false one, since there are institutions and system structures that successfully integrate the divergent views. This was evident to the review teams in visits and many examples of convergence could be given, from regional colleges in Norway, to university colleges in Sweden, to German *Fachhochschulen*, to the new universities in France, to state universities in Virginia and Australia. Just what successful integration means, however, is itself debated and it would be idle to pretend that all differences have been harmoniously reconciled. If indeed the objective is consensual policies, it is necessary, first, to pursue the differences a little further so that instead of an uneasy and unstable compromise, more solidly integrated policies can take root.

The "instrumental" approach treats the student as a consumer or customer who has wants and needs that service providers compete in seeking to satisfy. They can be defined in the form of competences or skills whose possession is certified in degrees or diplomas; they are varied but most often converge on employment opportunities in the labour market.

The consumer wants marketable skills and expects to acquire them with a minimum of effort, cost and time. Employers concur and policy-makers respond. Society needs its members educated to a high standard of occupational competence and citizenship. The institution or other provider makes bids to the funder to provide the programmes that lead to the qualification in ways that meet these expectations and yield positive returns. For the not-for-profit institution, returns for effort after costs have been met may consist of recognition and prestige, increased influence in the community and continuing support from government or funding agencies with opportunities for further expansion and growth. Many universities, whether public or private, in Australia, New Zealand, the United Kingdom and the United States, increasingly fit this entrepreneurial model. Others have usually not moved quite so far but the policy discourse in all countries is moving steadily in this direction, Denmark being a particularly good example. Where institutions are private and "for profit" they will expect trading returns on outlays in the same way as any other business enterprise. Whether public or private, in all countries and all institutions, there is evidence that some version of this instrumental model is beginning to take hold, even if often only a foothold.

Effective functioning of tertiary education markets in the market economies of the OECD is increasingly seen to depend on a number of interrelated factors, conspicuous among which are availability of a range of service providers, the consumers' ability to make well informed choices about the suitability and attractiveness of the services and to switch allegiance if need be, and the readiness of providers to tailor their service to client wants and to market them vigorously. Institutional providers (there are others such as the so-called "corporate quality universities" in the United States which are in effect the educational and training division or programmes of large private corporations) develop styles of decision-taking and management that are flexible, speedy in operation and designed to maximise the saleability of the service. Primary values include customer satisfaction, a good match between the labour market and courses and qualifications on offer, and efficient and cost effective delivery of service. As already mentioned, that service includes a growing interest in programmes either domestic or across national borders for fee-paying students from other countries. In these ways, education becomes a tradable commodity, a situation clearly exemplified in many private universities and colleges notably in Japan, Portugal and the United States but in some measure in all of the countries participating in this review. Germany, for example, would like to increase its "trade" and authorities there commented on the disfunctionality of very long study programmes whose costs and demands are unattractive to foreign students. In Australia, New Zealand and the United Kingdom, there is now explicit emphasis in public tertiary education policy on the market concept. This is quite noticeable in the recruitment of fee-paying overseas students, described in Australian trade reports as a significant export earner.

So much for the instrumental orientation or function, aspects of which are taken up again later in the discussion of costs and financing. The classical liberal position adopts a strategy whose starting point is neither economic or social utility, nor the student as consumer, nor the institution as service provider; it is, rather, the academic community's mission of knowledge creating and disseminating. This academic community is sometimes quite elevated: in the words of the historian of the Sorbonne, André Tuilier, "a conscience that poses all problems of knowledge and cannot be separated from its environment" (Tuilier, 1996). It is thus a civic conscience with moral obligations. Scholars and students – not suppliers and customers – make up the academic community so defined. The conceptual framework and language are not that of clients, service-providers, contractual obligations, management, efficiency, competence and skills and so forth but the qualities of the educated person, the self-governing or collegiate body of scholars, academic discourse and interchange, and the endless quest for knowledge and understanding. Using the old Oxbridge terminology, the student "reads" for a degree rather than is taught. Knowledge is structured through disciplines whose individual and distinctive characteristics provide the intellectual rationale for the subject-based curriculum and the departmental or faculty structure of the institution. Detachment from, rather than intimate engagement with, the world of commerce, industry, the professions, the schools and the government service is necessary to provide the right conditions for reflective, analytical, objective research, study and learning and, indeed, to provide a deeper level of service than meeting immediate wants and needs. Researchers and scholars, not public policy-makers, set the framework for inquiry since they alone have the requisite understanding and skills. Although active relations are maintained with other social sectors and institutions, they are on a basis of mutual respect. When there are contracts and regulations, their object is not merely regulatory; they protect the rights and freedom of the academics and preserve institut ional autonomy. Funding, from government or private sponsors, may be specified in considerable detail, but is nevertheless in a form that respects the academic traditions – the exceptions being periods of major political crisis or serious financial difficulties.

Often referred to as the Humboldtian tradition, in acknowledgement of Wilhelm von Humboldt's role in founding the University of Berlin early in the 19th century, or as liberal education in the manner proposed by John Henry Newman in 19th century England and Ireland, some form or other of the idealised classical liberal view became widespread not only in the several major European systems but throughout the English-speaking world well into the 20th century. It has had many notable exponents in this century from Ortega y Gasset in Spain to Robert Hutchins in the United States and has left a powerful legacy which continues to inform public policy, institutional and academic self-images and the practice of a great deal of tertiary education, not only in universities. Perhaps, of the institutions visited, the United States college of liberal arts and science is the best exemplar today. The ideal can be criticised as a kind or a form of nostalgia against which much contemporary policy and practices are judged and found wanting. The classical liberal view promoted a way of civilised life if only for a minority; it did not preclude education for the professions within the universities. Moreover, it was content to coexist with much more utilitarian orientations in the non-university sector; each had its place. What matters is that an ideal, an enduring type was established and used as a mean of judging actual practices.

This is not the place to enter a debate which, as already indicated, can all too easily give rise to false or misleading dichotomies, especially of the "theory" versus practice type. It is only necessary to point to the many different forms of knowledge and ways of advancing them. The classical ideal carries some of the connotations of the knowledge of the scribe and the supreme position he ("he" almost always) has occupied by virtue of his command of written language and mathematical calculation since the days of the ancient Sumerian kingdoms. The value of the many other kinds of knowledge now claim equal recognition. Is there, then, a basis on which these divergent traditions and viewpoints can

be reconciled in system policies? Need the functions of knowledge advancement, practical utility and sale of services be seen as contradictory or are there not demonstrations of their successful integration in institutional missions and practices?

2. TOWARDS CONVERGENCE?

The question that arose in every country is how far these divergent, sometimes contradictory positions so well articulated in debates, in the literature, individually or collectively inform policy and practice for example within the university in unitary, binary or multi-layered systems. We encountered stern critics of "instrumentalism" and equally stern critics of the aloofness of institutions. There are those who hope that the "market" is but a passing phenomenon in public policy, its impact to be constrained or subdued in time as more deeply seated traditions and beliefs reassert themselves. There are others who wish to see public policy take a more "instrumental" turn. Can public policy, purporting to reflect the wider interests of the community, while drawing on the critics' fire, succeed in taking the best from these ideal types, each with its vigorous exponents?

The challenge to countries, not just governments, is to formulate and implement policies that at best produce a resolution of these complex issues, including a new forward-looking synthesis, drawing constructively on the diverse interests. To be worthwhile, such a synthesis should operate on several levels, from that of fundamental purposes, missions and functions for analysis, to that of the many specific but chronic problems such as queues for entry to courses or deflected student choices, student financial hardship, attrition and failure rates or the prevalence of outdated laboratory and workshop equipment. There is need to pick up relevant features of the orientations and functions discussed above, putting them into a new or at least fresh policy orientation. That orientation, in all of the countries taking part in this review, would be most likely to arise not from a backward look at competing images of tertiary education but from the dynamics of society itself. Specifically it is the central argument of this report that the focus of policy, whether system-wide or institution-specific, should turn more towards analyses of the needs, interests and expectations of the clients and stakeholders and that the means by which institutions conduct their affairs should reflect this turn. The emerging consensus, undercutting conflicting images, is that highly-structured, formal and informal education is becoming or has already become the principal means of extending opportunity and the main engine or dynamo of sustained growth for individuals and society. This growth has several dimensions: economic, obviously, in view of the high intensity of new forms of knowledge and technology in industry, the professions and the service occupations, but equally socio-cultural and personal. It is a commonplace that societies and cultures are changing rapidly; less often remarked is that there is an underlying belief, still, in development and progress: change is believed – or hoped – to be on the upward incline of progress. Personal development is the acceptable face of individual ambition and striving to succeed even at the expense of others. To formal education is attributed the capacity to enable economies, societies, cultures and individuals to better themselves, to foster and sustain such social values as equity and cultural goals like the harmonious multicultural society and moral improvement.

Public policy has a major role to play in developing attractive scenarios and mobilising the enormous capabilities and constructive energies dispersed throughout the tertiary education system. In national or state policy documents, mission and strategy documents issued by individual institutions, and in the numerous dialogues between the reviewers and their many and varied interlocutors, what is striking is consistency across countries, types of institutions, staff and students, professional bodies and employers and unions in the view that the targets are growth – personal, social, economic, cultural. This cuts across if it does not fully reconcile the divergent viewpoints discussed above. Certainly there are differences of emphasis: finance and industry and employment department officials tend to focus more on economic goals, costs and efficiency issues for the system as a whole; academic deans, vice-presidents, deputy vice-chancellors and deputy rectors (academic/research), while very conscious of financial issues, tend to draw attention to the broader educational values, principles of academic life and objectives in their own institutional strategy plans. Teachers are worried about increases in student numbers, inadequate facilities and the growth of administrative chores. Students and families seek an entrée to employment and are increasingly concerned about costs including the often very large debts being accumulated as expenses are cushioned through loans. Students' organisations, however, are among the most vigorous proponents

of a broad philosophy of tertiary education. They see themselves as clients, but also as partners in progress.

There seems to be at least the following converging (and very demanding) viewpoints among the several major actors in the policy dialogue:

– The tertiary system has to change comprehensively: to accommodate large or increasing numbers of "first years" students, to address the expectations of its clients, to achieve reasonable economies, to increase efficiency and to continue the quest for high or better standards of teaching, learning, research and community service for all students, not the favoured few.

– Education in the "first years" can and should be responsive to economic and social change, student needs and public priorities; these priorities can best take the form not of detailed regulation but of strategic steering with the use of incentives and often indirect levers and with built-in monitoring and accountability procedures; such responsiveness need and should not entail the eschewing of the values and principles of free inquiry and the pursuit of curiosity-driven intellectual interests.

– Quite definite competences and skills are required for example to assist students in career entry or advancement; they can and need to be specified for the purposes of course design, teaching, learning, assessment and accreditation, but should be set in a broad framework of general education, variously defined, in which highly sophisticated knowledge structures continue to play a fundamental role.

– For students in the "first years" flexible forms of learning are emerging – in some instances are of very long-standing – but the principal providers are still the institutions, which themselves are increasingly developing more flexible learning opportunities and drawing on the new technologies.

– The collegial concept of decision-making in the institutions remains highly relevant and is necessary to ensure that responsibility is shared and that academic and professional decisions are academically and professionally informed, but "the college" includes students, non-academic staff and external representatives; inefficiencies and opaqueness of decision-making continue to need to be addressed.

- The introduction of a wide range of modern management and evaluation practices into those institutions not already familiar with them, not least in financial management, strategic institutional profiling and quality assurance, is needed in view of the scale and complexity of decision-making and the highly damaging consequences of errors, mistakes and inefficiencies; the requirements of transparency and accountability are the most frequently cited reasons.

- History notwithstanding, there need be no fundamental conflict between either so-called general/cultural education and vocational/professional education or between "collegial" and "managerial" styles of governance but considerable effort is required to develop new system-wide and institutional cultures that embody and interrelate these orientations.

While the foregoing is not of course exhaustive, it does indicate both widely agreed needs, irrespective of theoretical bearings, and converging directions of policy. The more detailed individual country notes prepared alongside this report draw attention to different emphases that naturally vary by country and to items which the reviewers, in close collaboration with country authorities, see as matters requiring further attention. In doing so, however, we and they have been mindful of national differences: the collegial tradition remains very strong in the university sector in Germany, Japan and in the United States liberal arts colleges; much greater emphasis in those countries is placed on labour market relations respectively in the *Fachhochschulen*, the special training schools, and the community colleges. In Australia, the United Kingdom and the United States, it would be difficult to say that modern management practices and labour market links are any less visible in one sector of tertiary education than another or less manifest than in many enterprises, private or public.

The argument over "useful" or "applicable" knowledge, often presented as a counterpoint in attacks on "irrelevant, self-indulgent" research topics or "useless theory", can be used to illustrate converging ideas not, as often affirmed, a strong divergence. Whether the knowledge developed, taught or acquired in and through tertiary institutions is "useful" can never be answered in general terms independent of context, participants and

potential users. The discoveries and constructions of 20th century nuclear physics, genetics, biochemistry and materials science have transformed modern industry and changed ways of life of whole populations. Yet the immediate use or possible application of these discoveries and intellectual constructions were mostly irrelevant to the inquiries being conducted and usually unknown to those making – or funding – them. Conversely, work on quite practical issues or industrial processes as developed to meet practical needs can be the source of theoretical puzzles and generate new lines of research. Researchers and teachers alone cannot be, indeed never claim to be, the sole determinants of topics for research and teaching; however, judgements about relevance and applicable knowledge certainly have to take account of their views.

This is not the place to embark upon a discussion of the uses in teaching of research findings and abstract theory; suffice to say that all and any knowledge has potential use, potential value. This does not simplify the issue of determining what research and which researcher to support, but it should induce caution in appraising what is taught, studied and analysed. With rapid knowledge growth including the dissolving of old disciplinary boundaries and the creation of whole new fields of inquiry and constant economic and social change, great care is needed in judging what is necessary, relevant, or not of any great value in teaching and learning. The relevant issue is whether or not the educational regimes are equipping students to acquire the intellectual apparatus and the habits of mind that turn them towards the uses they can and may make of knowledge and its applications, for which they have an ultimate responsibility. On this, the judgements of the market are of increasing importance as students express their preferences and evaluate their teachers and employers pick and choose. The market in tertiary education, however, includes the operations and mediations of classic kinds of knowledge and these, too, must be taken into account.

In all countries, a complex apparatus of political decision-taking and public policy-making relating to tertiary education is being built up where it does not already exist. New public policy instruments have been put in place or are planned and one of their tasks is to reconcile divergent, possibly conflicting values and interests. The State Council of Higher Education for Virginia is a very good example of the blending of representative government and professional expertise. The Higher Education Council in Australia, the German Conference of Ministers

CHANGING EDUCATIONAL VALUES AND NEW DIRECTIONS OF POLICY

for Education and Cultural Affairs and the other co-ordinating bodies, and the proposed Network Norway Council, all illustrate the value of and need for co-ordinating, consultative and advisory bodies. Where such bodies do not exist or have limited functions a heavier duty falls on ministries. In Denmark, for example, the need for a strengthening of monitoring and information gathering and the steering of funding at that level is recognised. The roles of a set of National Boards and specialised Councils as well as of the Ministry are evolving to meet these needs.

Many of the challenges to the institutions have already been identified in previous sections of this report. To them need to be added (or underlined) three broader, highly topical policy issues: devolution and decentralisation; partnership; and articulation of qualifications, institutional programmes, structures and learning pathways.

3. DEVOLUTION AND DECENTRALISATION

Devolution of authority and responsibility, and decentralisation of the agencies and processes of decision-making are trends which are more or less advanced and well accepted in all of the countries participating in the review. Not specific to tertiary education, they pervade modern society and seem to be popular with electorates. They relate partly to the perceived complexity and the inefficiencies of centralised decision-making by ministries and departments of state in very large systems, partly to changed fiscal and public financing conditions, partly to political views about individual or local freedom, choice and the virtues of "less government, more market" and, it seems, partly to what is fashionable and of the moment. A consequence for tertiary institutions is increased decision-making responsibility and the need for stronger management, including new procedures in institutional finance.

In the traditionally centralised Continental European systems and in Japan, institutions are welcoming devolution of authority and responsibility. Greater control over curriculum, personnel policy and financial management was welcomed by the institutions in Denmark. There have been very positive responses by the institutions in Sweden to the liberalisation reforms of the early 1990s; still more recently, those in Belgium (Flemish Community) and Portugal have achieved greater autonomy. In Norway, and in Flanders too, the extensive restructuring of the college sector is an added reason for

strengthening the management and decision-making capacity of those institutions. The reason for the centrifugal movement is not only the belief that local decision-making can cope with the exigencies of local situations and circumstance better than a regime of general rules from "head office". Devolved responsibility and increased authority are needed and, on the whole welcomed because they provide more space for local decision-taking and institutional management, in which institutions can not only stretch their entrepreneurial wings but also better exercise one of the classic liberal tenets, namely academic autonomy. However, there is an interesting convergence here between the classic liberal and the modern managerial philosophies: both agree that the locus of decision-making should be as close as possible to the immediate client. Students do not enrol in a system nor do they identify with national policies and programmes except when these policies appear to worsen their living and study conditions. Students' relationships are with particular programmes, departments and institutions, staff and, of course, one another. Staff, even when allowance is made for the very strong identification through research and scholarship with supra-institutional and often supra-national structures and organisations, tend to identify strongly with their departments and faculties.

The very local sense of identity of staff was well understood in Belgian (Flemish Community), Danish, Norwegian, Swedish and institutions which received the review teams. But not only those. In Australia, France, Germany, New Zealand, the United Kingdom and the United States many institutions, including large universities, now see their role as agents of regional development and this implies capacity to adjust their missions and use their resources flexibly.

Just as national level authorities are finding good reasons to devolve authority to the level of regional or local government structures and to individual institutions, so the institutions are carrying this process further by increasing the authority and responsibility of their sub-structures and units. What is intriguing is how, in this progressive shift of responsibility, it is possible to maintain coherence of policy whether at the level of the whole system or the individual institution. That balance is certainly needed if national priorities, including equity and increased participation levels, are to be met. The Nordic concept of steering, or autonomy within a national framework of policies and procedures, is one solution; another is the profiling procedures adopted in Australia, whereby institutions are steered in a process of negotiation over Commonwealth-funded student places, and the contracting process in Finland and France. The elements of steering by the national or state level agencies established to monitor and assess quality, and the direct and indirect mechanisms used to channel state funds are discussed below.

There are several cross-currents in the moves towards devolution. A greater concentration of decision-making in institutions is enabling them to relate their programmes more closely to the needs of students and to take into account the interests of other stakeholders. But more than devolution is required to achieve this. Policies which encourage or require wider partnerships, for example, may also be needed, a view advanced in some aspects of the new policy framework introduced by the New Zealand authorities. The exercise of financial responsibility requires a high degree of expertise, high standards of financial probity and new kinds of accounting procedures in the institutions. These are not always present. Greater responsibility for curriculum means more design and planning work by academic staff, yet staff numbers relative to students are being cut. There are also concerns, for example in Denmark, that central authorities need to reposition themselves so as not to lose the capacity to steer according to broad national policy objectives; in France, that local initiative can lead to programmes which duplicate existing provisions and impose additional obligations for public funding from the national budget; in Sweden, that institutions may adopt admission policies that, while they make sense at the institutional level, produce problems for the system as a whole. Devolution is not a panacea; it is but one element of a new, quite complex policy mix.

4. PARTNERSHIP

A further element in the complex of contemporary decision-taking and planning is the gathering momentum of partnerships within education and among education, industry and local community or regional bodies. This nexus is very well expressed for example in Norway and Sweden where, against a background of determined efforts at the regional level to sustain local communities and develop new economic structures, the institutions have joined with local/regional government and both long-established (fisheries) and sunrise (electronics, culture) industries in partnerships for teaching as well as

research and development. The contract policy framework in place in France explicitly requires just such links. In Australia, in the words of the country note, governments, industry and the professions "look to the universities not only to respond to their needs but to share creative and energetic leadership". In some countries, Belgium (Flemish Community), Germany, the United Kingdom for example, there is a complex set of public and quasi-public agencies which intersect with institutional decision-making. Belgium (Flemish Community) has a Flemish Education Council, a university council (representing universities), a recently established higher education council (representing colleges), philosophical or religious "networks" of institutions and a ministry; in addition there are various partnerships at the local level. Such structures, more or less elaborate, are common. Of increasing importance in all countries are the local partnerships of institutions with industry, in course design, planning and delivery. Impressive examples were noted in the United Kingdom and the United States where there are many programmes and projects aimed at fostering partnerships.

Just as devolution and decentralisation imply for central government bodies a vertical shift downward of responsibility and authority, so does partnership imply a horizontal shift whereby a new set of relationships is established, on a basis of shared interest in processes and outcomes of mutual benefit. Recent reports on the government-sponsored Enterprise in Higher Education schemes in the United Kingdom show just how extensive such partnerships have become. Reviewers were given first-hand accounts of local schemes in the North of England and in Virginia, and in the Minho region around Braga in the north of Portugal. The movement is developing rapidly in several countries and has extended well beyond the vocational sector.

Actors normally external to the institution are being brought in and the previously closed concept of collegiality is opened. This does not happen in all fields and, as may be expected, is most evident in those which have direct and obvious connections with industry and employment – the professional fields such as computing, nursing and health sciences, engineering, architecture, teaching, business studies, medicine and so on. There are, however, lessons to be learnt for the humanities and those social sciences, like anthropology or sociology, where professional links have not always been strong. As the Education Committee's activity on Higher Education and Employment showed, it is in such fields (but not only these) that employment has tended to be weaker and where partnership arrangements in system-wide and institutional policy-making and in study programmes have been less well developed. Arrangements whereby undergraduate students can include work experience in their degree programmes as in France, the U.K. and Virginia are a step in the right direction. The problem is much more acute in universities than in the vocationally-directed non-university institutions. Considerable progress is being made at the local and regional levels, although there are obvious disadvantages in piecemeal tinkering when the labour markets are national or international.

The partnership concept is an overarching one. For all fields of study and regardless of discipline, for all teachers and all students, there are fruitful avenues to explore if only the doors are opened. Partnerships have grown quite substantially in research, and new theories of knowledge creation and utilisation have been produced as a result of the boundary-crossing networks of researchers in tertiary institutions of different types, industry and free-standing research institutes (Gibbons *et al.*, 1994). Partnerships in tertiary education are a mixture of the quite sophisticated and advanced – in the professional fields – and the inchoate or sporadic in the others. There is no very good reason for this other than the direct links with employment in the former and the very indirect or undeveloped relationships in the latter. Students need exposure to employment opportunities, and experience of the world of work through partnership arrangements is a practical and well-tried means to provide it. Attitudes on all sides tend to be positive where there is open dialogue, good communication, a common set of interests and no partner is in a position to dictate outcomes or dominate the process. There is need, particularly in some areas of university education, to pursue avenues of co-operation more actively. These are likely to result in closer regard being paid by the institutions to skills for employment; no less important, they can assist employers to gain a better understanding of the competences of graduates and the uses to be made of them by enterprises.

5. ARTICULATION

Devolution and the growth of local arrangements including partnerships point towards greater variety and diversity of institutional decision-making and profiles. Students benefit from these but not if they lead to a disconnected system, each institution pursuing its mission independently of the others. There is an important issue of articulation. What this means, essentially, is the ways in which students may progress unimpeded from one sector, type or level of study, programme or institution to another that are clearly related to students' interests and needs. At the tertiary stage, such progression should not be assumed to be unidirectional. In Australia, for example, more university students and graduates are taking TAFE (technical and vocational) courses than *vice versa*; in New Zealand, students are taking the two concurrently. In Japan, the Sensho Gakko (special training schools) receive young university graduates sent by their employers and also enrol university students simultaneously in specially-developed programmes; in France, students from programmes offered in the vocationally-oriented short-cycle, *Instituts universitaires de technologie* (IUT) and *Sections de techniciens supérieurs*, often continue their studies at the second cycle in universities; in Germany, students travel both ways between universities and *Fachhochschulen*. However, students in several countries also make "involuntary" transfers, following failure in courses – arguably for their benefit, as they find other tertiary education programmes better suited to their interests and capacities.

Articulation is not a mechanical matter of formal recognition of qualifications, or of prior learning experience, necessary as these may be. It is also a learning concept, implying complementarity, continuous enhancement or development of competences, achievement and progression along a pathway that is personally meaningful and has social recognition and status. Articulation is necessary for several reasons in addition to the system variability that results from devolution and localism:

- learning is to be conceived as continuous and lifelong; learners need motivational reinforcement, to feel that they are progressing up "ladders" and not sliding down "snakes" or that learning is not a succession of discontinuous, unrelated events;

- students, particularly those of mature age, may be mobile; it cannot be assumed that a course or programme commenced at one location can be continued to completion at the same location;

- students who fail to meet the requirements of one institution or programme or whose interests change need to be able to move smoothly to another, with recognition of prior learning;

– institutions and their programmes need to be attentive to their complementarities as well as to avoid wasteful duplication of provision and the erection of arcane structures of regulations and rules;

– qualifications need to be transparent and portable, communicating in clear and consistent ways standards or levels of competence with a wide range of applications – across professions, economic sectors and regional, state and national boundaries;

– at present, due to a legacy of institution- or profession-based regulations and customs, there are too many restrictive practices in almost all countries regarding credit transfer and recognition of alternative modes of learning (for example, work experience); only thoroughgoing, system-wide, and transnational approaches will overcome them.

Consistency of practice and close institutional involvement are needed, but central control may not be the answer. Co-operation and a commonly used unit credit system for designating types and levels of courses work well in Virginia (United States). Barriers put up by institutions and professions, ministries, accrediting bodies and so on do not necessarily represent institutional inertia or sheer traditionalism. For effective credit transfer and recognition of what is, in every country, a multiplicity of formal qualifications (certificates, diplomas, degrees, etc.), a great deal of very detailed empirical work is required on just what is meant by the award of a qualification and the components that make it up. For this, some unit of comparison is needed. In Australia, over several years a national qualification framework has been constructed. It is a significant step in the direction of well-articulated levels and types of qualification. However, moves to establish an Australian Credit Transfer Agency foundered; institutions and faculties individually wish to retain control over intake and credit recognition. In New Zealand, a national qualifications framework is being put in place to establish competence levels independent of particular qualifications and institutions, to locate the requirements for all qualifications on the framework and to determine content-free units of credit which can be assembled according to different sets of rules for the award of qualifications. The universities, however, have resisted what they regard as unnecessary incursion into their procedures for attesting achievement and awarding degrees, and as an educationally unjustifiable

atomisation of the degree programmes. A compromise has been reached whereby whole degree programmes are recognised on the framework. This is one extreme, *i.e.* the capacity and determination of the individual university itself to determine standards and set requirements for the degree. The academic award of a degree or diploma does not always confer the right to practice a profession for which – in Australia and the United Kingdom for example – additional profession-set standards must be met. The Belgian (Flemish Community), Danish, German, Norwegian and Swedish systems also confer the prerogative to award degrees on the institutions, but with varying degrees of state surveillance and determination of broadly-defined requirements. The non-university systems are generally more tightly controlled, their awards usually being determined by state or system-wide agreements. However, the French approach which permits access to second-cycle university studies on the basis of any first-cycle diploma has had the unintended consequence of increased enrolment of those with the general *baccalauréat* in the vocational tertiary streams offered in *the Instituts universitaires de technologie* or *Sections de techniciens supérieurs* and widening the range of preparations of those subsequently embarking on second-cycle courses. It seems that in order to meet the need for articulation, clear, well-defined pathways and a functioning credit transfer system are needed in which the institutions across the different sectors and the professions play major roles but within a strong, uncluttered framework of national steering. No country has yet achieved this, although Scotland provides impressive examples of pathways from upper secondary through the further and into the higher education system; in the opinion of the review team visiting Virginia, overall articulation, especially credit transfer, is very advanced in that state.

Overall, the review teams concluded that, despite much progress and consciousness of needs, the articulation issue is unevenly and incompletely addressed. The different histories and traditions of sectors and institutions are a large part of the explanation: different administrative and financial arrangements, different approaches to decision-making, different system links, different categories of students. The lack of structures, including those for voluntary co-ordination, and of standard units of comparison reflect both history and the strong wish of institutions, in some countries, to set their own standards and control intakes and graduation. For students, however, when mobility is increasing and there is increasing need for individuals themselves to assemble personal portfolios of competences and qualification, there is clearly a need to strengthen articulation and clear away barriers, where they exist, to recognition and progression. Admittedly, this is not always straightforward: student mobility and the recognition of prior learning need to be reconciled with institutions' curricula and admissions procedures and there are resource issues. The devolution trend increases the onus on institutions to take decisions co-operatively, both within and across the separate sectors.

5

THE DESIGN AND DELIVERY OF THE CURRICULUM: TEACHING AND LEARNING

The curriculum is at the heart of the educational enterprise: the principal educational function of tertiary institutions individually or collectively is to design, plan, prepare and deliver the curriculum in ways that foster and support student learning. This remains true even allowing for the great diversity of routes and methods whereby students learn and teachers orchestrate conditions for learning. Experience of the curriculum is or should be the principal basis of student learning, and it is to that experience that the setting of standards and the analysis of quality are directed. Nevertheless, it has not been and could not have been the purpose of this review to attempt a comprehensive appraisal of curricula in tertiary education as designed, delivered and experienced. Such a task, even on a limited sample basis, would require the efforts of numerous teams of specialists in the huge array of disciplines and professional fields that, together, comprise the corpus of knowledge, skills, techniques, etc., in tertiary education. The magnitude of this task, far exceeding that required in either primary or secondary education, helps to explain why, in the national quality appraisals now so common, discipline and fields are usually reviewed not only individually but at infrequent intervals. We return to this point below. What we aim to make here are some observations on processes of decision-making, on overall frameworks or strategies that are being adopted, and on some of the crucial challenges being faced by students and teachers.

Responsibility for the curriculum and the processes of teaching at the tertiary level varies quite considerably both within and across countries. Whereas in many systems of primary, secondary and vocational education, curriculum is often prescribed at the national or state level, there is in tertiary education – the universities especially – a long and strong tradition of autonomy. This is not unconstrained. In Germany, among other continental European countries, there are state guidelines and requirements; in most, there is increasing consulta-tion and even very active partnerships, implying shared decision-taking, particularly in the professional disciplines. Architects and accountants, nurses, engineers and lawyers and many others through their professional bodies set requirements for professional practice, for example in Australia, New Zealand and the United Kingdom, which have a very definite impact on curriculum and teaching. In the United States, the regional accrediting bodies, in setting standards, have an influence on programme structure and organisation. However, there is for university programmes in many countries a tradition and a very clear sense that, whatever may be set forth in state regulations, contractual arrangements or the requirements of professional and accreditation bodies and whatever decisions may be shared through curriculum design teams, the final stamp of approval must come from or directly involve the institution itself. There is thus a complex interplay between institutional values and interests, accreditation procedures and state requirements. Devolution, now, implies leaving a greater role for the faculty board or committee (often strongest in continental European countries) or the university-wide academic board or senate (strongest in the English-speaking countries). The seal of approval for the award of the degree or diploma and approval of the course or programme and examinations require-ments naturally entail substantial academic judge-ment. This is an ancient, powerful prerogative which is jealously guarded; it provides the context for debates about relevance in the university.

In the non-university sector, the situation is often different. There are usually detailed state or employer requirements to meet and the role of the institution may be to deliver, not to design the cur-riculum. Nevertheless, a balance is commonly struck between system-wide prescription and local adapta-tion. The practice of a profession on a national basis and the partnership principle, combined with devo-lution, argue for a balance between externally-imposed requirements, locally-agreed arrangements and institutional dynamics. Through dialogue and consensus, at whatever level or type of institution, this balance needs to be struck. The growing convergence of the historically separate traditions of general and vocational education, while it does not of itself lessen outside control in the tertiary vocational sector, is leading to the restructuring of many programmes there. A related consideration is the regrouping of separate tertiary vocational streams, and the reduction in their numbers. The reduction of streams in the technological sector in Mexico from 55 to 19 illustrates a trend common to most if not all countries. Such trends, which reflect industrial restructuring and assist mobility, affect patterns of responsibility for decisions.

1. WHO IS IN CONTROL?

It is worth recalling that, for the universities in the European tradition – meaning all those encompassed by this review – the right to confer the degree and thereby to admit the graduate to the community of scholars and the learned professions was won only after the most bitter battles. In the Middle Ages, the battles were with the ecclesiastical authorities; in modern times, the clash of arms, when it occurs, is with the secular authorities. The growth of supra-national authorities, notably the European Union, brings in another dimension of control or significant influence. Current moves in Europe to achieve greater comparability of qualifications will certainly impact on institutions. Over time, the interest of the World Trade Organisation in cross-national professional recognition will also have an effect as the scope for international licensing of qualifications is investigated.

If there is pressure on curricula from the employment sector, there is also on the part of the students a growing realisation of their collective power as clients. This is obvious in those systems – Australia, Japan, New Zealand, the United States, and Portugal's private sector – where fees, fee increases, deferred charges and increasing loan repayment costs give a direct sense of proprietorship. However, nourished by the protest movements of the 1960s, in all countries student interest in the relevance and quality of curricula, teaching and the conditions affecting learning is evident if still uneven in its impact. The students are alert to the changing opportunities in the labour market. That significantly large numbers of them are of mature age and combining study with work makes them especially sensitive to the relevance of their

studies in economic terms and of the costs they are incurring in study. Due to the impact of the quality assurance movement and to the attention being paid by governments to reports on performance and general accountability, students are increasingly being encouraged or taking the initiative to provide evaluative feedback on courses. This, together with their interest in employment and the greater efforts being made by institutions to change and strengthen career and academic guidance, job placement procedures and internships (and the partnerships in course design, development and evaluation being entered into) means that there is mounting feedback from a wide variety of sources. From the student perspective, the curriculum is coming to resemble the substance of a contract, in which rights and obligations are specified as never before.

It would be a mistake to suppose that the student perspective on the curriculum is narrowly prescriptive or simply dictated by calculations of economic cost and benefit. The current UNESCO consultations with student organisations bring out a much wider range of interests and concerns. These students are uneasy over the diminution of a vision: the traditional model of the university as a community of scholars gathered together in the pursuit of truth and the common goal giving way to the "service station", "cafeteria" and "revolving door" models of higher education. In their reports, the students criticise continuing inequities (affecting women and minorities), the over-emphasis on the kind of commercialisation which instils individualism, materialism and competitiveness as the controlling values of society, and the "lack of depth" and of "wisdom" in the way specialisation has proceeded. However, the students are not arguing for lofty ideals detached from the needs of social and material life. On the contrary, a "holistic education" would develop capacities for critical thinking and moral judgement, a concern for justice and a sense of purpose and meaning, but also cross-cultural competences, the ability to access, analyse and review information, skills to undertake entrepreneurial projects, and competences for working life and successful careers in the global market economy (UNESCO, 1996). These students, in expressing such views, demonstrate a breadth of outlook and sense of purpose which need to be fully recognised in policy-making and the curriculum of the institutions. Their criticisms, which were echoed in the reviewers' country visits, include excessive reliance in teaching on impersonal lecturing and insufficient interaction with teachers. By contrast, in those institutions directly addressing these concerns, such as the smaller regional universities and medium-cycle institutions in Denmark, the university colleges in Sweden, the polytechnics and colleges of education in New Zealand, the liberal arts colleges and the highly-specialised proprietary "career" schools in Virginia and the polytechnics in Portugal, the students spoke very highly of the skills and attitudes of their teachers and of the care taken to produce highly-motivating learning-centred environments. Examples of this care were observed in all of the countries visited and were as apparent in off-campus programmes for adults as in initial induction programmes for secondary school-leavers. How far they are generalised to include all students is, however, another matter. Greater scope for the voice of students in the planning and delivery of courses by institutions and in the kind of consultation UNESCO has organised would draw in another dimension of partnership and broaden further the concept of control.

2. THE VALUE OF RESEARCH IN TEACHING

Even though the research function as such is not the subject of the review, mention has already been made of it earlier in this report and attention is now drawn to the interaction between research (R&D) and curriculum. The Humboldtian university tradition – intimately linking research, teaching and highly-concentrated study which from its Enlightenment origins has come to be widely recognised in most countries in the 20th century – has ensured a growing interaction between the research and education dimensions, however modified the earlier concepts are in today's practice. Of the many claims made for research in tertiary education, the least convincing one, however, is that all good teaching must be directly informed by current research undertaken by the teacher. This argument falls down empirically: even in the leading research universities not all the senior academics who teach are currently active in research. In at least one country, Sweden, much of the undergraduate teaching, even in the most research-oriented universities, is conducted by staff specifically appointed to teach, not to research, a practice which a government commission has now challenged. The Higher Education Funding Council of England and Wales, taking teaching and research as its principal criteria for funding, does not assume that all teaching in higher education or indeed in universities is or need be research-

based. Franchising or articulation agreements in Australia, the United Kingdom, United States, for example, are not predicated on research-based teaching. A subtly different point, which does carry conviction, is that a rich and varied research culture in the institution as a whole enhances teaching, and is valuable in eliciting student interest and motivation. Discussion in Sweden, the United Kingdom and several other countries brought forth examples including a three-way relationship: research, teaching, industry placement. The non-university sectors have sometimes been established on a "no research" basis. It does not at all follow that their teaching is inferior. Institutions in this sector, closely connected to industry and commerce, often now have a rich environment of consultancy arrangements and applications of research.

The policy intention to exclude research from designated non-research institutions seldom succeeds over time, but the reason for this is not that the staff see research as a necessary condition of good teaching. Rather, the issue is the status of research in tertiary education and the value that staff see in some kind of creative knowledge quest, whether "research" as traditionally understood or applied problem-solving, the latter included in what Ernest Boyer has termed "scholarship" (Boyer, 1990).

Although research issues were scarcely raised in the individual questionnaire to countries, they became quite conspicuous as the review proceeded. This subject deserves far more attention than is possible here but several points for further consideration arose in the country visits:

- all students, whether enrolled in university or non-university institutions would benefit from an active research and scholarly culture in which they participate both directly and indirectly, because research, broadly defined as structured, critical inquiry and its applications, provides the foundations for the acquisition and critique of knowledge; students' links with the research culture of the tertiary sector, as a whole and in its wider environment, are beneficial; all teachers should be *au fait* with current knowledge and major recent discoveries in their field;

- students readily identify with teaching informed by recent discoveries and fresh perspectives, and value a sense of being at the frontier;

- there are many different kinds of research and scholarship; the scientific paradigm is but one and it should not be treated as the sole benchmark; engagement in small group projects directed at solving practical problems is a valid way of introducing students to research conceived as structured, critical inquiry;

– a culture of research and scholarship implies not that all teachers are current, active researchers but that all understand and experience the ethos of critical, reflective inquiry and efforts to explore, construct and create knowledge;

– students need to understand that knowledge is not engraved on slabs of stone (or merely revealed in textbooks and lectures) but is the fruit of inquiry, that it is constructed and reconstructed through criticism, analysis and reflection and that being a student means being an active, reflective, critical inquirer;

– staff need the intellectual vitality, the refreshment, and the standard-setting associated with research and active scholarship.

Thus, the curriculum, teaching and learning should not be treated in isolation from research, nor were they in the review visits. Given the centrality of research, broadly defined, in the advancement of knowledge, and the heavy emphasis it receives in academic promotion and career advancement, notably (but not exclusively) in universities, it is indeed inevitable that research will be high among the factors shaping the curriculum. Students reflected positively on this, for example in United Kingdom and United States universities, paying tribute to their teachers for fostering a critical spirit, communicating their enthusiasm for their research and teaching methods of inquiry and data analysis. Other students, in New Zealand polytechnics for example, were appreciative of the ways in which staff build into their teaching the processes as well as the results of their consultancies and other links with industry.

It is not easy to judge how widespread are practices reported by particular groups in particular institutions or how well institutional goals are translated into daily practices. Certainly, review teams became aware of examples of teaching which appeared to be more routinely derived from second-hand experience and unlikely to foster a spirit of critical inquiry among students. To be a significant and positive force in education in the first years, research and scholarship need to be active and current, to be varied in context and method, to be widely diffused throughout institutions, to be equi-

tably supported by funding agencies rather than hard driven by rather narrow "national priorities", and to be of a kind where students themselves, as part of their studies, undertake projects and field work in which they assume some responsibility for formulating research questions, designing studies and evaluating results.

For the above reasons, the review teams were impressed by the many efforts being made to widen the access of students to research and to strengthen scholarship in the many different kinds of institutions visited. Whatever compromises occurred in practice and may be necessary, a distinguishing feature of tertiary education is the spread of the research culture traditionally associated with universities and often, even in them, confined to the postgraduate domain. Students do research and are exposed to research findings and procedures, so much so that it is not unreasonable to claim that research in some form or other is a defining principle, a means whereby the students' need for active, constructive, creative learning can be brought within the ambit of the ideal of the advancement of knowledge. We were therefore unsympathetic to the proposition advanced in some quarters that research combined with teaching should be reserved to institutions enrolling only students with the highest academic ability. This austere, exclusionist ideal seems to be based on a narrow and indeed unrealistic concept of research and it misses the potential benefit to all students of the research culture. The argument, from the perspective of high standards in national research policy, that resources should be concentrated in a small number of high-performing institutions, is another matter although the presumption that there may only be one particular type and style of research is open to debate. Obviously, there are different national needs to be balanced. Our point is that all students will benefit from research-informed teaching and that this cannot be achieved if rigid policies of concentration are adopted. Similarly, encouragement is needed for teachers to interrelate teaching and research rather than, as some studies have reported, to see them as competing priorities (Schuster, 1997). As Taylor (1996) notes in reviewing recent literature on the teaching-research relationships, the combined effect of national economic priorities, funding policies, institutional competition, career imperatives, and other forces leading to a concentration and specialisation of research "has been to weaken those tacit and informed forms of association among and between teachers and students that constitute the collegial ideal characteristic of elite higher education". The values in this elite ideal could be more widely diffused and overall tertiary education policies could profitably take this into closer consideration.

3. WHAT KINDS OF KNOWLEDGE?

It is not the purpose of this review nor would it have been within the competence of the review teams to address the kinds of questions raised by the single discipline evaluations which now play a major role in quality assurance. Our interest is necessarily of a different kind from the validity of particular kinds of disciplinary content, the question asked of students in assignments, tests and examinations and the specific learning resources at their disposal.

Putting these matters aside, issues of a somewhat different – but still related – character need to be addressed. The most pressing (if perennial) one is: what kinds of knowledge, what kinds of curriculum design and experience, what forms of teaching and what conditions for learning are needed and how are decisions on these matters taken?

How relevant, in an age of mass education, are curricula dominated by traditional disciplines separated from one another – or by the ambitions of particular professional groups? There is, of course, need for intensive work in single disciplines and professions. A separate question of particular interest is the place they do or might occupy in the all-round education of students in the first years of tertiary education. Many issues arise: some countries claim they have enough scientists and technologists, while others decry the lack of interest in these fields by students who seem not to care for the subjects or the professions they may lead to; engineers in several countries are unable to find engineering jobs; architects and builders look for work when the construction industry goes into decline; mathematics teachers are often in short supply, but there is a surfeit of primary school teachers – and so on. What do students need to know, to be able to do in a world characterised by rapidly changing needs and opportunities? Is the whole topic too large and diffuse, or are there general principles and curriculum designs that should inform specific decisions about what to teach – and learn – across the different disciplines and professional fields and with rapid change and uncertainty as a context? Prospective and current students make their own evaluations of what they need and find

useful, and these reflect a great variety of contingencies, personal as much as social and usually complex rather than simple. They combine courses and programmes, not always from the same institutions as the reviewers noted in Japan and Virginia, often in sequence, as in Australia, France, Germany, New Zealand and the United Kingdom.

Each discipline or professional field has its own criteria and procedures for determining what should be taught and these are often resistant to attempts to produce common courses and requirements for learning across disciplines. Attention to the interests and needs of clients might suggest a great variety of options among which students choose. There are many arrangements which encourage this, for example the New Zealand Qualifications Framework or the very wide array of programmes and course choices available in several different types of tertiary institutions in the United States. Rules govern the assembly of unit credits and requirements for awards, and these rules constitute a kind of generic curriculum framework which may be distinct from the rule sets imposed by individual departments or institutions which prescribe scope, combinations, sequences and so forth. Mapping provision, structure and pathways on this basis is an extraordinarily complex affair.

There is an immense field of activity as new courses are introduced and pre-existing ones discarded in the light of demand, whether by individual students at the institutional level, by professional bodies and employer groups or through national or state level priority setting and incentive schemes. Thus, in Australia in the 1980s and Japan in the 1990s, strong incentives were introduced to foster computer literacy; the academic upgrading of nursing and other health-related sciences in several countries, Australia and the United States for example, has meant more and more intensive studies in basic physical, social and human sciences and often a lengthening of courses to accommodate the additions; many other new subjects or areas of professional preparation have been introduced or transferred from one sector of tertiary education to another. New settings or combinations have arisen: languages combined with business studies; philosophy with environmental studies; mathematics with biology; computing with genetics, and with many other disciplines. There is indeed a constant shift in the disciplinary framework which is reflected in the patterns of course requirements and options pursued by students. These trends frequently entail more substantial and more systematic study of theoretical underpinnings and a wider purview of professional practice including, for example, professional ethics in business studies, nursing and teaching and the targeting of areas of professional practice for systematic, research-based analysis.

As already noted, the closer orientation of tertiary studies towards the workplace has meant that curricula have been modified to provide opportunities for work experience. A feature of the vocationally-defined sectors – for example the German *Fachhochschulen*, the former British Polytechnics, one-and-two-cycle colleges in Belgium (Flemish Community), IUTs in France and the former Australian Colleges of Advanced Education and Institutes of Technology, the American community colleges and, in several countries, the professional programmes in teaching, business studies, agriculture, etc. of the universities – is that work experience has been greatly expanded. The broader issue of education for competence has become more prominent across the whole spectrum of institutions and countries. Leading Japanese companies are beginning to seek evidence of this, and not only of success in secondary school examinations. There are many outstanding examples of efforts to broaden students' work experience which constitute part of the formal curriculum as is the case with United States co-op (co-operative learning) and internship programmes and with *stages* and vocationally-oriented study programmes in the French universities. These developments reflect an increasing awareness that curriculum designs must be more open to experience in the work environment, not confined to the classroom, laboratory, library or field station. Issues of how countries and institutions are structuring curricula in response to the tendencies either towards more diversity and free choice or more structures are taken up in the following section.

4. CURRICULUM DESIGNS AND STRUCTURES: MODULAR AND CORE

It would require far too much detail and would become tedious to attempt to document the great range of forces external and internal to the institutions that impinge on curriculum design. Research of this kind is needed, however; beyond single subject studies, there is relatively little analysis of tertiary curricula considered as the totality of structured learning experience of students and the goals, values and frameworks designed to articulate these experiences. Recent studies by Kogan and others in the United Kingdom and Scandinavian countries are promising in this regard (Henkel *et al.*, 1994).

In the countries reviewed, there is increasing attention to and interest in the links across disciplines and specifying overall requirements for study programmes leading to awards. The need for more strategic, institution-wide approaches is increasing as a result of the "pick and choose for convenience approach" students can adopt when confronted with an array of options, and of the increased institutional responsibility that follows on devolutionary policies. Constant growth of knowledge and changing employment needs result in new requirements to be met in curriculum design which cannot be adequately handled either by very slow moving or highly individualistic procedures for decision-making or the judgement of autonomous departments and faculties. Committees for general education programmes in Japan and the United States, the institution-wide undergraduate committees in Australia, New Zealand and the United Kingdom and the cross-faculty quality committees in Belgium (Flemish Community) are examples of institutional bodies drawing together a very wide range of subject disciplines and staff expertise. New directions in institution-level management would seem to foster more flexible, coherent and efficient responses, *e.g.* the "matrix" approach permitting institutional managers to "supply" appropriate teaching in specific subjects across a range of study programmes as noted by reviewers visiting newer regional universities in Belgium (Flemish Community) and Portugal. However, it is in the individual departments and faculties that these planning structures still appear to be strongest. In most countries, the reviewers suggested that there would be considerable benefit in strengthening institution-wide structures for the evaluation and design of first-years' curricula conceived as the overall framework for student-learning.

The information provided and the field work for the review disclosed many different ways of conceptualising and framing curricula. For purposes of analysis, they may be reduced to two basic types or ways, which respond to student preference and needs and provide some form of coherence external to the students' own conceptual mapping and learning preferences. As ways of analysing curricula structure and organisation, they apply equally to vocational/professional fields and to the academic structure of disciplines regardless of particular vocational uses. These two types are: *modular*, providing scope for many different combinations including optional or elective studies and *core*, setting forth a structure of required learnings usually in sequential form.

The advocacy of electives as part of the modernisation of the university curriculum by President Eliot of Harvard University towards the end of the 19th century was instrumental in breaking down the rigidities of the discipline-based curriculum in which practically all courses for the degree were required and set forth in lengthy sequences. The *modular* approach is not new. During the 20th century, the principle of student choice of subjects to be studied has been combined with new ways of organising subject matter, as pre-specified modules in which subject matter is presented in standard, relatively short, time blocks and levels (units), which are taught and at least to some extent assessed one by one. The qualification is awarded on the basis of an accumulation of these units. United States tertiary education has fully incorporated the unit/credit system: degrees are typically structured through course modules with an assigned credit value and formal qualifications are awarded on the basis of a specified number of credit points accumulated through successful performance in required and optional courses taken in specified time periods (semesters, trimesters, etc.). This confers a high degree of flexibility, facilitating new combinations, student choice and cross-crediting. It has also been criticised for atomisation of subject matter and undermining sequential learning. Australia, Japan New Zealand, and Sweden have developed comparable systems and it is being developed for first-year studies in France. Indeed, in most countries there is something resembling a modular system if the term module is taken to signify a curriculum block or sector taken over a specified time period (*e.g.* a semester in the United States or a year as in Flanders), used as a basis for assessment and cumulatively towards a formal qualification. Key features of the modular system, as it operates today for example in the new British universities and the New Zealand Qualifications Framework, are that:

- any kind of subject content can be built into modules, which have standardised dimensions;
- subject matter is reduced to uniform or comparable quanta, and rules or pathways indicate those combinations and sequences of modules which are acceptable for the award of a particular qualification;
- these pathways are numerous and often provide very wide scope for student choice, including choice over sequence of studies;

- student performance is usually assessed progressively, on completion of individual course modules, but this may also be combined with more programmatic, overview-type assessments;
- modules may be and usually are provided by institutions, but under the appropriate rule set, any learning experience in any setting can be given modular status.

Modular systems have as principal justifications flexibility and adaptability to changing needs and priorities. In principle, a very large array of combinations is possible and often in practice this is the reality.

There is, however, another approach to curriculum design in tertiary education which often has its own non-modular structure although it can also be developed through strong sets of rules applied to modular systems. It is based on the concept of holistic education through an essential *core* of knowledge and competence from which a substantial body of compulsory courses is derived and study sequences are set. In Germany and other Continental European countries, professional programmes have a large core with limited scope for elective student choice and broken learning sequences. The core may consist of knowledge or competences drawn from any domain. Thus, there is normally in professional degrees a core of, say, engineering or medical or accounting knowledge. That core may also, as in Japan, include a required general education component to ensure that specialised study provides a rounded education. There can be cores within cores; thus these professional degrees typically include a core of basic sciences, physical or social, and within each of the specialisms, *e.g.* electrical engineering, a further core is defined and compulsory courses are built around it. But we need not enter into these details. The key point is that judgements about combinations and sequences are made for, not by, the learner and that the resulting curricula have a high degree of internal consistency governed by principles or criteria of the required organisation and structure of knowledge.

Such cores are of a technical nature. They reflect received views about what a technically-educated person needs to know both as a general practitioner in the field and as a specialist within it. In the domain of professional education, they are of considerable importance as a means of controlled development. The core concept has another related set of meanings which derive from the tradition of liberal education discussed above. Theories of human development and social and cultural competence rather than professional expertise provide the basis of a tradition that is today, among all the countries visited, most visible and vigorously alive in the United States. As we observed in Virginia, a core of liberal studies for all students in college or university, regardless of discipline or future career, is a requirement. In the United Kingdom, forms of general education are also provided, for example through courses which are based on generic skills or cross-disciplinary concepts or modes of inquiry to which attention is increasingly drawn in both goal statements and quality appraisal reports. The efforts of the Higher Education Quality Council to define "graduateness" as an overarching set of qualities or generic competences point in this direction. To the extent that these are or were to become a feature or required part of the study programmes of all students, they constitute a core curriculum. But in none of these is there the same persistence of the view found in the United States that there are not only cross-curricular competences but also subject content in the sciences, social sciences and humanities which all students should continue to study, regardless of their disciplinary or professional specialisation as a required, quite explicit and substantial part of their undergraduate programme.

An important difference between the United States and practically all other systems is the postponement of professional specialisation to the next stage beyond the first-years, certainly beyond the first two years of an initial qualification. Japan, which in the period following the Second World War remodelled its education system along the United States lines, appears recently to have softened the requirement of a core of general education in the first two years of the degree. From having been relatively integrated requirements within the first two years of the undergraduate programme, general education courses there can now be dispersed across the whole four-year period of the degree. The intention of policy-makers was a shift of responsibility for curricular matters to the institutions, a shift that has resulted in some institutions weakening their commitment. Several senior academics voiced their concern to the reviewers over these possibilities, yet the aim of tertiary education policy in Japan remains the improvement, not the dissolution, of general education for undergraduates and some very interesting examples were observed. In Virginia's colleges and universities, the general education core is not taken for granted. There is today a wave of reviews as programmes are being recon-structed and revitalised with greater attention than hitherto to rigorous interdisciplinary courses and team teaching and to improving communication skills both oral and written. Requirements for study of mathematics and modern foreign languages are being stiffened. These changes have a dual focus: first, across the whole undergraduate programme and therefore falling evenly on all individual disciplines in which students major (writing as a task for science students, computing for a history major) and second, as a feature of the remaking of the required general education programme for which there may be a structure or division separate from the major disciplines. Although each institution is going about this in its own way, the revitalisation movement is part of a long-running nation-wide debate about liberal education.

While this is the case in Virginian universities and four-year colleges, the situation is, however, not so clear cut in the community colleges where the internal structures do not make such direct provision for a core general education programme. Even there, however, the idea that general education should continue for all students beyond the secondary school into tertiary education is still current. If there is a gap, it is in the so-called career or proprietary (private, profit-making) schools. These highly-specialised establishments offer short courses as direct preparation for jobs, comparable in that respect to the short-cycle (one- or two-year) programmes in the vocational schools in Continental European countries. The degree of specialisation in these institutions contributes to their success in placing graduates on the labour market. Nevertheless, an issue raised by the review team in Virginia is whether a broader range of competences and general education combined with subject specialisation has better potential for longer-term success on the labour market, including job mobility, or whether the shorter more specialised courses perhaps followed some years later by another specialised course has more lasting value. Students who were interviewed were, however, uniformly favourable towards the high degree of specialisation for its immediate practical utility. Their views may be compared with the university students who participated in the UNESCO study discussed above. The issue is broader: the advocates of general education do not confine their arguments to labour market success; they treat education as both part of and preparation for life with many potential benefits both individual and social and for the longer as well as the short term.

The case for a core of general education is not restricted to the university sector but very little was heard about it in the non-university institutions where professional and technical specialisation is the dominant interest of students, employers and the institutions. As already mentioned, there are vestiges of general or liberal education in several countries and, often, a required, common set of subjects, *e.g.* language and mathematics.

Some critics of the notion that there should be a substantial core of general education studies for all students claim that its continuance at all in the tertiary sector demonstrates the inadequacies of secondary education. The Continental European tradition, for its part, assumes that, a broad general education having been provided in primary and secondary schools, students at the tertiary level should embark directly on specialised disciplinary and professional studies. This tradition, however, is having to come to terms with the highly variable attainments of secondary school-leavers. Critics of a core of general education for all are also troubled by what they see as the danger of superficiality and the risk of student indifference or hostility. These are among the considerations that led the Japanese authorities to relax their requirements. In Virginia, by contrast, the movement has been to modernise and strengthen the core of general education and to make it more stimulating for students. This is in reaction to concerns which have had widespread publicity about cultural illiteracy and the steady reduction over the years of the breadth and "common core" of the general education as actually experienced by American students in their degree programmes.

In Australia, very few universities have in recent years aimed to include a required core of general education for all students but one that we visited, originally a university of technology, has continued its early commitment. There are moves in other countries, mainly as a reaction to over-specialisation, but also to student failure, to broaden the base of first-year studies (as is now under discussion in France and Portugal). In the United Kingdom, another approach has been taken. With some exceptions, a core in general education has not been a requirement in universities and polytechnics, although in the further education sector there is a tradition of liberal studies as a required part of vocational preparation, and Scottish degrees have been more broadly based than English ones. As mentioned above, an arm of the universities, the Higher Education Quality Council, in part building on the core skills/core competence movement that has been a feature of the attempted reform of vocational preparation, has explored the concept of "graduateness". What are the distinguishing features of graduates: their generic skills and basic knowledge? Can a composite be created, whereby a "graduate standard" might be defined as one of the criteria for assessing the quality of teaching and learning? This work is still proceeding. Together with the formulation of the desired qualities of graduates and of generic learning outcomes which are to be found in sectoral and institutional mission and strategy documents, these are promising if as yet incomplete and controversial efforts.

Altogether, the mixture across countries of reform measures to improve general education, scepticism about its value, and the specialised professional programmes reflects widely divergent views about the purpose and nature of tertiary education. Among the many unresolved issues is whether a more holistic approach to the undergraduate curriculum, incorporating a core of multi- or cross-disciplinary studies, is preferable to the increasingly popular "cafeteria" approach. As noted above, international students' organisations (including highly-specialised professional fields) participating in the UNESCO consultation favour more holistic studies with a strong emphasis on values and socio-cultural issues. To put the matter more precisely, should curricula be built around a substantial body of required studies, defined as a core either within one or more disciplines or as a general education, or should there be student choice from a wide range of modularised offerings? Beyond this question is the background of world-wide communication networks, whereby computer-competent students can access information and knowledge as a supplement or alternative to the specifications of the institution in which they are enrolled. This access will increasingly yield a multiplicity of informal curricula and diverse learning experiences. Technology thereby becomes the handmaiden of choice and diversity; but it leaves unresolved the issue of curriculum coherence.

In all of the country notes prepared as part of this review, examples are given of initiatives which are being taken to reform the curriculum for the first-years of tertiary education. Their range is quite extensive, evidence that curriculum reform is high on the agenda everywhere:

- whole new degree programmes or components are being constructed, for example general sciences and general education in

Virginia, and new subject combinations introduced;

- new components or dimensions are being added, *e.g.* internationalisation, information technology, communication skills in Australia and Belgium (Flemish Community);
- short- and medium-cycle vocational programmes are combining and regrouping vocation-specific programmes in Denmark and Germany;
- opportunities exist for combining degree and specific vocational qualifications in France, Germany, Japan, New Zealand, United States, either concurrently or consecutively;
- business and employment bodies and government departments in Australia, Sweden and the United Kingdom are liaising with institutions to achieve a sharper curriculum focus on the changing realities of social and economic life, second language proficiency and effectiveness in communication;
- project-based curricula in combined science have been developed in Denmark and the United States;
- several leading Japanese universities, public and private, are reconstructing their general education programmes;
- in the relatively new fields of study in Swedish tertiary education – telecommunications and hotel and restaurant service – course planning is jointly conducted by academics, industry representatives and students; in New Zealand, aspects of course planning in courses offered through polytechnics are being influenced directly by the expectations and objectives set down by Industrial Training Organisations;
- in the United Kingdom independent study programmes to foster student initiative and inquiry are a well-established feature of several of the new universities;
- as institutions, in the United States for example, develop the scope and increase the accessibility of information sources and communication technologies, students are enabled and encouraged to make their own curriculum enrichments and extensions; in some French and Portuguese universities, student associations organise workshops and activities which foster the development of work-related skills and contacts.

These are among numerous and highly varied innovations in the design and development of curricula to meet new needs or readdress long-established ones. As for the overall frameworks of which they are part, whether clusters of modules or the longer, more predefined sequences of the core curriculum, there is no consensus and often no meeting of minds. Different interest groups, institutions and whole sectors go their own ways. A purely impressionistic judgement is that learning outcomes appear to be less dependent on overall structure than on the actual content taught or selected and learnt and on the uses students are able to make of it. The current debate does not really focus on structure, or even on content as such, but on relevance and quality: are institutions and systems providing opportunities to study courses that have social, economic and personal relevance and are these courses being taught and learnt to appropriate quality levels? These questions are central, for example, in the curriculum debate which is taking place even in such long-established professional fields as medicine and law. The answers being given are extremely diverse. There is a lively curriculum dialogue in many countries, fuelled by the introduction of quality appraisal procedures and in most countries by the greater involvement than hitherto of the professions and employers in educational decision-making and by the cross-disciplinary modes of research. The demand for a better educated workforce is having a profound effect, indirectly through student choices and motivations, and directly on the formal curriculum and on the services institutions provide: orientation to study, counselling, career guidance, mentors, work placement, etc. While government direction and oversighting of curriculum is becoming less direct and detailed, the involvement of other client and stakeholder interests is providing a melange of new insights and opportunities.

But it is not in all countries or all programmes and discipline fields that these debates or changes are occurring on any significant scale. The first-years curriculum has been the subject of several major reports and studies, perhaps the most comprehensive being those of the US Carnegie Commission on Higher Education and the Carnegie Council on Policy Studies in Higher Education in the 1970s. Sweden has a national council to advise on undergraduate curriculum issues; in France, the États Généraux de l'Université (a public consultation) and the National Evaluation Committee (CNE) identified problems in and possible reforms for teaching and learning in the first years; in the United Kingdom, the recent government inquiry into higher education has several relevant curriculum-related references. Nevertheless, a holistic approach to the undergraduate curriculum is very difficult to visualise given the very wide diversity of programmes, courses and electives; it is still not a central theme in policy discussions, nor does it always feature in institutions' strategic plans. This is due in part to the scope and complexity of the topic and in part to the reluctance of system policy-makers and institutional managers to enter the famous secret garden whose surrounding walls are made even more insurmountable or mysterious by virtue of specialisation which achieves its apogee in single-subject departments in universities and technical institutes. With some exceptions, as already noted, countries or institutions tend not to have overall statements of curriculum objectives and frameworks for tertiary education in the way they do for primary and secondary education. It is only the general education movement that has made serious inroads into this tradition, and that is because general education is itself a philosophy of the overall curriculum as distinct from a set of explanations for or justifications of what is being taught in separate subjects or fields. There does appear to be a need for more substantial analytic work to be initiated, in the context of mass participation, the critiques of secondary education outcomes and the evident difficulty large numbers of students are having in their studies.

5. A NEW FOCUS ON TEACHING AND LEARNING?

Some of the most important moves to open up the curriculum garden are rather indirect: first, the exposure of teaching – its quality, relevance and effectiveness – and, second, the quality assurance movement. That movement will be taken up in the next chapter, but of course it cannot be separated from a discussion of teaching and learning.

On the one hand, teaching has usually been even less transparent in tertiary education than the curriculum; on the other hand, the need for making it more visible, for evaluating its quality, for procedures to support and improve it and for recognising success and effectiveness, is gaining acceptance everywhere. The potential challenge of the new information and communication technologies to much conventional teaching and customary learning is enormous. Yet very few examples of significant innovation in the content and manner of teaching were encountered by the review teams. Theory in this domain is generally well ahead of practice. The

reviewers encountered several innovations – new interactive distance education programmes in Virginia; campus-wide networking embracing all students in a purpose-built private university campus in Japan; the Open Learning Agency in Australia which draws together distance education courses from a number of institutions and others. Nevertheless we were rather disappointed, in France and elsewhere, by the widespread rather mundane if not limited use of communication and information technologies. As a recent CERI report indicates, there are many exciting opportunities but very considerable efforts are needed to take advantage of them (CERI, 1996*b*).

The impetus for changing many established practices, centring on the lecture, the seminar, the demonstration, the tutorial and the field trip, arises from several considerations. The rapid and substantial growth in numbers; increased diversity of students of all ages; the particular requirements of part-time students and those unable – or unwilling – to receive campus-based instruction; the results of research and evaluation studies on effectiveness; the potential of the new information technologies: all combine to challenge many long established beliefs and practices in the field of teaching.

Calls are coming from various quarters, employers seeking more creativity, initiative and problem-solving ability in new graduates; the Japanese University Council regretting nation-wide weaknesses in teaching; German students, critical of didactic methods, calling for *"mehre Ehre der Lehrer* – more honour, more valuing of teaching"*. Sometimes, the sheer pressure of numbers, resulting in overcrowded lecture halls and unmanageable quantities of assignments to assess, has proved sufficient to stimulate the introduction of new methods. France, Germany, and New Zealand provide examples of student complaints about overcrowding and highly impersonal teaching but also the beginnings of creative and responsive ways to address the complaints while improving teaching and learning for all. Improvements in the physical environment on campuses in Virginia and in some institutions in the United Kindgom have encouraged part-time students to identify more closely with the institution and to broaden the concept of academic study.

Acceptance of the value of sensitively designed new buildings and equipment in fostering learning and positive attitudes towards study lies behind some highly imaginative projects visited by review teams – in Denmark, Japan, Sweden, the United Kingdom and the United States. A marked feature is the overall quality of design and materials, for example in the new libraries cum learning cum social centres. The combination of advanced technology with a welcoming ambience of the multi-purpose complexes, which are increasingly becoming the main centres of institutions, is impressive. In Norway, the combined forces of education and national and local government have resulted in a complex of multipurpose buildings for education, sporting, recreational and cultural activities in a small town which not one of the co-operating parties by itself could have produced.

In Australia, the United Kingdom and Virginia, major innovations in the design and delivery of curricula and in teaching have resulted from the development of distance learning, an "innovation" dating from no later than the first decade of this century and traced by some historians much further back. Some of the recent innovations, such as teletutorials and interactive telecasting, have brought about a much more direct and personal relationship between teacher and students – who are often part-time – than is possible in correspondence courses or in large lectures for full-time students on campus. Summer and weekend schools and other short, intensive periods of residence are very important. In principle, and on a rapidly growing global scale, high speed networks, full-motion video, flawless data transmission and impeccable audio are available. They are of undoubted significance given their potential for improving communication in both "real" and "virtual" time, reaching audiences worldwide, facilitating interactive learning and enabling students increasingly to structure their own curricula and modes of learning. But the difficulty of restructuring education to take advantage of these opportunities is very great indeed. It is not just the habits of a lifetime but the structures in which practice is embedded and the costs entailed which combine to explain what many have criticised as too slow and too uneven progress. The pedagogical potential of the new technologies is being explored in depth in some specialist centres but the results are not widespread in practice. There are public agencies and programmes, for example the Committee for Undergraduate Education in Sweden which influenced the establishment of the Committee for the Advancement of University Teaching in Australia, and in Denmark the Centre for Technology-Supported Teaching, which are designed and funded to foster innovation. Nevertheless, the reviewers frequently remarked on the rather limited and unimaginative uses being made of the new technologies. Very

interesting exceptions were observed in Australia, Japan, Virginia and elsewhere, but they are still exceptions. Systems with great technical potential are being built into institutions whose human capacity to make full use of them is quite uneven.

The transformation of tertiary teaching is of course not universally needed: excellent lectures, seminars, tutorials, demonstrations, laboratory exercises and field visits continue to take place and will still play highly important roles in the future as technology use increase. The issue is not particular methods, but rather the capacity to define and implement policies grounded in a critical and reflective approach to teaching. In the words of Gerhard Casper (1996), President of Stanford University, "no university in the world, not even the best, will be exempted from reviewing in a searching and comprehensive manner, department by department, the quality of its teaching programmes". Teaching is the chief, though not the only means of fostering student learning. It is the main, but not the only, component of the academic career. Yet recruitment to that career, in universities but not always in other tertiary sectors, is typically based on research and scholarship; promotion and recognition are mainly through research performance or success in institutional management; and academics are not usually, in their preparation for a teaching career, taught anything about teaching or curriculum design and development. There is a clear need, especially but not only in the universities, which is now beginning to be widely recognised, to focus more on the enhancement of teaching and new designs for learning and on the selection, career development and reward system for the tertiary teaching profession.

The prestige and power achieved by research, including the highly advantageous position it has acquired in funding regimes, is no more than a reflection of its fundamental importance in technical, economic and social development. Consequently the research endeavour itself is often not well balanced, or at least is weighted not towards the advancement of knowledge per se but its potential industrial applications and uses in everyday life and the competitive advantages it is expected to confer on national economies or multi-national businesses. In its relation to teaching, research in tertiary education institutions can become a significant goal or preoccupation so absorbing as to complicate the teaching role and draw time and resources away from it. Research also has the potential to support and strengthen teaching as we have already pointed out. The importance of research in tertiary education is not in contention, but what does need review is the way in which priorities, balances and relationships are established within the institutions and across the whole sector. Too often these are occurring with insufficient attention to the requirements and needs of first-years teaching. But there are hopeful signs that the teaching function per se is being given closer attention and more support.

In several countries, Australia, Germany, New Zealand, the United Kingdom and among others, units have been established to assist teachers to evaluate their teaching and to carry out measures to improve or modify it when that seems to be needed. In Norway and Sweden, student evaluation of teaching is now an accepted part of institutional life and teachers are encouraged to engage students in discussing the results of their evaluations. This approach is also being introduced in Portugal. Such dialogue is probably of much greater value than tabulated report sheets, scaling and the like. In Australia, teaching featured strongly in the three-year programme of Commonwealth-funded national quality reviews; in addition, a programme of small grants to foster innovation in teaching has been in operation for several years (Committee for Advancement of University Teaching). There is a similar arrangement in Sweden through the National Agency for Higher Education and in Denmark through the recently-established small grants committee to support innovation in the use of technology, as already mentioned. In Belgium (Flemish Community), the need for wider adoption of new methods is acknowledged and there are good examples of innovative practice in many institutions, including induction courses for new staff.

Despite or perhaps because of such innovations, the challenges to further improve teaching have grown. But the infrastructure usually falls short of the need. The teaching development and support units neither exist in nor are accessible to all institutions, even where countries have them at all; where they are institution-based, it is unusual for them to draw in all, or a majority, of the teaching staff. There is need for more sophisticated methods of selecting and preparing teachers, including industry-based, part-time teachers. The introduction into some US Ph.D. programmes of experience-based courses in teaching is a recognition of the academic career path many doctoral students have in mind. Also in the United States, the national foundations, respectively for the sciences and the humanities, support designated university teaching chairs. As far as we are aware, this is not paralleled by similar schemes in other countries. Increasingly, institutions and systems require or provide, on an optional or sometimes compulsory basis, induction courses for new staff. Yet a number of questions remain:

– Is the widespread introduction and spread of the new information and communication technologies being accompanied by systematic schemes not merely to train staff in their uses but to explore new teaching and learning models? On the evidence of the review visits, and materials provided by countries, the answers are either no or only partly so. Despite very promising innovations, no system-wide investment comparable to the costs of installing the new technologies is yet being made in experimentation and carefully evaluated innovations in teaching.

– Do institutional procedures for career advancement, promotion and recognition in teaching match those in research? The answer to this question is usually and unsurprisingly no, in the major research universities, but, in many others, steps have been taken to formalise the criteria for selection of staff and for promotion there is explicit reference to teaching potential and performance. Nevertheless, except in those institutions and sectors in which funded research is not a significant element, the research criteria prevail. And in those other institutions and sectors, it is not clear that there is a career in teaching as distinct from institutional management and external relations (including contracts and consultancies).

– Have sound and well-accepted procedures for identifying teaching quality and relating teaching to learning outcomes been developed? Work is proceeding on these difficult matters, but is nowhere at a stage where learning outcomes can be confidently and extensively related to particular kinds of teaching. This may seem a surprising observation in light of the very long history of tertiary education in some form or other. That history has not, however, provided much scope for rigorous and systematic studies as distinct from anecdotal or personal accounts or, occasionally, philosophic critiques of the teaching-learning relationship. Teachers teach; learners are expected to learn, and whether at this stage they do or do not is as much a matter of their choice and behaviour as of what teachers do. Indeed, in the European university tradition there has long been an expectation that the university provides opportunities and that students can avail themselves of these if they wish. If they fail, that is a confirmation of their unsuitability and demonstrates that the vital screening function of elite selection is being well exercised. Failure in universities or non-completion of studies in the past carried no particular stigma, by contrast with the vocational tradition in which the young student-workers were apprenticed and gradually made their way up the ladder. Failure or non-completion in this system incurred severe penalties both economic and social.

Together with meeting the costs, the development of effective teaching is perhaps the greatest challenge arising from the continuing expansion of student numbers in tertiary education. Students, employers and the professions have high expectations which, at least by their accounts, are often not met. For students, the most oft-stated needs are for a more active, personal style of teaching and learning. Their quest for meaning and purpose and for social and cultural relevance and intellectual stimulation are very positive indications of their educational values and an effective rebuttal of the frequently-made observation that students are interested only in the immediate, practical and material benefits of learning. These are indeed included in their expectations but are a quite incomplete measure of them. The tertiary teachers also have high expectations and often spoke of their frustration in being unable to realise them. The teachers' associations in several countries, for example, wished to see formal reward processes and career advancement more clearly and closely related to good teaching reports. Consequently they value attempts to specify the nature of good teaching and to assess it in a comprehensive fashion. Although there are some counter-indications, to which we have referred, it is widely accepted that a more systematic approach to teaching – its recognition and improvement – is needed and would be welcomed.

6

ACHIEVING QUALITY FOR ALL

As the normal experience of everyone comes to include some kind of tertiary level education, there will be need for new educational concepts and strategies. The concept of "successful performance" has to be redefined in more inclusive terms; new approaches are required now for defining and assessing quality. Thus, new demands fall upon teachers and system and institution officials, leaders and managers. These demands are manifold; they are already the subject of innumerable national and international conferences and projects, including those of the OECD's programme of Institutional Management in Higher Education. To date, much of the interest in quality appraisal and improved management arises from requirements for transparency and accountability and from the increasingly entrepreneurial roles of institutions. Equally important are appreciations of the quality of the educational experience of students and of the capacity of institutions and whole systems to provide conditions for a high standard of teaching and learning for all students, that is, quality appraised for the purpose of educational development.

In their country visits, the reviewers took a particular interest in three of the several qualitative issues which stand out in the management of the transition to mass tertiary education: drop-out and failure rates; system-wide quality evaluation; and newness in management and leadership.

1. THE PROBLEMS OF FAILURE, DROP-OUT AND NON-COMPLETION

The problem of high failure, drop-out and non-completion rates has already been considered in the context of increased demand and more open access. Now we turn to issues of quality in relation to teaching and learning.

Many of the problems already discussed have their issue in what is politely known as student attrition rates. "Attrition" is a useful if rather bland term, since in a non judgemental way it encompasses many different aspects of non-completion of courses and programmes by students. Students may withdraw or not complete for quite different reasons, as in Norway, where "stop-out" may be more applicable than "drop-out" since students may withdraw only temporarily or they may never have intended to complete a whole programme, but take only a course or two. Students also change their plans and interests, move, assume new responsibilities domestically or at work, or find better opportunities elsewhere. In Belgium (Flemish Community), we were informed that high attrition rates at the end of first or even second year are a consequence of delayed screening, students being enabled to have a year or so of exploration, trial and error, before they or the tertiary providers decide what is most appropriate. While all these considerations are undoubtedly valid up to a point, there are limited data on rates of success in courses and examinations for which students present themselves, presumably or most often with the aim of succeeding, but in which they drop out or fail. Moreover, even in those systems where access is open many students and tertiary educators express concern about high drop-out and failure rates. Are these rates simply to be accepted, or can they be reduced by improved teaching, more relevant learning assignments, better support for students – and improved study habits? The position taken by the review teams is that there can be improvements and that they should be set as targets in policy directed at teaching and learning.

Student failure, drop-out and weak performances vary as between courses, programmes and institutions, but they are now of concern everywhere, regardless of the type of institution or programme or country. However, for a variety of reasons, including privacy rights and the cost and difficulty of system-wide tracking of students and graduates, it is not possible to present a reliable, accurate picture of what is really happening. "Drop-out", for example, for reasons given above, can be a misleading term. Drop-out from one course or institution into another, as happens for instance in Belgium (Flemish Community), Denmark and Germany, when students transfer from university to college of higher education and complete a programme there, cannot be equated with failure overall even though the cause of the move may have been failure in the university course. In Virginia as elsewhere in the United States, a mature-age student may take two or three courses but not complete a degree – not because of failure or dissatisfaction but because these courses meet an individual need, perhaps for professional updating, to take up employment or simply to pursue an interest. Data on length of study time can be particularly misleading since even when a student is enrolled full-time, as in Denmark, Germany, Sweden, the reality often is that study is being combined with a job, family responsibilities, travel, and other forms of study. In these circumstances, what is to count as a reasonable target for time to complete the degree? The issue has, of course, implications for financing policy, and countries are seeking to tighten up. Denmark and Sweden set limits on funded study time; they are by no means alone in this. Favourable loan regimes are normally linked with specified completion time. Data relating to completion of individual courses and programmes, to the length of study period and to grades or marks in examinations are usually kept at the institution or system level or both.

Improvements in success and completion rates are widely conceded to be needed, but on what scale and of what kind are often unclear. There is obviously need for more research and analysis, including longitudinal studies of particular categories of students, and in different disciplines and kinds of institutions. The reviewers were seldom informed of the existence of research or of plans for it, except for data emerging from quality reviews which are extremely variable in this respect. While considerable caution is needed in interpreting such figures, as was pointed out in discussions in Belgium (Flemish Community), Denmark, France, Sweden and the United States where failure and drop-out issues have been the subject of considerable debate, it is widely agreed that there is cause for concern and the review teams strongly endorse this. There is no agreement on what might constitute an acceptable failure or drop-out figure expressed in terms of percentage of an entering cohort who complete a degree in a specified period, say six years for a four-year degree. The figure of 80 per cent given in some United States institutions is usually regarded as very satisfactory and may be put forward as a target by individual institutions. Through targeting, efforts can be concentrated on a better

understanding of why 20-30 per cent have not completed. Targeting also encourages institutions to take steps to remedy such shortcomings as may be identified – in selection, orientation, counselling, teaching, curriculum, assessment, study finances, etc. But where it is not 10-15 per cent but 30 per cent and more that drop out, fail or do not complete, as happens in some courses, there is cause for more immediate concern and action. It was not clear to the reviewers that problems on this scale were being treated with any sense of crisis.

Well-targeted approaches, at the institutional level where there is opportunity to identify very specific functions as they relate to individual students, are necessary; they would benefit from surveys which both quantify trends and highlight issues which need to be addressed system-wide since many of the problems are not institution-specific. Entry requirements are usually common or commensurate across a system; when there are very high levels of completion of upper secondary education, substantially based on school assessment of performance, there can be very considerable variability of standards. It may be that system-wide, co-operative approaches are needed to strengthen transition procedures; for example, in several countries, communication between secondary and tertiary institutions is tenuous. While tertiary teachers commonly complain about poor standards in basic skills among entrants, and secondary school teachers about the impersonality of teaching methods in tertiary education (especially the universities), it is too often the case that teachers at neither level have more than rudimentary and often out-dated knowledge of what the others are doing or expect. Career counsellors, admission tutors and recruiters in the tertiary sector do of course meet with secondary school teachers and counsellors, and this is a very worthwhile development (even if links to non-university tertiary institutions are limited). But the crux of the matter is the continuity of teaching and study requirements. The often severe break at the point of transition needs further attention, particularly in the matter of study skills which should bridge upper secondary and tertiary education.

Many different conditions affect student performance and in different ways according to the kind of student – young adult, mature-age, first generation student, non-native speakers, male/female, the discipline studied and where and when study takes place. Some of these conditioning factors, such as personal home and family circumstance, may be – and should remain – beyond the purview of the institution or the system authorities. Nevertheless, the rapidly developing movement of quality appraisal and the research literature point to changes that are within the competence of the providers and, among them, knowledge of student traits and expectations together with possible modifications in curriculum and in teaching deserve closer attention. It is increasingly recognised that, to improve learning outcomes and reduce failure and drop-out rates, more systematic efforts are needed to improve the selection of teachers, their initial training and orientation and their continuing career development. The latter is particularly important in consideration of the inadequacies of past arrangements which affect the large bulk of those now teaching in tertiary education and are likely to continue to do so for many years to come. The question still remains as to whether tertiary teachers and institutions uniformly and consistently see successfully learning students in study programmes of high quality, interest and perceptible relevance as a fundamental objective. Where they do, a further question is whether conditions for successful study are being provided, at least in institutions, in a comprehensive and equitable way for all students. Financial constraints are an important consideration and there would be considerable benefit in cost effectiveness studies which relate closely to curriculum designs and teaching strategies, both actual and hypothetical.

Institutions recognising these student study needs are providing counselling, advice and means to improve study skills. In New Zealand as in most other countries, individual departments as well, sometimes, as whole institutions are providing study skills coaching. Belgium (Flemish Community) has a ten-point programme to provide better information and orientation in the final year of secondary schooling, improve guidance in the first year at the tertiary institution and in other ways to smooth the transition. But it was reported that implementation has been weak. However, some institutions visited have made notable progress. In France, considerable effort has been made to extend widely guidance and counselling services and peer tutoring with as yet uncertain effects. In Germany, numerous proposals were made in a key issue programme in 1993 to reduce the time taken to complete the university degree, make study programmes more transparent, mentor students and generally improve teaching. While some progress is reported, it falls short of expectations. Yet, as various programmes testify, for example the support given to African-American stu-

dents in the "historically black" colleges in the United States, significant improvements in student success rates can be achieved. But the schemes, depending on the commitment and expertise of dedicated professionals, tend to be highly institution- or department-specific and they are costly. It will require very considerable effort, resources and system-wide approaches to bring about a general improvement. Institutions individually have the main responsibility and progress depends on their giving the issues of failure, drop-out – and stop-out – higher priority than is now common.

There is a particular issue of the standard of performance that is expected. All agreed that standards must be maintained, but which and whose standards? It is unrealistic to expect that "standards" will mean the same thing in circumstances where not 10-12 per cent, but 70-80 per cent, of the age group are participating in tertiary education. As mentioned earlier in this report, curriculum designs need to be more closely adapted to students, not idealised through expectations that cannot be met.

In several countries, student performance needs to be seen in relation to preferences for institutions. For whatever reasons, the university is oversubscribed and large numbers of students crowd out certain courses. This problem, particularly acute in Germany, is being addressed through expansion of the *Fachhochschulen*. Students and families will need to see the value of this; in some institutions and for some programmes, that value is already recognised. In Portugal, an approach which encourages individual polytechnics to develop further distinct profiles could help to address the problem of the weak perceived status and value of their programmes. Perhaps a closer articulation of the university and non-university systems and cultures will be needed. At any rate, in all countries it is the whole of tertiary education in its variety of structures, institutions and programmes which needs to be accessible, to have full public recognition and support and to play a full part in ensuring successful learning by all students. That is an ideal – practice will always fall short. But now it often falls well short and steps can be taken to narrow the gap.

2. STANDARDS, QUALITY AND ACCOUNTABLE PERFORMANCE

During the past few years, the issue of quality – of teaching, curriculum, institutional management and student performance – has quickly moved to the foreground whether in the perspectives of system-wide policy or institutional priorities. Reasons are not hard to find: greater visibility and higher overall costs as numbers continue to rise; growing recognition of the vital role of tertiary education in economic and social advancement; community-wide movements of consumers' and citizens' rights; the diffusion of business practices; the shift in the political spectrum towards informed choice by individuals; and greater competition among providers. There is now in many countries a pervasive mood or belief that all aspects of tertiary education, from the overall system to the work of teachers and students, shall be open to scrutiny. A thoroughly critical or evaluative spirit is abroad; responses in institutions range from indignation and defensiveness to thoughtful and wide-ranging appraisals and improvements; governments are introducing or strengthening system-wide methods of quality assurance and accountability.

"Quality assurance" covers a multitude of activities ranging from intensive national level reviews of curricula, teaching and assessment procedures and research in single disciplines, to periodic audits of the self-evaluations being made by single institutions. The international movement of quality assurance has gathered momentum, with the establishment of new organisations and co-operative projects such as those of the Association of European Universities (CRE)/European Union, the quality assurance project of the Institutional Management of Higher Education (IMHE) programme within OECD, and the International Network of Quality Assurance Agencies. Several of the countries participating in this review are playing leading roles in these and other international activities, from which further changes within national systems may be expected. In Denmark, the Council for Quality Assurance in Higher Education, after a trial period, is being firmly established. Its focus thus far has been the quality of individual subjects taught. In Belgium (Flemish Community), universities are under a legal obligation to carry out a mix of internal and external quality reviews. Similarly, in Portugal, recent legislation has called for discipline-based evaluations in all public and private tertiary education institutions; at present, the new evaluation process is being implemented for public universities in co-operation with a foundation established by the universities. Australia, for three years until 1996, maintained a national review which rewarded institutions for their progress in setting up quality reviews; a new scheme of quality appraisal is now being prepared. Sweden's Higher Education Agency, a relatively recent establishment, is in process of setting up comprehensive appraisals. France's National Evaluation Committee has undertaken over 90 reviews organised at the institutional level.

Everywhere, observations are being made, interviews conducted, notes taken and volumes of reports produced. When these evaluations are scaled, as in the United Kingdom, the media are quick to produce league tables. The value of such tables is a matter of debate. They may sell newspapers and please the high scorers, but their critics are not convinced of the overall benefits or, rather, point to a wide range of concerns, such as the increasing differentiation of institutions not by virtue of a valued variety of missions but on a simple performance scale with clearly-demarcated winners and losers. This can distract attention from the now urgent question: what do we mean by quality in education in a universal system? Why do some institutions, programmes, students and teachers succeed while others do not? How can quality improvement, when needed, be best achieved? Supporters, however, argue that highly visible competition including published tables sharpen the competitive edge, highlight quality issues, and bring about real changes through "benchmarking". Nevertheless in several countries, policy-makers do not agree that publication of comparisons institution by institution, is necessary or even desirable. They prefer to establish frameworks whereby institutions regularly evaluate themselves and introduce a variety of measures for improvement as needed.

Quality is an almost ineffable concept; its several dimensions can be meaningfully expressed only when related to specific activities, the aims and values that inform them and their discernible effects or consequences. Highly generalised definitions are usually banal, of little use for the individual and for the different quality assurance procedures that are being adopted. Several of the academics who were interviewed, including rectors and vice-chancellors and their deputies, were troubled by what they thought is the undue influence of business practices. Not all resistant to quality appraisal, they wished to see greater emphasis on the distinctive features of academic life and sought an approach which explicitly acknowledged them. Conversely, there is a risk that quality assurance mechanism may freeze curricula and teaching around lines that are "academically correct". Procedures that bring to bear multiple perspectives including those of the students are, on the whole, preferable to those which highly privilege one set of players.

For functions as diverse as teaching, research, academic management and decision-taking, costs and financial arrangements and the various support services, quality has to be separately defined. Indeed, the use of the singular is misleading: qualities in the plural is more helpful since this use acknowledges the need for and value of diversity and variety. One common, if still evolving, approach to determining quality in institutional review is the ends-means-results analysis: are the objectives or purposes appropriate? Who takes part in defining them? Are they being operationalised in the activity and what are the discernible effects? What adjustments or changes are needed and how feasible are they? Thus, for teaching, there are objectives both individual (the single teacher or small teaching team) and collective (the department, the institutions, the discipline community, the profession, etc.) and there are expected effects in student learning. What then is the adequacy of the means: the methods, techniques, materials and settings? Are they the best possible to meet the objectives and are they facilitating and supporting student learning? Who will be responsible for making changes? Such questions are relatively unthreatening, helpful in starting a dialogue and opening the frequently closed domain of teaching to new ideas and fresh insights. Teaching is very much to the point since in the course of the review it was more than once asserted that teaching cannot be assessed, or that only the teachers themselves or the academic department know enough to make valid judgements. But national-level quality agencies or bodies, among them Australian, Danish, French, Swedish and British, have systematically reported on the quality of teaching and, in order to do so, have established procedures and criteria that transcend the individual teacher or department. The adequacy of these national-level procedures is certainly contested, but this is not a reason to abandon the task of developing them. They are helpful not only for quality assurance purposes, but in order to extend and strengthen the work of the growing number of teaching development and support units. Not least to meet expectations regarding the use of public resources, better means of informing the community are being introduced.

A particularly difficult issue, however, is whether financing should be directly related to public judgements, including indicators, of teaching performance. In Denmark and Sweden, institution funding is partly based on one aspect of teaching performance, namely rates of student success in examinations. This approach has caused institutions to consider their own efficiency. Are standards jeopardised by institutional manoeuvres to meet these finance-linked targets? Review teams were assured not, but the question will remain pertinent. In Australia, New Zealand, United Kingdom, Virginia (United States), high-quality teaching is acknowledged in prizes and awards and sometimes in salary increments. "Post-tenure" review for all staff has been mandated by law in Virginia; this review must give attention to teaching. As already noted, teaching performance is increasingly being built into selection and promotion procedures. For all of this to be possible, there must be clarification of, and a good level of agreement on, criteria of good performance (quality) and acceptable procedures such as peer group appraisal for reaching conclusions. One topical issue is whether it is appropriate to reward individuals or groups. In the United Kingdom and the United States, some institutions are recognising the teaching efforts of whole departments, as is frequently done for research appraisals. Quality appraisals and career development for tertiary teachers are often seen as quite separate, whereas the one can readily feed the other.

Well established, especially in Nordic countries and the United States, is student evaluation of teaching and teachers. Most countries if they do not already have such arrangements are now introducing them. Yet the trend is still debated. How much impact do student evaluations have? What kind of validity do student judgements have? Who designs and implements the evaluation procedures? Should the reports be public, confined to a small number of individuals (department head, dean, etc.) or private between the class and the teacher? Should evaluation be made only by present students or should not graduates, after a period in the work place, make judgements in light of their experience? All of the practices or reforms implied by these questions are to be found in some systems and institutions visited by review teams; practice is very diverse and there is no established body of opinion or substantial research base to provide something of a benchmark. What is evident, however, is that the student role, already well established, is growing.

On quality issues more generally, there are several conclusions to draw from the experience of this comparative review:

- Quality assurance, combining both external and internal procedures, has been widely adopted to the point where, variations notwithstanding it can now be regarded as part of the norm of expectations regarding the functioning of both institutions and the overall system. This is a very considerable change in the culture of tertiary education, accomplished in a relatively short time.

- After a few years of intensive efforts, innovation and experimentation in which a very wide range of quality assurance procedures has been tried, there would be value in further international work to consolidate, draw conclusions and pinpoint issues of common interest. The international efforts mentioned above are a contribution to this consolidation but in several countries ambitious programmes are still at a relatively early stage and in others, decisions on future policy are pending. The Norwegians, for example, acknowledge that a more systematic national approach should complement the procedures that are at present internal to institutions. International exchange of information will continue to be of value as national procedures are introduced, assessed, and further developed.

- It is widely agreed that the national or state-level moves to introduce quality assurance have made very heavy demands on institutions, thereby increasing administrative costs and requiring burdensome documentation, the full detail of which cannot be subsequently handled through national-level analysis and reporting. Countries, mindful of the costs of procedures, are exploring ways to reduce and lighten demand for documents and reporting. Australia's annual cycle seems to have been too demanding (and costly since it provided financial incentives). On the other hand, reviewers several times questioned the infrequency of other quality surveys, for example in Belgium (Flemish Community) and Denmark which follow a seven-year cycle of discipline reviews, because of the difficulty of ensuring follow-up action on the results and recommendations of the surveys. In most countries, it is not clear just what is expected to result, how results are to be assessed and any action that might follow poor or insufficient follow-up by institutions. Monitoring of follow-up is often very limited and is generally a weakness in national schemes although such procedures do figure in the Inspectorate's evaluation of one-cycle programmes in Belgium (Flemish

Community). These are not easy matters to address, but they need to be taken up especially by national or state-level quality assurance agencies.

- In some countries there is a strong – but not uniform – body of opinion that national or system-wide measures should take the form mainly of quality audits. That is, the responsibility of the system is not itself to conduct detailed evaluations but to be assured that adequate arrangements are in place. That is the view, for example, of the quality audit unit of the New Zealand Vice-chancellors' Committee and the Flemish Interuniversity Council in Belgium. But the recently established Agency for Higher Education in Sweden is itself conducting system-wide evaluations, as has been the case in France and the United Kingdom. In Virginia, the Council of Higher Education, with substantial expertise in evaluation, invites institutions to evaluate themselves and then offers comments on findings of the evaluations. This approach, a combination of audit and direct evaluation depends for its success on a close knowledge by the Council and its staff of the working of the institutions. It does not require massive documentation by institutions and results in quite brief reports. The Australian system of profiling, whereby Commonwealth agencies negotiate a development profile with each university using this as a basis for funding, is not a formal evaluation but the procedure includes means of assessing quality, for example of provision and personnel for teaching particular subjects. The development and use of such profiles and contracts may be found in Finland and France as well. The Finnish Ministry's effort to streamline the negotiation of "performance agreements" with institutions warrants attention as an attempt to make procedures more cost-effective and efficient.

- A significant weakness in many procedures for quality assurance in common use is that little practical use is found for much of the data produced. There are exceptions: reviewers in the United Kingdom were informed of data used by the vice-chancellors and senior staff of universities and colleges. Deficiencies are followed up by the funding councils. This was a clearly expressed aim of the new evaluation process in Portugal. In Belgium (Flemish

Community), the chair of a discipline review also was confident that follow-up based on careful appraisal of findings does occur. Yet monitoring of the follow-up seems to be quite modest by comparison with the initial review. Implementation is primarily – and appropriately – a matter for the individual institution, faculty department and teachers. Detailed monitoring and follow-up by system-wide agencies could be intrusive, costly and perhaps have little effect since it implies a lack of trust and conveys a sense that "outsiders" know best. "Outsiders" certainly have a key role, but it may be best performed using the audit model where the major work is in the hands of the institution itself, perhaps with consultant help. Self-evaluation has its well-known weaknesses, however; if this becomes the norm, further studies of its operations and effects will be needed. As for system-wide analysis of the data produced by a number of evaluations, over time and in different subject areas and institutions, the reviewers received little information. This is a topic that warrants attention by agencies and ministries, since there may be valuable policy uses on the one hand and, on the other, ways of reducing redundancy.

– Questions arise as to whom are academics accountable, and for what. The principle of institutional autonomy might seem to suggest "to the institution, department or faculty". Academics are also members of communities that transcend institutions: the community of the discipline or profession, for example. This implies accountability to subject and professional peers. Institutions are funded, publicly or privately or, nowadays, from both sources, and the funding and support agencies have a significant interest in the quality of the work, so there is an element of accountability to them. In Virginia and the Nordic countries, the legislators seek close relationships with tertiary institutions, for example through finance committees of the parliament. These bodies are often well informed and have a responsibility and a definite interest in public accountability. By no means least, academics are accountable to the students they teach, in the sense of fulfilling an implicit contract to meet students' expectations and needs qua students. Hence, the legitimate

growth of student evaluation of teaching quality.

Accounting for quality of their performance by teachers, even from this incomplete outline, demonstrates that accountability is to multiple audiences and requires a range of procedures. Each audience has different, if related perceptions of quality, of teaching, curriculum, resources for learning, environment, support services and so on. Thus, the appraisal of quality and the reporting of its results cannot be reduced to simple formulae or a neat set of indicators.

One difficult and still unresolved question already alluded to is to know what "standard" and "quality" mean in an age of vastly increased and diversified participation in tertiary education. Who is to determine them? Can all institutions usefully be rated on a single scale or does the wider experience and diversification of tertiary education suggest the need for several scales and multiple concepts of quality? Can there be a uniform, minimum standard even within single subjects or areas of study, against which the performance of all students is measured? Such scales and standards do exist, for example national secondary school examinations and/or qualifications in France, Germany, the United Kingdom, or tests of graduate aptitude in the United States, or tests set by professional associations for entry into a profession or recognition of a level of attainment within it, as in accountancy in Australia and New Zealand. These measures provide comparative rankings, determine entry or progression and set a threshold standard. They are a widely used, valuable but also criticised indicator of quality. The long and very powerful tradition within the universities of autonomy seeks to protect their definitions of standards of performance from what is often seen as illicit or external interference. Similarly, professional bodies jealously guard their prerogatives. "Interference" in universities and colleges comes mainly from the state or professional bodies and agencies governing entry into vocations, and employers (an increasing influence). The primary form this institutional self-protection takes is control over the awarding of the diploma or degree and academic judgements which inform these decisions. This is a prerogative into which some inroads are being made, as already mentioned. Institutional autonomy means, *inter alia*, that the academic concept of quality prevails in the vital matter of awarding qualifications; academic accountability is thus perceived as a purely academic matter with, in the more extreme form, the quality controls over rules, curriculum, teaching, core learning resources, assessment and qualifications in the hand of the academics. Among the countries participating in the review, none is so extreme but several are well towards that end of the continuum. The various moves to open up the institutions, to introduce alternative sectors or programmes to the university sector, to experiment with non-formal learning, all carry with them challenges to those forms of quality control vested in the principle of exclusive autonomy. This concept of quality is, more and more, becoming diversified as it is informed by different audiences, clients and interest groups.

7

DECISION-MAKING, LEADERSHIP AND MANAGEMENT

The key questions arising from this review for decision-makers and those responsible for institutions centre on the quality and relevance of the services provided. Are the needs of clients being comprehensively addressed? Are they understood, and met effectively and efficiently? Are the stakeholders well engaged and are their interests taken fully into account? Whether or not this uncompromising focus on service to clients and stakeholders is fully accepted (indeed, it is not in some quarters), it is generally agreed that more and more complex, varied and numerous decisions are required at the system level and that of the individual institutions. Wide-ranging considerations and interests have to be taken into account, yet there is increasing need for speed and precision. Clarity and firmness are called for; so is flexibility and the readiness to change course. Decentralisation and devolution which are resulting in new relationships between central administration and institutions, and within institutions, imply not only new kinds of responsibility but a greater dispersion of that responsibility. Yet there are also well-established structures and practices which the academic communities understand, value and wish to retain or modify rather than abandon. It is not always easy to maintain the client perspective in these complex decision frames.

1. STREAMLINING MANAGEMENT AND GOVERNANCE

In all systems, there are moves to transpose to educational institutions principles of private-sector business management with heightened executive responsibility and authority and sharper forms of accountability than hitherto. Within institutions, this tendency has resulted in moves to strengthen the hand of rectors, vice-chancellors, presidents, to cluster small executive teams around them, to streamline committee structures, to invest individual office holders with increased authority and to sharpen competitiveness internally and externally. Contract appointments and performance-based remuneration have emerged in several countries, tending to differentiate those holding high-profile executive positions from the main body of teachers and researchers. However, maximising profit is not the purpose in education and it is necessary to ask whether the adoption of practices from the business world is consistent with the multiple services expected of educational institutions. The two purposes or orientations need not be inconsistent with each other, but they can be. For example, an institution might find it unprofitable to devote substantial resources to assisting weak students to improve their performance whereas the service principle would indicate that – having first enrolled the student – the institution has incurred an obligation to provide those resources, consistent with its overall mission and resource base. This example, not at all fanciful, illustrates the need for considerable sensitivity in decision-making where a balance of forces has to be established among several considerations. The point is also relevant to helping students with special needs – physical, psychological and so on – where services are very labour-intensive or costly (CERI, 1997). We have already referred to the problems of a similar nature raised with the introduction of "the market" or market influences. The argument for a "businesslike'" approach is that there are vital lessons to learn in the efficient use of resources, financial management, personnel policies, marketing and so on. A concern that review teams encountered was that these lessons, valuable as they are, would not be sufficiently contextualised within academic environments with their distinctive values and missions.

Governing bodies in several countries have come under scrutiny and their size and composition changed in the drive for more efficient and leaner forms of governance; reduced size and more external membership are among the targets. Recent moves in this direction have provoked criticism, for example in Australia and in New Zealand, from students, teaching staff and unions. "Instrumentalist", "economic rationalist" and "managerialist" are not complimentary epithets in the mouths of academics who are uneasy about what they see as a greater concentration of executive authority and scant regard for academic values in the constant quest for cost-cutting, efficiency and utility.

In some countries, Germany for example, where academics in established posts are civil servants, efforts have been made over many years to improve the complex patterns of decision-making as between state and federal authorities and institutions. Yet, decisive action has proved extremely difficult: structural reform often remains elusive for a variety of legal, political and cultural reasons. In Continental European countries generally, the collegial tradition of elected department heads, deans and rectors contrasts with the more common appointment and increasingly contract-based system in English-speaking countries. It is an open and debated question as to which yields a better or more effective and efficient decision frame, but there are moves in both to adopt the mode of strategic planning with clear roles and well-defined authority positions. Institutional managers are under constant challenge to respond to and indeed anticipate wider environmental changes: to scan and forecast, assess the capabilities and responsiveness of their institutions, develop communications systems, prepare business plans and so on.

In all of these moves, there is, however, an unanswered question: what kinds of leadership roles are best exercised by governments, system-level authorities, institutional governing bodies, academic councils, the senior-most institutional officers, deans, department heads and the various interest groups, student associations included? In both governance and management, what is the role of leadership, of such qualities as clarity of thought, imagination and foresight – and values, such as empathy, consideration, conviviality? There is a kind of authority, transcending the position held, which distinguishes leadership from management and it can work for good or ill. There may be a tendency to neglect these considerations in the prevailing discourse on efficient and effective management which focuses strongly on roles, structures and resources. Although there are important differences in the public sector between universities on the one hand, with their strong internal cultures and traditions of autonomy, and the more regulated non-university institutions, on the other, these questions are relevant to both and were discussed with both in the visits made by review teams.

High-order skills in strategic and financial management become of crucial importance as institu-

tions take greater responsibility for their affairs and, as many do, extend the range of their activities beyond teaching and research and consultancy. No less important, however, is the leadership and management of the human, social enterprise that is the institution. Staff costs form the largest part by far of institution budgets and the leadership and management required to maintain the quality and make the best use of this human resource is crucial. In their visit to Virginia (United States), the review team was impressed by the recognition – in the legislation, the State Council of Higher Education, the institutions and the various representative bodies – that a combination of educational leadership and management is essential if the institutions are to carry out their missions and relate constructively to the environment. Very difficult, at times unpopular, decisions are required and institutional leadership can be a hazardous occupation.

At the national or state level, ministers and senior administrators develop, articulate and implement policies that may be highly contentious and that fall heavily on large numbers of people. Their rationale needs to be strong, to be clearly explained and well expressed in decisions and action. At the same time, politicians and officials need to demonstrate understanding of the wider impact of policy; they are challenged to provide motivation, encouragement and a sense of common purpose as well as to act decisively and courageously when opposition may become strong and heated. Tertiary education, now directly involving and affecting the bulk of the community, is a major political force to be reckoned with. Parliaments and governments need to be very well informed and lines of responsibility, modified through devolution, need to be redrawn. In Sweden, the reviewers in a meeting with the all-party parliamentary education committee were impressed by the depth of knowledge and interest of members. At the same time, the committee impressed upon the reviewers the need for national decision-making to draw more fully upon the resources of parliament.

Experience in all of the countries participating in the review (and more widely) indicates that changes are overdue; with difficulty, they are now occurring in long-established practices of governance, management and decision-taking. In some countries, changes have been rapid and dramatic – Australia, Austria, Belgium (Flemish Community), Denmark, Finland, New Zealand, Sweden, the United Kingdom; in others, France, Germany and Japan, for example, they have been more gradual and limited in scope; in yet others, such as Portugal, changes are in their initial stages. New players have been brought in to institutional governance, for example in France, New Zealand and Sweden, on advisory committees and in teaching or support roles, notably from enterprises, regional government and professional bodies. Student and staff unions have achieved increased influence on governing bodies. Others, notably the discipline-based professors in the older universities, have experienced a diminution of their institutional authority and roles. Part-time staff, very numerous in the non-university sector but also in the universities, often play a minor role. As their numbers and proportion of the teaching force increase, governance and management practices will need to be further modified in order to forestall the rise of a new caste system: the "real" staff and the "others".

The strengthening of governance and management involves both downward and upward "turns": keywords for the former are devolution, consensus and partnership, enhanced responsibility, efficient and effective management; for the latter, keywords are steering, transparency, monitoring and accountability.

2. CHANGING PATTERNS OF DECISION-MAKING

Changes that are occurring in the patterns of decision-making and responsibility for them range from subject-based national advisory boards independent from, but closely related to, the Ministry in Denmark to general university or higher education advisory councils in Australia and Japan to quasi-autonomous funding agencies in the United Kingdom, respectively for the higher and further education sectors, to a highly-influential higher education advisory council in Virginia (United States). Each country has policy advisory and consultative procedures, sometimes informal through ministries and ministers and sometimes through formally established "arms' length" bodies. In Sweden, the National Agency for Higher Education, with monitoring responsibilities and a significant evaluative role, does not advise on or channel funds. It is not superior to the institutions which receive their assignments directly from the parliament and government (as do public institutions in Virginia, from the state's legislature). There are also, in Sweden, commissions which or who (some have one-person membership) can play a highly significant role in seeking consensus over recommendations that result in legislation. In the United Kingdom, periodi-

cally a "blue riband" committee is established (Robbins in the 1960s; Dearing in the 1990s) to advise on matters which for one reason or another government needs the authority of independent experts and representative interests. In Australia, a broad advisory role is performed by the Higher Education Council, a quasi-independent body which works closely with the Department for Employment, Education, Training and Youth Affairs. The government in 1996 appointed an independent Review of Higher Education Policy and Funding which, following the Dearing Committee in the United Kingdom, reported in 1998. New directions and structures are expected to follow in each country.

It is not necessary to enumerate the details of within-country structures for decision-making and advice at the national or state levels. Many are ultimately subject to the legislative body and, usually, the government of the day; all function with a framework of laws, regulations or terms of reference; each has a network of relations with institutions and with other agencies. The decentralisation process has not diminished the roles of central or state government or of system-level agencies but has changed them. One change is the strengthening in several countries of the consultative, advisory and steering bodies; another is the enhancement of strategic policy-making, including the introduction of financial levers which are discussed below. Balances among interest groups have changed, sometimes radically, and are not settled. The review team in Virginia understood that partners may dilute the established lines of control by government through their own lobbying mechanisms. By contrast, in the United Kingdom, education legislation in 1992 specifically prohibited interference by the Secretary of State in allocations by the Funding Councils to individual universities and colleges. The Funding Councils have this as a statutory responsibility. There are no clear, obvious advantages in a system of buffer bodies or diffused authority, as in New Zealand or the United Kingdom, over one where the lines are fewer and more direct, as in Belgium (Flemish Community), Norway, Sweden. Preference for one rather than the other seems to be more a matter of national style. It is not so much the particular kind of structure that counts as the capacity for well-grounded advice and decision-taking. In most countries, such a capacity is at present inadequately supported by research, particularly research on the consequences and effects of strategies adopted by these bodies.

In many countries, policies being considered or implemented could eventually have the effect of changing many established patterns of governance and decision-making at the institution level. These vary from the highly participatory to the highly executive-directed; from the model of community and industry partnership to that of the self-governing academic corporation. The nature and scale of changes now in process or emerging point towards a clarifying of roles and relationships: a strengthening of the policy-making and monitoring role of governing bodies; enhancement of the authority to be exercised by senior institutional executives; the specification of responsibilities of institution-wide academic boards or senates; and a general – but not uniform – increase in stakeholder involvement. Efficiency in process and effectiveness in the use of resources are the criteria that have come or are coming into common parlance and in procedures for evaluating the performance of these roles by individuals and committees.

Large governing bodies, dominated by internal interests, often find difficulty in reaching conclusions, taking decisions swiftly and incisively and finding effective linkages with other social, cultural and economic actors. However, there are many considerations to take into account: the plurality of interests; the wish to share responsibility for decision-making in an academic environment where quality of thought and experience are widely dispersed; the complexity of many issues; and the academic capacity for analysis and seeing several sides to these issues. On the other hand, the rector/vice-chancellor/president/director is not always privileged to act as chief executive with extensive delegated powers, and the authority of other senior executives such as registrars, finance officers, deans and department heads is frequently constrained. Reviewers were told both within the institutions and outside them that it is in the interest of the institutions, as of government and the numerous bodies with which institutions have dealings, that clear, unequivocal and timely decisions are made and institutional positions widely communicated. There has, indeed, been a growth in internal and external communications: bulletin boards (electronic and otherwise); newsletters; promotional material; round tables and so on abound, as institutions compete for attention and support not only with one another but in the wider socio-cultural milieu. Advantage has been taken of the facilities of full colour printing, CD-ROM, television advertising and local TV and radio in their self-promotion by institutions and programmes. Complex relations with the wider environment, including institution-industry partnerships, contract research and the increasingly elaborate networks of international relations, require simple, powerful structures and direct operating procedures. Moreover, the roles of governing bodies and executive officers are closely interrelated and must be examined together. Reforms in institutional governance and new patterns of management and communication go hand in hand, as shown in structural changes made or underway in Australia and New Zealand.

While experience in several countries suggests that there is a compelling case to review governance and management at the institution level, this should be done in full acknowledgement of the particularities of the academic environment, its patterns of decision-making and institutional culture and history. There is a complex interplay between those considerations, demands being made by stakeholders and the not always well-articulated client expectations and stakeholder views. Reformed structures, as we were often informed, need to incorporate procedures for widespread consultation and dialogue both internal and external; the interests and the expertise of the whole organisation need to be systematically drawn up and brought more directly into decision-making. It is widely believed that procedures for determining policy, monitoring performance and communication need to be even more transparent. Few, if any, institutions in modern society are faced with such a challenging set of relationships.

In their visits to Norwegian regional colleges and higher education colleges in Belgium (Flemish Community), review teams observed that it is of greatest importance that institutions fully understand, accept and come to "own" new structures of governance and management. For this purpose, close attention is needed to the varied nature of decisions and the relationships between types of decisions and structures for working and implementing them. Academic decision-making, in the context and organisation of studies, evaluation of learning, research procedures, staff appointments and staff development, belong to the academic staff, to academic bodies or committees and to those at the level of the faculty and department, all with good student and stakeholder representation. Here the collegial principle reigns. Its exercise does not preclude streamlining of structures, greater use of delegated authority and the development of institution-wide plans, for example by small specialist committees and with the use of external experts.

The collegial principal does not stand in the way of improved procedures for the councils or supreme governing bodies which must reconcile the multiplicity of interests and concerns of a modern institution and forge policies that do justice to them all. The size of governing bodies has become a hotly debated issue in some countries. Reduced in size and opened to increased outside membership or influence by government decision in Australia and New Zealand, elsewhere large bodies have been retained with full academic control. Small bodies have been criticised: they cannot incorporate all of the major interests, both internal and external. But bodies can be too big, bringing into question an institution's capacity to define and articulate functions and diversify structures accordingly. There is no agreement on an ideal or appropriate size, even for broad categories of institutions. A slight majority of either internal or external members – and there are good arguments for each – seems preferable to an overwhelming majority of either since that precludes or diminishes rich and effective dialogue between the institution and its environment. However, some very prestigious and successful universities function well with no external members on their governing councils. Whatever the size and composition of the councils, the chief executive and senior managers need authority in order to exercise their increasingly demanding and onerous responsibilities, but must be accountable to the governing body for the exercise of that authority and they have duties as well as rights in respect of their colleagues and staff. The modern management style of limited-term contracts, with a performance element in remuneration and emphasis on entrepreneurial flair, can be quite consistent with the collegial tradition and the principle of peer-based academic leadership, but considerable care – not to say vigilance – is needed in introducing reforms of this nature.

3. COUNTRY TRENDS

The foregoing general directions and considerations are reflected, albeit unevenly, in reforms undertaken in several countries.

In Germany, there is agreement at government levels that greater autonomy is needed at the institution level if institutions are to be more responsive. But as the review team noted, institutional autonomy in a real sense can be complicated not only by the individual freedom of teachers but also by the traditions of civil servants and their relationship to the state, and of the institutions and their relation-ship to the state. This means that ministries treat universities as part of public administration, regulating and filling positions and calculating, more or less in detail, line-items for different types of expenditure. The enhancement of institutional autonomy implies increased responsibility for all kinds of institutions, some diminution in autonomy for individual teaching staff and academic units within institutions and a new orientation of work within ministries.

In Australia, reforms in the late 1980s which led to amalgamations and the emergence of a number of very large, multi-campus institutions have raised new questions about governance and management arrangements, to include the perceived loss of a style of life ("collegial") and its displacement by modern business-related practices ("managerial"). Contract appointments and remuneration packages along business lines are the order of the day. Similar changes have been under consideration in New Zealand, where criticisms of institutional "inwardness" and a view about the efficiency or otherwise of large, complex, academically-controlled councils led to the proposals already mentioned to cut the size of governing bodies and to change their composition by reducing academic representation and increasing representation of the government's "ownership interest" partly through the involvement of outside interests with business and management experience.

In Denmark, the University Act which came into force on 1 January 1993 introduced new powers for senior officials and collegiate bodies of the universities. The Act sets down clearly defined responsibilities for decision-making among rectors, deans, heads of departments and course supervisors. The authority of the rector is enhanced, and he or she will have a management structure with delegated authority. The management of education and of research are to be separated. The Act calls for reconstituted collegiate bodies and, for the first time, requires university senates and faculty councils to have two external representatives as well as representatives of different staff groups and students.

The limited influence of institution-wide structures for academic governance and management also may be found in Austria, Belgium (Flemish Community), the Czech Republic and Poland, but for different reasons in each case. In the latter two countries, for example, reforms following the political changes of 1989 provided increased decision-making powers for departments and faculties which in practice weakened the positions of institution-wide academic bodies as well as rectors and deans.

In Austria and Belgium (Flemish Community) as in Denmark and Sweden, steps were taken in the early 1990s to transfer greater responsibility to individual universities. In Austria, new legislation has led to the creation of advisory boards which operate independently of the Ministry and a strengthened role for the rector.

Substantial decentralisation took place in Finland in the early 1990s in a series of moves to install "management by results." A new University Act envisages refinements in present arrangements for university administrative bodies, requiring only that they must include representatives from concerned groups within the university (external representatives are permitted, but not required). It is anticipated that personnel decisions – the appointment of professors – will be moved from the government (appointment by the President) to the individual universities. This is not the case in France, where the Comité National des Universités (CNU) reviews the qualifications of candidates for university posts. Such a process, while intended to assure uniform quality, tends not to take into account the programme, teaching and learning contexts and needs in individual institutions.

The newly-elected government in Sweden in 1993 expanded the autonomy of institutions to organise themselves, to use their resources more effectively, to develop curricula and to attract students. While there is debate about whether decentralisation has gone too far or not far enough, institutions have responded to a new sense of autonomy by a variety of initiatives. Thus, consideration is now being given to how to strengthen the functioning of institutions operating with a greater scope for decision-making. The university/university college board does not deal with academic matters. This strengthens the position of the rector/vice-chancellor, who both chairs the governing board and in principle has authority to appoint (following an internal election process) or dismiss deans or heads of departments.

Countries differ in the extent to which approaches to and developments in decision-making and management in universities apply to other, non-university institutions. In Denmark, changes now in place for universities are being extended to the colleges which provide mostly "medium-cycle" programmes. Governance and management of the technical and commercial schools which offer "short-cycle" tertiary education have been the subject of a separate reform which differed in detail but moved in the same direction. In Austria and Finland, new non-university institutions and programmes have

different ownership arrangements and structures, so specific adaptations have been made. What is interesting, however, is the extent to which the new tertiary institutions incorporate the "downward turns" identified earlier.

Generally speaking, no substantial distinctions are made in decision-making and management arrangements between public and private universities and colleges in Japan, Korea, and the United States. But in these countries, there are differences in contexts which are reflected in management style, for example when institutions are parts or an outgrowth of religious and cultural foundations. A small private institution which was visited in New Zealand is family owned and run, and may be contrasted with the relatively large profit-making technical and career schools in Japan and the United States, as well as with some (but not all) private universities in Portugal, which operate as commercial enterprises (some are attached to larger commercial enterprises) and so follow large-scale commercial business practices with regard to decision-making and management. In this respect – and as with Austria – it could be said that some of the "downward turns" identified as the most promising directions for decision-making and management for all tertiary education institutions are more apparent and more widely implemented in institutions other than universities and other "conventional" institutions of higher education.

In several countries, tertiary sector-wide governance, broadly defined, takes place through a mixture of statutory and less formal advisory and decision-making groups, mostly working in close association with the ministries when not already part of them. These include the University Council in Japan, subject- and profession-specific national advisory boards in Denmark, the Council of Higher Education in Virginia, the United Kingdom Funding Councils, and in all countries, bodies representing the institutions and/or their chief executives, staff and students. Some of these bodies have executive power, including control of funds; others are advisory and others still aim to use political means to advance their interests. A particularly noteworthy development is the establishment in France of an Agency for Modernisation, supported jointly by the Ministry and the Council of University Presidents (CPU). While the tasks of the agency are being worked out, it is expected directly to support change and the development of management capacity at the institution-level.

4. STUDENTS AND PROVIDERS

In the new tertiary education environment, responsibility and responsiveness more than ever before need to be addressed at the level of delivery, of contact between students and providers. Reforms at the national or state system level are, on the whole, designed to enhance or highlight these more immediate loci for action. This is appropriate. Students collectively have a role at this level and have been very influential in reform, for example in France, Germany, and Norway, either in gaining acceptance for their own proposals or those of government or others which they believe serve their interests or in resisting those government initiatives or other proposals with which they disagree. On matters of fees, grants, loans and resourcing, it is also at the state or national level that the student voice is most effective. It is at the institutional level that the students' interests in the quality and relevance of their studies and the conditions affecting teaching and learning are being increasingly recognised. Not all student organisations accept that this recognition has proceeded very far, but the student voice certainly is being heard in the highest decision-making bodies, in institutions and in ministers' offices. The transient nature of the student population, part-time and deferred study and the growing number of foreign students can make a consistent and clear student view very difficult to obtain. Many representative groups of students have quite small active or engaged constituencies. By contrast, in some institutions of which the University of Uppsala in Sweden is a striking – and, it must be said, unusual – example, the role of student bodies (in this case, "the nations") in enriching the experience of the undergraduate years is highly significant. "Governance" in the sense of the formal governing bodies of the institution is not the only relevant consideration. Residential institutions have a big advantage in this regard as do institutions where student clubs and societies are numerous and active. There is thus a very diverse and uneven pattern of student responsibility for and involvement in the decisions that frame their lives as students.

For the institutions, the principal providers of tertiary education, the task of adaptation and adjustment in governance, management, leadership and decision-taking cannot be too strongly emphasised. The ultimate test for them is not so much management efficiency – whose need is well recognised – but whether insightful, knowledgeable and imaginative forms of leadership are emerging and being cultivated. Through such leadership, the difficulties can be overcome of reconciling "collegiality" and "managerial" styles, of reconciling highly local, regional, national and international perspectives, of distributing decision-making and enhancing the sense of responsibility of all the stakeholders towards the clients.

8

COSTS AND FINANCING

The evolution of large-volume participation has led to new patterns in the costs and financing of the first years of tertiary education. The broad comparative picture is conveyed by OECD education indicators; more detailed patterns and trends are documented by information supplied by countries taking part in the thematic review.

For the participating countries, total expenditure for tertiary education institutions as measured relative to Gross Domestic Product ranges from 2.4 per cent in the United States to 0.9 per cent in the United Kingdom (see Table 5). The Minister of Education in one of the participating countries has recently stated his wish to set a target of 3 per cent. Many factors could account for the relative position of countries on such an indicator: high expenditure countries may be enrolling larger numbers of students while low expenditure countries may claim greater efficiency owing to low rates of drop-out or high rates of progress to degree completion; the distribution of enrolments across sectors and fields of study may differ; the scale and organisation of

Table 6. **Tertiary educational expenditure per student (US dollars converted using PPPs) on public and private institutions, by type of programme, 1994**

	All tertiary	Non-university	University
Australia	9 710	6 320	11 030
Belgium**,[1]	6 390	x	x
Denmark	8 500	x	x
Germany*	8 380	4 960	8 560
Japan	8 880	5 760	9 600
New Zealand	8 020	8 200	7 970
Norway	–	–	–
Sweden	12 820	x	x
United Kingdom**	7 600	x	x
United States	15 510	x	x

–   Data not available.
x   Data included in "All tertiary".
*   Public institutions.
**   Public and government-dependent private institutions.
1.   For the Flemish Community (1993), All tertiary: 6 585; Non-university: x; University: x (data supplied by the Ministry of Education of the Flemish Community).
Source: *Education at a Glance* (OECD,1997), Table B4.1.

linked research activity may vary; there may be some uncertainties on the validity of data on private expenditures; and so on. Some of these differences are reflected directly in measures of unit costs, *i.e.* spending per full-time equivalent (FTE) student (see Table 6). A common experience over the 1980s was for educational expenditures per FTE student to fall, in some cases markedly. The trend has continued in some, but not all countries. Nonetheless, a question frequently encountered is whether per-student education expenditures can be reduced still further.

These data refer to educational expenditure at tertiary-level institutions; students, their families or other third parties incur additional expenses for living costs and miscellaneous expenses such as books, etc. Comparative information on such costs are available from various sources, but some indication of their scale is provided for several countries in the OECD indicators database (compare last four columns of Table 7).

Table 5. **Tertiary educational expenditure from public and private sources for educational institutions as a percentage of GDP, by type of programme, 1995**

	All tertiary	Non-university	University
Australia	1.8	0.3	1.5
Belgium	–	–	–
Denmark	1.4	x	x
Germany	1.1	–	1.0
Japan	1.1	0.1	1.0
New Zealand	–	–	–
Norway	–	–	–
Sweden	1.6	x	x
United Kingdom	0.9	x	x
United States	2.4	x	x

Note: Expenditure may cover levels and activities other than first years teaching.
–   Data not available.
x   Data included in another category
Source: *Education at a Glance* (OECD, 1997), Table B1.1d.

Table 7. **Educational expenditure as a percentage of GDP for tertiary education, by source of funds, 1994**

	Direct public expenditure for institutions	Public subsidies for institutions via households and other private entities	Private payments to institutions	Total expenditure for institutions	Total expenditure for institutions (including international sources) plus subsidies for households	Other private payments	Financial aid to students NOT attributable to household payments to educational institutions for educational services
Australia	1.2	0.16	0.45	1.8	2.0	–	0.19
Belgium[1]	1.0	n	–	–	–	–	0.19
Denmark	1.4	n	0.01	1.4	2.1	–	0.71
Germany	0.9	0.01	0.1	1.1	1.1	–	0.09
Japan	0.5	–	0.59	1.1	1.1	–	–
New Zealand	1.1	0.29	–	–	–	–	0.29
Norway	1.4	n	–	–	–	0.75	0.75
Sweden	1.5	n.a.	0.11	1.6	2.2	0.68	0.54
United Kingdom	0.7	0.27	0.005	0.9	1.2	0.26	0.27
United States	1.1	0.02	1.24	2.4	2.4	0.12	0.02

Note: Expenditure may cover levels and activities other than first years teaching.
n   Magnitude is either negligible or zero.
–   Data not available.
n.a. Data not applicable.
1.   For the Flemish Community (1993). Direct public expenditure for institutions: 0.95. Public subsidies for institutions: 0.95. Public subsidies for institutions *via* households and other private entities: n. Private payments to institutions: –; Total expenditure for institutions:–; Total expenditure for institutions (including international sources) plus subsidies for households: –; Other private payments: – (data supplied by the Ministry of Education of the Flemish Community).

Source: *Education at a Glance* (OECD, 1997), Table B1.1c.

Countries differ in how all of these costs of tertiary education – for tuition, student maintenance, books, supplies and other expenses – are financed. However, even in Japan, Portugal and the United States among other countries with large-volume enrolments in private institutions, tuition fees and charges or student loans, public funding remains significant and substantial. In all countries, public expenditure, both direct and indirect, continues to be the principal source of funding for tertiary education.

Participation in the first years of tertiary education is increasingly being regarded in policy terms and by learners as an investment, yielding both public and private returns. So long as the returns on that investment, measured crudely by likely productivity increases for economies, regions or enterprises and earnings gains (reflecting also reduced rates of unemployment) over the working life for the individual, are sufficiently greater than the relevant costs, a rationale exists for numbers to expand and overall investment to increase. Students as already mentioned do take a broader view of the learning experience – regarding it as an engagement in which to pursue and develop their individual interests in the course of their studies, to engage in a stimulating social and cultural life, to broaden their intellectual horizons and reflect on their values, and to open up more opportunities later on. Keen attention is, however, given to access to employment, to stable jobs and to likely longer-term economic and employment outcomes of study at the tertiary level. Thus, there is widespread recognition that an important part of the underlying growth in individual demand can be attributed to the potential earnings and employment returns perceived by learners to result from participation in tertiary education. This is reinforced by the views expressed by representatives of business in every country: a workforce with increased levels of skills and competences contributes to the ability of firms to compete in their product and service markets.

Such an investment perspective does not diminish the strong public interest in tertiary education, with regard to such matters as access, the quality of the student experience and outcomes. The public interest is seen in every country participating in this review to require a predominance of public funding. Far from implying a reduction in public funding, development towards near-universal participation in the first years of tertiary education can be seen to strengthen the case for the substantial public stake in the overall costs of investment. However,

at a time of increased competition for resources on the public budget, a challenge facing governments is how to marshall and make best use of public funds made available. Realising the scale of the tertiary education enterprise and the costs to be financed, countries have adopted or are considering methods of financing which serve strategic purposes of mobilising additional private and public resources (the latter from other functions in the budget and from regional and local levels), improving efficiency (with an accent on reducing costs of teaching and learning for providers, participants and governments and third parties who provide the finance), and stimulating responsiveness to the demand.

I. MOBILISING THE RESOURCES

An emerging position underlying new approaches to financing is that on-budget public expenditures are being distinguished from overall levels of investment in tertiary education. Thus, public financing is increasingly seen as providing for only a part, albeit a very significant part, of the investment. Financing mechanisms are being used to leverage the participation of the learners and third-party payers in the financing of tertiary education and in providing needed resources. In this respect, countries are taking into account a much wider concept of investment than institutional costs of instruction. The tertiary education investment to be financed includes student maintenance costs and miscellaneous expenses, if not all of earnings forgone. As it was put to reviewers in one country: "students are busy, too". Several options have been pursued to bring about a wider sharing of the costs, in one or more countries.

One option is to define an appropriate level of tuition fees, financed in different ways. The Higher Education Contribution Scheme in Australia obliges every student to repay about one-fourth of the costs of instruction for each year of study leading to the first degree. By 1995, HECS payments provided more than A\$ 250 million towards the budgeted costs of tertiary education, or 15 per cent of the total. In New Zealand, the formula for core funding provides about 80 per cent of the "fully budgeted" level of support per student, leaving to each institution the decision to establish a schedule of tuition fees. Students can finance the tuition fees through student loans, to be repaid in instalments in periods when incomes exceed a threshold. In the United Kingdom, the government proposed a fee of £ 1000, to be reduced for students from low-income families. In most Continental European countries, efforts to introduce fees or levy charges (apart from modest service fees) have not been considered or, when proposed, actively resisted. However, the newly-established *Fachhochschulen* in Austria do impose fees, and modest charges for public tertiary education have been introduced in Portugal and recently increased in Italy.

The Australian HECS permits prepayments or repayments of the contribution on behalf of students by parents, grandparents or employers. Such a payment of tuition fees on behalf of students by family members or third-parties is not unusual in Japan or the United States (both countries having long experience with tuition fees); further third-party participation in financing tuition fees could be encouraged through favourable tax treatment. New legislation in the United States provides such favourable tax treatment for parents, grandparents, employers or charitable groups who contribute to a prepaid tuition plan which guarantees that tuition fees will be paid on behalf of the student at the time he or she enrols in tertiary education (regardless of fee increases between the date of purchase of the tuition-fee contract and the date of enrolment). Under the legislation, such plans can be used by employers for the benefit of employees or their families.

A second option is to shift part or all of the responsibility for financing student maintenance costs from the public education budget to the student and his or her family or to other ministerial portfolios, for example onto unemployment or training funds. In Germany and Sweden, student financial support is provided partly in the form of grant and partly in the form of subsidised loan. Debate continues in both countries on the appropriate balance between the two components, although the principle of some level of student repayment obligation is not in question. In the United States, where funds advanced through loans are used to pay both tuition fees and other student expenses, the ratio in the volume of federally subsidised loans to federal grant aid has shifted markedly over the past twenty years from 20:80 to 70:30. In the Czech Republic, students now pay 23 per cent of the costs of accommodation and 40 per cent of the costs of meals. In France, proposals to rationalise further indirect support for students have figured in the public debate on financing and reform. Recent changes in social insurance eligibility criteria in Denmark have already brought otherwise inactive beneficiaries into

tertiary education; for these new tertiary education learners, social insurance budgets will bear at least some share of the maintenance costs. In the United States, recent changes in regulations have limited the eligibility for beneficiaries to continue to receive benefits while participating in tertiary education. Newly-ineligible beneficiaries could receive support for living costs through various student financial aid programmes.

For reasons both external to and resulting from tertiary education policies, changes in patterns of attendance in many of the countries visited also have served to mobilise private investment from students and their families. Among them: a greater tendency for learners to commute from their family homes and the increased share of part-time and mature student enrolment, which in some countries is subsidised at a lower rate than full-time enrolment.

A third option is to develop further the earning capacity of institutions in providing both teaching services and a range of other activities. The trend towards such income-generating activities was noted in the Education Committee's work on financing higher education in *Financing Higher Education - Current Patterns* (see OECD, 1990). Such activity increases the scope for "cross-subsidy" of first years teaching, as when activities such as contract teaching, international programmes and research – funded through other sources – can help to underwrite administrative overhead but also directly to support teaching and learning (to different degrees in different institutional settings). Complementarities can be exploited in contract teaching, such as that provided in business schools in Belgium (Flemish Community), Denmark and the United States, and in United States community colleges, United Kingdom further education colleges or Australian TAFE institutes among others. Building on such complementarities requires expertise and decision-making authority at the institution level, covering broadly both substantive aspects of teaching, research and community service as well as administrative and financial aspects of institutional management. The risk is that attention will be deflected from first-years teaching and learning to income generation. However, the acquisition of expertise at senior levels of institutions and the steps taken to ensure strategic development in each institution (*e.g.* through "contracts", "performance agreements", "strategic plans", as found in several countries) and to institute quality assurance procedures may have reduced this risk.

A fourth option, related to the previous one, is to promote the development of new forms of teaching and learning in partnership with business and industry as in the British Enterprise in Higher Education initiative and Virginia's inter-institution/inter-sectoral co-operative effort in the Jefferson Labs particle beam accelerator facility. These initiatives not only build on the expertise and contexts for learning residing in the partner organisations, but draw on financial, human and material resources provided by the partners (both private and public, in the latter case from other budget functions and regional and local authorities).

A fifth option is to draw systematically on full- or part-time student earnings, in part building on changes in study programmes which cater for alternate periods of work and study. While earnings generated through concurrent or consecutive work permit learners to shoulder a larger share of the investment in tertiary education, there are both opportunities for and challenges from expanding the blending of work and learning. Among the opportunities, tertiary education programmes conceived with work experience in mind may be seen as a means to introduce a lifelong approach to learning through greater emphasis on such programme initiatives as the bachelor's degree in Denmark; modularised curricula in Scotland; "cycles" in the first degree at a university in England; new approaches proposed for first-year study in France; associate or occupational degree articulation in the United States and articulation with special training school programmes in Japan. Among the challenges, engagement in work during the course of tertiary education studies could put student progress and success (as gauged in relation to full-time study) at risk, unless there is further adaptation in the contexts, contents and methods of teaching and learning in the first years.

A sixth option is to exploit further the possibilities afforded through student mobility. It should be possible, for example, for systems having excess demand in particular fields to accommodate that demand, in part through an increased cross-border outflow. The mobility of students opens up possibilities for the generation of income, although the precise allocation of gains and costs is not straightforward. In some instances, these matters have been negotiated between systems, *e.g.* among the Nordic group of countries or, within a country, *e.g.* through the Southern Regional Education Board (a voluntary structure which promotes co-operation among a group of southern states in the United States). Gen-erally, systems and institutions hosting fee-paying students gain financially up to a point; those assessing low tuition fees or charges incur, without compensation, most of the marginal costs of administration and instruction but may gain financially in other ways (expenditures on lodging, meals and miscellaneous items) as well as in terms of broader, long-term economic benefits for the region and enhanced curricula for the institution (CERI, 1996a). A case can be made for public funding from "host" regional authorities in partial support of students from other systems/countries. Countries which finance domestic students through means which require student repayment may not receive the repayments from students or graduates who move abroad (and fall outside of collection processes within the country, such as the national tax system as is the case of Australia's HECS; it should be noted that mobility does not absolve the learner's obligation to repay).

As the pressure on resources continues to mount, these and no doubt other options will assume greater policy relevance even in countries where one or more of them are at present rejected. The argument of this report is that it is not too soon to set in motion studies and discussions with increased overall individual and social investment in view.

2. PROMOTING EFFICIENCY INCLUDING INNOVATION IN TEACHING AND LEARNING

A second position underlying new approaches to financing tertiary education is the drive for efficiency, both to reduce unit costs and to increase effectiveness as measured in various ways: reduced drop-out, more rapid rates of progress to degrees and increased rates of degree completion as proposed in earlier sections of this report. Some of the financing mechanisms used in several countries which implicitly or explicitly work to improve efficiency are listed in the Box.

Of the countries reviewed, Denmark has moved the farthest to encourage more rapid progress by students towards completion of degrees though its "taximeter" funding mechanism. Two features of the "taximeter" operate in this direction: eligibility for student stipends is limited to twelve terms of enrolment and institutions receive appropriations on the basis of the number of "passes" on examinations. Similar performance criteria are applied in Sweden; likewise Finland, where part of the public funding provided to institutions is based on the volume of completed degrees (especially advanced degrees),

Encouraging Efficiency through Approaches to Financing Tertiary Education

For providers:

i) consolidation" in Australia and Belgium (Flemish Community), in which steps have been taken to bring about a reduction in the number of institutions, to permit the realisation of anticipated economies of scale within institutions;

ii) institutional "profiling" in Australia and "contracts" in Finland and France, in which financing geared to differentiation and specialisation among institutions permits larger average enrolments across institutions for study programmes in specific fields;

iii) funding mechanisms which favour development, relatively, in less expensive provision at the tertiary level, to include alternatives to universities (as in Germany and the United Kingdom), secondary schools (New Zealand and Virginia in the United States), distance learning (Australia, Flemish Community in Belgium, Germany, Japan, Norway, United Kingdom) and part-time study (Australia, United Kingdom, Virginia in the United States);

iv) funding mechanisms which provide for a ceiling on funding, as in the application of the new funding formulae in Belgium (Flemish Community), the United Kingdom and in the allowance for a "self-financing" expectation for institutions in Australia and New Zealand;

v) funding mechanisms which tie public funds to performance indicators or service standards, to include funding on the basis of exams passed (the "taximeter" system) in Denmark or the "production of credits" in Sweden, "contracts" in France and accreditation in the United States.

For "consumers":

i) funding mechanisms which directly affect participant eligibility for support, as in limits in Germany on the number of terms for which public support is made available (8-10 terms, in universities; 6-8 terms in *Fachhochschulen*) and Denmark (twelve terms of eligibility), requirements for progress in the Flemish Community of Belgium (students must succeed in year exams to receive stipends in the subsequent year), and additions to the annual student contribution for students who do not complete their studies within a fixed time period (Higher Education Contribution Scheme in Australia);

ii) funding criteria which indirectly encourage "consumers" to be efficient, in particular tuition fees (a direct application of the market model), in Japan, New Zealand, the United States, and (at modest levels) Portugal; Australia (via deferred charges); and the United Kingdom (tuition fees for full-time students);

iii) guidance on the contents, methods and likely results of participation in programmes of study, in process of reform or review in Belgium (Flemish Community), New Zealand and France, and discussed in Germany, for both students and parents.

Within institutions:

i) extending autonomy within institutions, in which there are consequences for programmes or faculties from the choices they make in organising instruction and research. A number of large, private universities in the United States have adopted such an approach, which includes "gain-sharing" through which a "unit" (faculty, department or centre) keeps a portion of the surplus it generates;

ii) benchmarking" of costs, in order to evaluate the variation among institutions for identified services.

Source: Adapted from Wagner (1996).

and Belgium (Flemish Community), where stipends are provided only to students who have succeeded; those retaking course work because they have failed the year exams do not receive stipends.

In those countries where students pay tuition fees or incur debt (to finance fees, maintenance costs and miscellaneous expenses), such obligations are seen as incentives which promote careful choices among programmes and more rapid completion of degrees. There is very limited comparative evidence of the effects of fees or lo ans on the patterns of choices or transfers among programmes or time to degree, in part because policy changes in several countries are recent and the effects are difficult to estimate.

Encouraging institutions to introduce more cost-effective means for study represents another approach to promote overall efficiency. Several of the developments in teaching and institutional organisation discussed in preceding sections of this report have considerable potential in this regard. Part-time and distance study options now are more common, and more widely used by students. In several countries, public funds cover a smaller share of the education expenditures and maintenance costs of students enrolled in these study options than is the case for students enrolled in full-time, residential courses. There also is expanded offer and use of articulation arrangements and recognition of prior learning. Institutional arrangements exist to a significant extent, in the United Kingdom (*via* "franchising" in further education colleges), in Virginia (*via* community colleges; secondary schools which provide advanced placement courses that permit, on successful completion, initial enrolment in tertiary education beyond entry-level; and so-called "dual enrolment" arrangements for students to pursue classes in the community college while still enrolled in high school), in Australia (*via* tertiary-level courses in TAFE institutes and secondary schools), in Japan (*via* options for earning both a diploma from a special training school and a university degree) and in New Zealand (*via* tertiary-level courses in secondary schools). These arrangements have the advantage of reduced costs for students, through lower indirect costs as students continue to live at home while participating in such courses, lower total tuition fees and charges (as appropriate) and, in some cases, less time required to complete a degree or diploma course. Such arrangements tend to hold down claims on the public budget, among other reasons because public funding per student is lower in secondary and non-university tertiary institutions or the time to degree is shorter.

Efficiencies may be achieved through the use of new information technologies (NITs), both to hold down unit costs and to maintain if not improve learning outcomes. This view is often expressed and was several times encountered in the course of the country visits, but reliable national figures to verify it are not available. It is also argued that unit cost savings are available through distance education, whether technology-intensive or not. Preliminary and very approximate calculations based on figures provided by three of the countries participating in this review (Japan, the United Kingdom and the United States) suggest that the on-budget unit costs of NIT-based distance learning approaches could be in the region of one-fourth to one-third of the per-student costs in on-campus study programmes. The figures need to be cautiously interpreted, for three reasons: *i*) costs for NIT-based distance learning approaches and traditional forms of residential study are not necessarily comparable, reflecting often different mixes of disciplines, fields or modules (science vs. social science or humanities); *ii*) some of the costs of NIT-based distance learning may not be reduced, but rather are shifted from the programme or system budget to learners or other parties (raising questions of equity, which are discussed more fully below); and *iii*) possible differences in learning outcomes attributable to NIT use in distance learning have not been gauged (the "effectiveness" side of efficiency). This last point merits emphasis: attention to wider use of NIT-based approaches should keep the aims in view – learning in the first years – as well as means (level and distribution of the costs).

3. FINANCING EQUITY FOR LEARNERS

In countries recently undergoing expansion – Australia, New Zealand, Norway, Portugal and the United Kingdom among them – financing and resource allocation for expansion have been seen to serve equity purposes. In Australia and New Zealand, it is argued that the expansion has by definition served to promote access and equity, as those who were excluded owing to prior limits on the number of places are now participating. In Australia, it is argued that the expansion was made possible through funds generated by the Higher Education Contribution Scheme (HECS). While it is not possible to judge whether HECS-generated revenues replaced funds that otherwise could have been provided from general tax revenues of the Commonwealth, it is probably the case that the rate of increase in student numbers over the 1988-93 period would not have been possible without this additional, non-public source of funds. What is not clear is the extent to which financing expansion partly through the imposition of student contributions has restrained participation from under-represented groups. Various analyses seem to indicate that enrolments from these groups have been maintained in the course of expansion. It is reasonable to ask, however, whether they should have been increased in relation to enrolments from other groups – at a time when differential rates of access to higher education persist (children from wealthy families being twice as likely as those from poor families to enrol in universities, but this difference could be partly explained by reverse patterns of enrolments in TAFE institutions).

In Japan and the United States, where there is long-standing experience with large-volume participation in tertiary education, those from lower socioeconomic families continue to be under-represented in the full range of tertiary education options. In the United States, with substantial public funding provided to institutions for tuition and nearly thirty years of federal-level student aid aimed primarily at ensuring access to tertiary education for young people and adults from under-served groups, participation rates from low-income families continue to lag behind those from middle- and high-income families. Access to different forms of tertiary education vary according to student characteristics: those admitted to flagship public universities as well as elite private institutions tend to come from high-income, professional class backgrounds. In Japan, participation in the more prestigious higher education institutions is also lower for those from the lowest income groups. Even though the family income distribution of students in the more highly subsidised national universities corresponds more closely to the distribution of family income for the relevant population reference group, it appears that those attending the flagship University of Tokyo are even more likely to come from higher income, professional class backgrounds. To some extent, these patterns reflect earlier differences in the allocation and use of resources – to include variations in private spending by families for cram schools, parent choices of schools at lower levels which are known to produce "well-prepared, hard-working" pupils for entry into the best schools at the next stage and the encouragement and direct involvement of parents.

Failure and drop-out patterns, as discussed earlier in this report, raise equity as well as efficiency issues. In the omnibus of explanations and remedies put forward, some have implications for costs and financing. Most obvious is the pressure of student costs of attendance (including necessary books, computers, etc.). But there is a need to give attention, as noted already, to adaptations in teaching, learning and support services if the success of those at risk of failure is to be promoted. The most promising directions for policy in this area appear to be partly based on a re-direction of resources towards certain programmes and student support initiatives and – in some instances – towards individual learners. Under the 10-point programme adopted in Belgium (Flemish Community), each university is required to apply 5 per cent from its academic staff budget towards study support in the first year with the aim to improve success rates.

One further issue in financing for equity should be noted, namely the position of the part-time learner. As mentioned above, in a number of countries, part-time enrolment in degree-credit programmes continues to be funded from public sources at levels below that of full-time enrolment. In the United Kingdom, such enrolments are fee-bearing; in New Zealand and the United States, many institutions implicitly impose higher per credit hour fees for part-time when compared to full-time students. Moreover, study arrangements and financial support for part-time students remain weak relative to the needs of these students, many of whom work and provide for their families. In these cases, the assumption appears to be that the public teaching mission should be directed at full-time students, and that part-time students are therefore marginal to that mission. Such a position should be challenged on its merits. There is, further, in countries where fees are imposed, an inconsistency between this position and the funding and pricing policies in place. If part-time students are indeed "marginal" to the institution's instructional mission, then the fees charged to part-time students should reflect marginal, not fully-allocated average costs per equivalent unit of instruction.

Among the implications of these patterns of financing related to equity in a context of large-volume participation in tertiary education, three should be noted here: i) expansion *per se* does not ensure equity in access to tertiary education; ii) further investment in schooling or a reallocation of resources at the tertiary level (beyond financing retention to include support for the implementation of new contexts, contents and methods of teaching and learning for young people from under-served groups) may be needed if those newly accessing tertiary education are to succeed; and iii) equity needs to be re-interpreted in relation to a lifelong perspective of learning and against a view of tertiary education which is based less on the "hierarchy" of institutions or programmes and more on the range of opportunities at this level. In this regard, it is the functioning of pathways, via articulation arrangements or part-time study, not the existence of such pathways, that needs to be assured.

4. FINANCING CHANGE AND ENCOURAGING RESPONSIVENESS: FINDING THE BALANCE IN FUNDING MECHANISMS

As noted above, countries are mobilising resources and seeking to foster change and promote responsiveness, not necessarily through additional overall funds for education but by internal shifts.

Adaptation and change are easier and, arguably, more rapid when "lubricated" with additional resources. Such a situation was evident in several participating countries, Australia, Denmark, New Zealand and United Kingdom among them. In these countries, student numbers increased more rapidly than decreases in public funding per student, leading to additional resources on overall institution budgets. Those additional resources backed up changes introduced by governments. In Denmark, for example, the government implemented broader reforms in governance, management and funding regimes (the "taximeter" system) at the same time as overall levels of funding increased.

In several other countries, among them Finland, Japan and the state of Virginia in the United States, overall funding specifically for teaching declined in the early 1990s (as did per student expenditure). Nonetheless, authorities and institutions continued to pursue change. An underlying view, expressed in one of the countries visited, is that "scarcity creates its own creativity". In Virginia, a "restructuring" process already underway was strengthened with the requirement that institutions of higher education prepare strategic plans which both addressed the missions of teaching, research and service and indicated how the lower absolute level of resources would be applied to achieve the objectives set out. In Japan, particularly at private universities and in junior colleges, steps were taken to revise curricula and adapt programmes to a wider range of student abilities and interests, partly in order to sustain enrolment (and revenue from tuition fees). Similarly, private universities in Portugal offer interesting examples of innovation in programmes, teaching and learning, partly in efforts to be responsive to the needs and interests of students paying full fees and partly to hold down costs (and fees) in a highly-competitive environment. In Finland, institutions were expected to use the greater autonomy newly

available to them in taking decisions on how to manage the decline in overall funding.

Authorities in all countries will need to rely to an even greater extent on decisions taken at the institution and programme levels, for such reasons as the complexity and range of activities of institutions; the wider range of provision at the tertiary level, to include both a blurring of boundaries among tertiary education institutions and the presence of more, and more varied, options, outside formal education institutions, for learning at the tertiary level; and even more diverse sources and forms of funding, weakening the position of any single funder solely to set the aims.

In a number of countries taking part in this review, one trend is to provide funds to institutions in the form of a block grant over which institutions have greater discretion in how the funds are spent. Still, the criteria used to allocate funds in relation to outputs, in fact, are intended to influence choices on internal allocations within institutions. A crucial issue is how criteria in the funding formula can or should be used to encourage responsiveness and steer provision in institutions afforded greater autonomy over the management and administration of programmes. More specific criteria in formula-based funding may appear to be a good way to "steer" provision; however, in practice, such criteria can combine to introduce new incentives, leading to arrangements which may be inappropriate or wasteful and to poor-quality programmes. A challenge is to introduce transparency so that all concerned can see and understand the criteria, but also sufficient subtlety to acknowledge unique circumstances and the different approaches taken by different institutions. This is not easy to achieve, because those responsible for setting the criteria cannot direct providers or students to respond in the ways intended. A second challenge is to preserve sufficient scope for institutions to develop programmes and courses, even as some governments have taken steps to shift the basis for funding from detailed control of inputs to more fully specified outputs or outcomes. Experiences in different countries reflect attempts to achieve the balance.

In New Zealand, the Ministry establishes the number of students it wishes to support and the allocation of these enrolments among broad groupings of fields. Institutions are funded on the basis of actual enrolments, in relation to the targets they set for themselves and accepted by the Ministry. In this sense, funding is demand-led. Each institution is free to alter the mix of specific courses within the broad groups, but those institutions which fail to reach the agreed "target" in a broad group must return that portion of funds for students not enrolled. Australian universities – but not the Technical and Further Education colleges – are funded on one-line budgets; accordingly, the institutions are largely free to alter student mixes. Similar discretion is afforded in Belgium (Flemish Community), Denmark and Sweden, where funds follow student enrolment and the institutions are free generally to allocate resources among faculties and programmes, even from instruction to research, as they see fit. In most of these countries, as students generally may enrol in the institution or programme of their choice, institution-level decisions to allocate resources among programmes and activities will have consequences both on student choices and institutional budgets: institutions which draw funds from a highly-subscribed programme to support an under-subscribed programme may eventually affect the conditions of study in both programmes and, therefore, the relative attractiveness of each when compared to similar courses offered in other institutions.

Programmes and institutions in the non-university sector of tertiary education are positioned to be even more responsive to demand, in part because of funding provided directly by third-parties, not least employers. For the short term, advanced technical and professional training of specific interest to employers, TAFE institutions in Australia, further education colleges in the United Kingdom, short-cycle programmes in Denmark, community colleges in Virginia (United States) are particularly well-suited. In most of these countries, enterprises are willing to pay (and often do) and, in some cases, learners also are willing to pay modest fees. Such programmes, whether offered in these institutions or by universities or university-level institutions, widen the scope to build links to and further nourish first-years teaching and learning.

Such internal resource allocation decisions may well be appropriate, serving the broader development interests of each individual institution. But, as yet, there is limited evidence that the scope for reallocation of resources has been strategically used. In some cases, multi-faculty or multi-programme institutions continue to operate as a "collection" of faculties, programmes or activities rather than as institutional entities. In other institutions, the inertia of past practices and some limits on the scope for redeployment of existing resources have

meant limited real innovation in programmes and resource allocations. The new management and governance arrangements in many countries have yet to bring about decisive changes in this regard. As important, senior administrative management frequently lack the expertise to undertake the kind of strategic and financial planning and decision-making so vital in institutions being afforded even greater autonomy in these fields.

The strategic development of institutions must evolve partly in response to broader system-wide interests. These broader interests can be served through requirements that institutions develop or respond to plans, profiles or contracts setting out the proposed allocations of resources, both public and private. In Virginia, each public institution develops its own strategic plan which sets out objectives in relation both to its unique intended profile and clientele and to broad goals advanced for the state as a whole. These plans include financing proposals, consisting both of the costs (according to the volume and composition of student enrolment) and sources of revenue (broadly divided between state appropriation and tuition fees), which are developed on the basis of incremental budgeting in consultation with the State Council of Higher Education for Virginia, and submitted to the legislature and relevant state executive officers for approval. "Performance agreements" in Finland and "contracts" in France are the counterparts of the strategic plans used in Virginia. In each case, governments "negotiate" the balance between institutionally-identified aims, outputs, means and resource needs and system/national priorities, desired outcomes and available resources.

In this respect, most of the countries visited could make more use of incentive funding for targeted opportunities for reform and development in first years teaching and learning. What is needed are "carrots" as well as the "sticks", the latter as reflected in the requirements and regulations which institutions are obliged to follow. Such incentive funding has been usefully targeted on quality improvement, through initiatives which encourage institutions to undertake their own evaluations and demonstrate quality improvements. In Australia, the Committee on Quality Assurance administered three rounds of competition for funding, one of which was based on quality in undergraduate teaching. In the United Kingdom, institutions were obliged by the Higher Education Funding Councils to pay for and participate in reviews and studies of the Higher

Education Quality Council (organised by the Committee of Vice-Chancellors and Principals). The HEFCs (now merged with the HEQC in a new Quality Assurance Agency), undertake their own reviews and the results of these reviews as well as those of professional accreditation processes applied to some fields of study carry implicit funding implications: withdrawal of accreditation may mean a loss of enrolment, threatening both public and private (*via* tuition fees) funding.

Curriculum development represents another important target for incentive funding. There is recent experience in several of the countries participating in this review with initiatives to strengthen links with business, to encourage innovative uses of new information technologies or to promote internationalisation through better integration of international activities. That experience suggests that relatively modest amounts of incentive funding have generated considerable reflection and activity within institutions on matters related to teaching. Examples include, for Australia: Committee for the Advancement of Undergraduate Teaching; Denmark: Centre for Instructional Technology; Japan: Educational Research Centre; Sweden: Council for Renewal of Undergraduate Education within the National Agency for Higher Education; Virginia: Center for Innovative Technology and the Jefferson Labs; United Kingdom: Enterprise in Higher Education initiative.

5. THE MARKET: ADDRESSING CLIENT NEEDS

As indicated earlier in this report, for a variety of reasons (not all financial), a number of governments have moved towards more client- or market-based approaches, in which programmes expand, contract or are modified in line with changing student preferences or interests, taking into account industry needs and as a result of a widening of participation in decision-making. Changes in student interests and aspirations partly reflect prospects for employment and careers, partly perceptions of quality and partly shifts in students' views about how the organisation of teaching meets their needs and backgrounds. Those changes are given weight in funding mechanisms which, directly or indirectly, allocate funding on the basis of student choices and student outcomes rather than resource inputs.

Notwithstanding the active role of students, no country taking part in this review has given over all of tertiary education to market-based provision. All provide some kind of regulation or provision and most control the "output" of degrees. Even though in a number of countries, fully private tertiary education providers may operate outside the regulations and controls for public institutions (*e.g.* special training schools in Japan, career or proprietary schools in the United States, data processing and commercial or business schools in a number of European countries), there is often a regulatory structure for the private sector. In Japan, for example, public standards are set and qualifications regulated for the special training schools which are privately operated. In answer to the question: who is the "client" to be served – employers, students, the broader economy and society – countries have sought different balances in part to build on the complementarities and minimise any adverse effects arising out of the competition of interests. But the balances are changing and can be expected to change further as tertiary education becomes more visible, more widespread and more open to the pressures of the market. In this respect, all countries are recognising that clients have a major role in shaping policy and practice.

A key requirement is information. In most systems, there are information gaps and imbalances, for policy-makers, institutional managers, potential and current tertiary students, teaching staff and third-party payers. New efforts to provide more systematic information to learners and their parents (where appropriate) on career prospects and the suitability of programmes figure prominently in Belgium (Flemish Community), France and New Zealand. In these and most other countries, teaching staff at both secondary and tertiary levels appear to need more knowledge about new developments in job destinations and careers of tertiary education graduates and in subsequent education and training paths. The wide range of backgrounds and interests of potential tertiary education learners increases the need for more information, advice and counselling not only with regard to the types and nature of tertiary education opportunities available but also what will be expected of students in the first years and, not least, in the labour market.

Such information would enable both learners and prospective employers to better understand the qualitative diversity in programmes and/or institutions, even where all programmes lead to the "same" degree, *e.g.* bachelor's. On this view, the "market" would permit – and could lead to or even promote – a range of qualitatively different programmes rather than a single, common degree standard imposed by controls or inter-institution agreement. Students might choose different routes to qualifications, in line with their capabilities and interests. Such qualitative differences do, of course, exist and are not new; in several countries, the differences are believed to be broadly understood by learners as well as employers. In Germany, the United Kingdom and the United States, the media have played a role in disseminating comparative information at the national and regional level. In Virginia, for example, one institution referred in a brochure provided to prospective students to its position in ten separately-published rankings or informal evaluations of colleges and universities. Rankings such as these often take into account – and provide information on – costs, programmes of study, characteristics of the student population, teaching resources and perceptions about the quality of teaching, student services, the student experience and post-graduation experience. Although useful, this information is not sufficient. Governments and institutions have a responsibility to assume a much greater role in ensuring that clear statements of objectives and expectations as well as anticipated outcomes for all programmes are provided to all potential students and other interested stakeholders.

Large-volume participation in tertiary education introduces new information requirements for employers. A key concern is whether the qualification still represents a recognisable and acceptable range of "standards". Higher qualitative variation in programmes is seen, for example by the Confederation of Business and Industry in the United Kingdom, as an impediment to the functioning of the market for graduates: simply, it is argued that it is not possible to know what constitutes a "degree". This position argues against the view, developed in earlier parts of this report, that there should be more "product differentiation", including differentiation of standards and degree requirements. On the whole, the non-university sector has aimed to avoid such differentials within (as distinct from between) programmes and qualifications. The issue is at its most acute in those university programmes which are loosely coupled with occupational fields, as may be seen in the development of new, more specialised study programmes in Portugal's private universities. Interestingly, students in the United Kingdom – particularly those in other than the "old" universities – saw the qualitative differences as a good thing: employers could no longer evaluate job applicants solely on the basis of

a university vs. other higher education degree but rather would need to look further into the programmes and student attributes and accomplishments of those completing courses in universities as well as in other tertiary education settings. That employers may be willing to do so seems to be indicated by the interest of some Japanese employers to depart from the traditional recruitment practice, in which they recruited graduates from one or two institutions and, within those institutions, from particular faculties. It must be said that those employers who recruit more widely remain exceptions to the common practice.

It has been argued that market influences might operate better if learners had a significant stake in their investment in tertiary education. As suggested above, students in most countries already invest to some extent in their own learning, through the use of their time (immediate forgone earnings), reflected partly in their out-of-pocket expenditures. Even in those countries where a substantial share of all expenses are covered by public funds, some increase in the student's stake in the investment might be foreseen as participation continues to expand towards a majority and more of an age cohort.

In this respect, concern is expressed in all countries about the adverse consequences arising from high or increasing financial demands on students. The impression gained in the countries visited for the thematic review is that these demands are well understood and taken seriously by students and their families and that, for the most part, they are being reasonably managed in relating career aspirations, choices of subjects, attendance options and debt levels. Questions remain about how far and how fast such demands can be placed on students and their families; about whether, in some countries, the student/family share is already too high; and about what combination of new and old means might be used to harness best this "market influence" on students while not introducing or reinforcing adverse effects on access, career choices, concurrent work and study success.

Other market influences are introduced when business and industry interests, whether individually or collectively, request tertiary education institutions to produce graduates with specific profiles. In some countries, such requests are reflected in quite specific ways in intermediate tertiary-level programmes, for which business and industry might be expected to pay. In an increasing number of cases, they do pay – in part because they appear to account for a smaller share of the direct provision of training than before (at least in the United States). The challenge is to establish an appropriate balance of demands from the range of "clients", having on the one hand short-term employment and enterprise-specific benefits in view while, on the other hand, taking into consideration long-term career prospects for individuals and overall productivity gains for the economy.

Market influences – including competition among institutions/providers – may encourage both a "client" orientation and the development of strategic alliances in the form of co-operative agreements among institutions. However, these market incentives seem to work against other forms of inter-institution co-operation which could provide gains in both effectiveness and efficiency. At present, existing linkages are from secondary schools to tertiary institutions and between different types of tertiary providers; they involve articulation and "feeder" arrangements or sharing the use of facilities (as described above). Such arrangements certainly extend the reach of all of the institutions involved, and arguably contribute to improving the efficiency of the system as a whole. The co-operation could go further, within as well as among sectors, to improve the choices available to, and the quality of teaching and learning for, students. Such co-operation could be used to sustain small, high-quality offerings; other forms of co-operation in teaching and learning also could be envisaged. Governments could encourage, with targeted funding at the margin, more jointly-offered programmes or "linkages" which encompass a larger number of institutions/providers.

Governments already intervene to a greater or lesser extent in the market, among other ways, by supporting expansion, or capping enrolment, in particular fields. Experience in OECD countries with "managing" supply in this way is not, on the whole, positive: witness the inability to maintain a balance in teacher demand and supply. There would appear to be merit in considering a more flexible application of public funding mechanisms, perhaps to allow for a rolling cycle of public funding and adjustment which takes into account the need to maintain institutional capacity in all (or most) fields and to provide a margin for management within individual institutions to better sustain programme quality and effectiveness (beyond the funding needed to cover certain core administration and overhead

expenses). Such an approach would recognise that adjustment to year-to-year fluctuations in demand by field, unlike adjustments in the supply of other goods and services, can be accommodated within limited margins. It is not so easy for institutions or the system as a whole to achieve this on a larger scale; importantly, this applies to expansion (or re-establishment) of capacity (as in the teacher training case) as well as reduction. Arguably, greater flexibility in the funding mechanism would introduce no greater mismatch of places by field with student interests and employer demands. In this regard, there is value in the approaches of Finland (negotiated four-year plan for universities), France (contracts negotiated over a four-year period), Flemish Community of Belgium (part of the institutional subsidy is fixed, part is variable) and Virginia (incremental budgeting, coupled with revenue variation arising from student fees). Such approaches would be consistent with supporting the consolidation or mergers of institutions (as in Australia, the Flemish Community of Belgium and, possibly in the near future, the United Kingdom) rather than closure.

In summary, means to introduce or sharpen the operation of a "market" or market influences in tertiary education can be found in nearly all participating countries. The developments in this direction follow broadly an intention to promote responsiveness to student demand and other stakeholder interests; indeed, it could be said that such responsiveness is being stimulated through the various incentives arising from markets in tertiary education. However, in all participating countries, tertiary education is seen as an integral part of public policy and it should remain so. Thus, in most countries, governments are proceeding in ways that allow markets or market influences to operate within a broader policy framework. That broader policy framework, in the light of the trend to devolve decision-making and management, should aim to give institutions more control over their funds (e.g. carry-over, investment and retaining income, owning property). Such a framework also incorporates other instruments to promote informed decisions by the clients, providers and stakeholders (quality assurance, guidance and counselling, institutional management and governance); to enhance the positive messages from the market, in relation to demand, benefits and costs (monitoring, data collection and analysis, and dissemination of information and good practice); and to intervene with both regulation and incentives to ensure that wider public interests are being served, in relation to equity, coherence and efficiency (targeted funding). It is in these policy areas, where the "conditions" for the effective operation of the market and market influences are established, that the most promising directions for policy will be found.

6. THE PUBLIC POLICY INTEREST

In a period of growing and more diverse demand from students and more intensive expectations from business and industry, the professions and national as well as regional and local governments, it should not be surprising that countries are grappling with matters of tertiary education costs and how these should be met. Governments regard tertiary education as a matter of high public interest, and accordingly continue to see public funding as the substantial basis on which tertiary education is financed and resourced – "the government's inevitable financial responsibility", as expressed in the Portuguese Ministry's new Guideline Document for higher education policies. However, in the light of the scale of the investment required, financing policies have taken on strategic foci, seeking to mobilise resources from private and a wider range of public sources; to improve efficiency; and to stimulate responsiveness to demand. A key feature of the most promising approaches is the wider use of targeted incentives which are aimed at students, providers or third-parties such as businesses, the professions and local governments. Such strategic uses of financing are being conceived within a broader policy framework which seeks to enhance the effectiveness while limiting the adverse consequences of the incentives for potential and current students as well as largely autonomous institutions. The introduction or refinement of market influences, embraced to a greater or lesser extent in different countries, represent the manifestations of this more general approach.

If client needs are to be met, the market philosophy and devolution argue for greater institutional autonomy and responsibility. This includes more autonomy over financial and resource allocation decisions as well as in the organisation and content of programmes, teaching and learning.

In every country, the case for sustained and better managed public funding is overwhelming. This applies with equal force in those countries with substantial enrolment in private institutions, as students in these institutions benefit directly or indirectly (through institutional funding, tax abatements and so on, provided to the institutions) from public funding.

The pressure of demand and growth has given rise to deliberations and development on tertiary education finance policy. The underlying trends set in a new frame the more fundamental question: who pays? There was wide acceptance of the rationale for full public funding (and modest, or no, tuition fees) when the elite selected and educated at the tertiary level followed careers in the "public interest", in government, teaching or management in enterprises in which the state had a substantial direct interest. The argument for increased private participation in financing the costs of tuition emerged at a time when enrolments were expanding, employment destinations widening and graduates benefited from being in short supply relative to demand. Completion of tertiary education conferred in practice, if not in law, a virtual entitlement to secure and highly remunerative employment and careers. That relative advantage, coupled with the large costs involved and competing demands on the public budget, has reinforced the argument for increased private participation in the costs of tuition.

However, if participation grows beyond half to three-fourths or more of each generation, there will be good reasons for public funding to be the substantial base on which tertiary education will be financed and resourced. At such levels of participation, education at the tertiary level will become even more widely regarded as a social and cultural entity, with even greater social benefits. This is not so much by way of the contribution of an elite to serving the "public interest" as in the past; rather, an emerging view encountered in the countries visited is that tertiary education "is the place to be" for everyone – a society-wide view that all should have the opportunity, and be supported, to participate. Such a view parallels earlier experience at the secondary level: presently, with an OECD-wide norm of 80 per cent or more of an age cohort completing secondary education, the principle of public financing of education at this level is accepted without question. Further, if participation approaches three-fourths or more of each generation, those benefiting will also form, over time, the majority of those making relatively higher tax payments owing to relatively higher incomes. Thus, sustained high levels of participation for successive generations would work, under certain assumptions applied to the benefit principle of taxation, to reduce an often asserted inequity arising when non-participants pay, through taxes, for participants in tertiary education: it will be the participants, as graduates, who pay the large share of the public investment. Public funding as the substantial base for financing tertiary education need not apply to all studies and activities. The principle of public funding could be established to cover a large share of the investment only in the first years of tertiary education; for those wishing to pursue studies beyond this minimum, a large share of the costs of the additional studies could then be covered by contributions from students, their families, enterprises or other sources. Public funding is already widely used to ensure that a potential barrier of substantial costs of attendance is not put in the way of those at the margin. This rationale for public funding is likely to become even more prominent, as rates of participation in the first years of tertiary education increase: those left behind will be even more at risk and more marginalised than their counterparts without tertiary education in the 1950s and 1960s, even in comparison with the cohorts of the 1980s. The financing barrier could be addressed

through means-tested grants or tuition charges as well as a range of debt or deferred payment schemes which rely more on non-public funding sources. However, although often highly targeted through the application of detailed eligibility and payment criteria, these financing mechanisms tend to be more complicated and less transparent. As a result, they may be less effective than direct institutional subsidies and generally available grants in overcoming the perception of lack of affordability by those at the margin.

If the public policy interest now favours a continuation of growth in participation in the first years of tertiary education beyond half to three-fourths or more of each generation, this implies that there should be no disincentive for anyone wishing to participate. If approaches can be implemented to reduce the costs and mobilise all available resources, the argument of this report is that means exist to extend even more widely the opportunity for tertiary education, at a manageable cost to the public budget.

9

CONCLUSIONS AND FUTURE POLICY DIRECTIONS

We have argued that tertiary education in some form will increasingly become a normal expectation of most if not all young adults. For them, as for mature-age students, and whether full- or part-time, the tertiary institution will be "the place to be" although that "place" will have various meanings reflecting the diverse needs and interests of different categories of students. The needs of students, the principal clients, and the several stakeholders in the wider community can only be met if the institutions show a readiness to adapt, to innovate, to evolve, as many – but by no means all – are now doing. A readiness by institutions to review their missions, policies and procedures openly and critically is a precondition of meeting the requirements of large-scale tertiary education. Responsiveness to demand, diversity and a client orientation are keys to the successful adaptation of systems to the changing environment.

The transformations in demand and expectations now occurring and likely to continue call for highly-sensitive and intelligent leadership at all levels: the onus on institutions and systems to demonstrate alertness to social and individual demand and flexibility has never been greater. In their continuing development, systems and institutions need to balance the functions of research and scholarship, post-graduate and advanced studies, continuing professional education, community service – and study and teaching in those "first years" which not only underpin the research, advanced study and other functions but also relate ever more closely to the employment market.

Clearly, tertiary education policy overall must address all major functions and goals. In singling out the area of the years of initial study leading to a first degree or diploma, we have signalled the importance of one of these functions – the one that most immediately involves the largest numbers, touches all parts of society and, we think, presents the most immediate challenges to policy. We have drawn attention to many specific issues; several are the focus of current policy concern and the subject of

intensive efforts, others much less so. These issues as presented are both quantitative and qualitative: the scale and diversity of demand, the problems of access, the quality and relevance of educational provision, the challenges to governance, management and leadership and ways of meeting the inevitably increasing costs as participation in tertiary education shifts inexorably from "minority" to "majority".

Growth in demand for tertiary education, already at record levels, can be expected to continue, even if in some countries there are fluctuations and platforms (possibly temporary). If, as expected, demographic decline in the younger age cohorts is counterbalanced by increased numbers of qualified youth and by mature-age students, the sector will continue to grow and the pipeline effect of growth in student numbers in the first years will put great pressure on graduate programmes and other tertiary education roles, thus sharpening the issue of overall national and institutional priorities. However, governments must decide whether growth should be further encouraged since policies, especially financial ones, can be inhibitory or stimulating, i.e. they can slow down or accelerate growth.

Precise targeting seems unrealistic except in a few study lines or professions, so the issue is of a more general nature: is participation by all or most people, at some stage in their lives, a worthy goal of policy? The conclusion of this review is, first, that it is and, second, that governments cannot reasonably stand in the way of the deeper forces which, on the evidence available to this review, continue to drive growth. Thus, countries will need to strengthen their capacity to meet demand for access and, we suggest, should adopt positive policies to foster participation.

There is a particular problem of "steering" demand. On the one hand, some professions and subjects of study can be over- or under-subscribed, but on the other, detailed forecasting has proved unsatisfactory as a basis for policy actions which, in the event, have had limited overall effects on supply and demand. Moreover, it is questionable whether governments in democracies should take upon themselves the right to direct students and determine careers. The client orientation adopted in this report argues for a different approach: one which acknowledges a great diversity of interests and motivations, which focuses policy on ways of understanding and responding to these needs and motivations, not in isolation but as part of a web of interests. Hence the argument that neither existing institutional structures, policies and procedures, nor the controls exercised by governments should be the starting point. Rather, the needs and interests of the clients, the students, and the stakeholders should frame the debate while governments hold the ring and make strategic interventions. This requires that policy-making be in a new key: flexible, open, and finely tuned to those needs and interests and centred on the student. The argument for continued expansion is threefold:

- individuals are increasingly seeing the value of continued education and training of a high standard;
- the advanced, industrialised democracies for both economic and social reasons require highly-competent, responsible citizens;
- there is an increased risk to social structure and cohesion and a threat to equity and social justice if a significant proportion of the population is excluded or discouraged from participation in a stage of education which clearly confers benefits.

Very impressive adaptations and developments have occurred in response to the volume and diversity of demand in a context of social, economic and technological change, yet many policy areas require further attention. Transition from school to the tertiary institution is often a weak link: no one has direct responsibility and there are discontinuities in learning which seem to disadvantage many students. Too many students are failing, dropping out, or undertaking studies that do not meet their own or society's needs.

The growth and diversity of demand has generated enormous pressures and not all groups in society in practice have equal opportunity for access; inequalities and distortions continue to exist. In all countries participating in the review, lower-standing socio-economic groups and certain ethnic minorities continue to be significantly under-represented among tertiary applicants. Moreover, for some who do gain access, disadvantage is reflected in performance and subsequent job placement. These and other obdurate problems have not yielded to earlier ameliorative efforts. Since the inequalities are deeply embedded in the structure of our society, more comprehensive and co-ordinated policies – health, housing, and employment among them – are needed. These will help to build up a climate of opinion in which inequities have no place. Participation and success rates in tertiary education provide evidence of the need for policies which take effect at a much earlier age than young adulthood. Tertiary education cannot be treated in isolation from what comes before.

One of the most striking phenomena in many countries is the substantial if uneven growth of demand from mature-age students. The "first years" can be entered at any age from late adolescence to old age. Part-time study opportunities are especially important in this respect since many mature-age students are unable to participate full-time. But most institutions have been designed not only for "less traffic" but for the school-leavers studying full-time on campus. The needs of these two groups overlap but there are important differences. Where the volume of participation by mature-age and part-time students is high, provision tends to be more comprehensive and varied. Thus institutions encourage part-time students by designing programmes and facilities to meet their needs. Hours of opening are long, access to libraries and equipment is flexible and teaching is specifically geared to a very varied clientele. Inclusive policies for the first years of tertiary education need to start from a recognition of the full scope and variety of students seeking or needing access. This will require many changes of values, attitudes, institutional organisation, modes of teaching and the provision of resources and facilities.

Of great potential significance, but still far from being fully developed or utilised, is distance education. The costs of initial design and development are very high, which may explain very limited provision in some countries, but probably the greatest barrier, a persistent attitude, is that off-campus, part-time study is regarded as "second best" or even quite inapplicable in certain fields. Successful experience over considerable periods of time in several countries should be sufficient to refute these opinions, yet the spread of distance education with its pioneering use of a variety of technologies to facilitate learning, has not been rapid across the

OECD area. Those countries not already well advanced could gain considerable benefit from studying the experiences of those that are. "Distance education" is not only for the students at a geographical distance – its main value is flexible study: at the students' own pace and at the workplace or at home. The innovations in teaching, learning, assessment, institutional management and technology in distance education programmes have applicability as well to full-time, on-campus study. Of all the innovations in teaching and learning, it may be the one that offers most as a way of reconceptualising mass tertiary education, because of its efforts to individualise the teaching-learning relationship with very large numbers, its readiness to assess established practice and its experimentation with a wide repertoire of teaching and student support strategies.

Funding policies in some countries have been less favourable to part-time than to full-time students. In the perspective of lifelong learning for all, it is essential that part-time study and various combinations of work and study be given greater encouragement. Conditions of study need to be highly attractive in order to foster a community-wide mentality of continuing education. Through the current mandate of "lifelong learning for all", the Education Committee may wish to undertake co-operative international work on this important but relatively neglected topic.

A major consequence of the growth of demand and increased access is pressure on staff and facilities in institutions. This, combined with constrained budgets, has resulted in deteriorating staff-student ratios, overcrowding and very great unevenness in the quality of teaching and learning. These are serious problems which are likely to worsen unless new ways can be found to strengthen the resource base. The option of increasing or imposing direct charges for students (fees) is supported by many arguments, but our conclusion is that this is not a sound basis on which to further extend opportunity. Instead, governments need to be more active in mobilising a wide range of financial sources, both public and private. There are costs which fall upon students, often quite high even in "no-fees" regimes, as well as benefits that accrue to them, and the balance should not be so tilted as to lead students away from instead of towards tertiary education. Greater efficiency in resource utilisation, for which there is scope if institutions are prepared to appraise their practices and to innovate, and a community-wide approach towards resource provision should be the underpinnings of a continually expanding sector. Our fear is that undue preoccupation with student charges deflects attention from the wide range of options to mobilise the needed resources and to use them more efficiently. Some countries, some institutions and some parts of institutions have demonstrated great flair and innovation in new designs, system reconstruction and the efficient use of resources. The problems therefore are not universal and much can be learnt by studying what has been achieved under demanding circumstances. As stated in the report, the new contexts are disturbing but rich in opportunity.

There is a very definite challenge to institutional management to establish new structures since the old – and existing – ones are so often insufficient to meet the needs. We reject the argument that there are "too many" graduates or that growth should or even can be constrained, although it can be fostered and, to a degree, steered. When the quality of education, in its several dimensions, is at risk due to rapid growth and constrained resources – as it plainly is – governments, the major stakeholders as well as the institutions and the students themselves need to combine forces, resources and ideas in a concentrated effort to maintain and strengthen quality in the face of growth, large volume participation and competition for resources. Thus far, there is little evidence of significant decline in standards of student performance resulting from growth. However, such a statement must be treated with caution since reliable measures of performance over time are notoriously difficult to devise and use. Our evidence is the reported views of policy-makers and institutional representatives. It will become more substantial as quality assurance measures are more widely adopted. But there is a major area of concern: student failure, drop-out and extended periods of study.

The drop-out and failure phenomena, only partially documented and seldom resolutely addressed in policy measures, seem often to be accepted as an inevitable consequence of large numbers, resource limitations and the myriad conditions affecting study by adults. However, even allowing for all of these, failure and drop-out rates in all the countries reviewed are generally unsatisfactory although there are wide variations across and within countries. More detailed and sharply-focused studies than were possible in the course of the review are required to pinpoint specific difficulties. Nevertheless, several steps suggest themselves. The scale of the problem needs to be determined. Not all students who fail on programmes or courses drop out. Not all who drop out have failed. Many students transfer from one programme to another, but are not "tracked"; some who drop out return to study and this "stop out" may be a planned phase in an individual's life cycle interests of study, family, work, travel, etc. But since no country could provide statistics sufficient to understand these movements, policies to address problems are difficult to envisage. Even lacking such data, individual institutions in their self-evaluations, and individual teachers in appraising their own and their peers' teaching, need to question current assumptions and practices. Are entry procedures, initial orientations and guidance, monitoring of student progress, learning assignments, curricula and assessment procedures satisfactory? Is teaching appropriate to the clientele? Are the conditions in which students study and learn appropriate? Are there arrangements for credit transfer, recognition of prior learning and of experiential or work-based learning? And so on.

In short, while there will be an irreducible number of failures, there is certainly need and room for improvement. While some students enrol for poor reasons, or may have no intention to complete a study programme, the investment made by the overwhelming majority suggests that success rates of a much higher order than are common at present, across countries, institutions and programmes should be actively sought by all parties. Similarly, more needs to be known about the lengthening of average study completion times, a tendency in several countries. The data, again, are not always available or are often difficult to interpret. Prolonged study may be a less appropriate term than interrupted or combined study as students combine study with paid employment (often necessary to meet costs and keep indebtedness to manageable levels), family life and travel. Such combinations can be extremely valuable, even if they mean that many years elapse before the target qualification is achieved. Again, however, there are serious drawbacks for the individual – inefficiencies in use of time, and associated costs, thus accrue. These problems are more likely to increase than diminish as numbers continue to rise; together with failure and drop-out, they constitute a major set of continuing policy concerns. The introduction of intermediate qualifications in long-cycle study programmes, of more frequent assessment, of closer supervision or at least monitoring of student progress and the

points as already made about curricula and teaching, would result in improvements. In several countries, heavy financial burdens falling on students are a contributory factor and policies are needed to better relate these cost regimes to conditions under which students study and their assessed performance. If countries wish to reduce these problems – and there are very good reasons to do so – more vigorous policies than are commonly in use now will be required.

With some countries having moved towards "unified" systems by combining previously separate (university/non-university) systems, others remaining firmly "binary" and all in reality having several sub-systems which function either separately or under an umbrella, a question naturally arises as to which seems to be the best direction for future development. Our conclusion is that there is no clear set of relationships between the overall organisational structure of systems and the quality or efficiency of the resulting educational provision in the countries reviewed. Decisions about changes or new structures have gone either way – towards a unified system in Australia, Sweden and the United Kingdom, towards a strengthening of binary systems, in Norway. These decisions reflect the internal political environment and/or traditional values and national self-images. It is less important that countries should have a "unitary" or a "binary" structure than that learners be provided with a diversity of learning structures, pathways and programmes which are nevertheless sufficiently interrelated to permit ready movements between them. Considerable effort is required in most if not all countries to strengthen credit transfer arrangements and the articulation of programmes and institutions. Some are very well advanced; many are not. Information and advice for students may be lacking and pathways may be unclear or very complex; nonetheless, students are increasingly making their own mixes and combinations, need further encouragement to do so and require options which are more than the ad hoc, "second-best" choices now available.

Curriculum and teaching are the subject, increasingly, of quality appraisals for which impressive new agencies and procedures are being put in place. Further investment in those agencies and procedures and more comprehensive and systematic sectoral and institutional strategies directed at the overall curriculum and teaching arrangements will be beneficial. The need is widely acknowledged and while there are many examples of reforms, the overall impression is of variable performance and interest. Not all countries have national or state level quality appraisal agencies and it may be too soon to conclude that the innovation warrants universal adoption. But there is little disagreement on the need for more systematic appraisals of performance and better and wider communication of the results as an aid to decision-making by policy-makers, institutions, students and the various interested parties.

There is some risk of quality review procedures becoming both routine and unduly resource demanding. There is widespread, but not universal, agreement that the emphasis should shift towards institutions and programmes evaluating themselves, within a system-wide framework of criteria and general principles. That framework needs to be firm and clear. It should call for rigour and consistent behaviour. Weaknesses in follow-up and especially in staff development have been frequently noted. While it would be unrealistic to expect swift and comprehensive changes in large, complex institutions when there is no unanimity about the desirability or direction of such changes, quality assurance procedures are among the relatively few instruments available to systems to address issues of curriculum, teaching and learning. Much patient, diplomatic work will be required if the quality assurance agencies and procedures are to achieve the role in system-wide development that is expected of them.

On curriculum matters at the institutional level, no attempt was or could have been made in the review to appraise the quality and relevance of the vast and varied array of content in tertiary education provision. Instead, attention has been drawn to the value of an education which promotes breadth, initiative and a capacity to work in different ways and different jobs over the life cycle. The old idea of specific careers for specific types of education, while still valid in many occupations, is under increasing challenge. It is not that we will have "too many" graduates – on the contrary we may have too few – but that tertiary education should be developing wider capabilities, more entrepreneurship and a more flexible attitude towards working life. There are criteria and evaluation procedures which seem relevant regardless of content: that students' interests and needs should always feature in decisions; that relevance to future (or present) employment and social needs and expectations be addressed, for example through open door policies towards the

community; that greater attention be given to coherence, especially in modular systems; that cross-curricular and generic competences be given more attention, together with the claims of advanced general education; and that the value of partnerships, for example with industry, in providing for more experiential and problem-based learning be more widely recognised. These issues are of paramount importance to address, based on our discussions in all countries.

Ways of improving the quality of learning and success rates in study are of concern everywhere, not only with reference to the issues of failure, drop-out and delayed course completion. Progress will depend not only on the tertiary institutions but on the schools. As participation in tertiary education moves towards becoming universal, the secondary schools in particular will need to give increased attention to their role in preparing students to continue study in environments where greater onus is placed on the learners and there is a higher expectation of self-directed study.

As the use of information and communication technologies spreads, students will have a wider repertoire of learning sources to draw upon and will be able (and be called upon) to exercise more choice, to self-pace their learning and to qustion the authority of their teachers. These opportunities could, but will not necessarily, foster a more creative and critical approach. Mechanical and unimaginative uses of the technologies as an aid to unreconstructed classroom teaching and unreformed curricula could stifle creativity. Thus far, with some elegant exceptions, innovative curriculum designs, teaching and learning strategies have not kept pace with the technologies.

In order for institutions to respond in the ways indicated, teaching as a function of the academic career needs to be more highly valued and recognised in institutional policies. The preparation of tertiary educators for a career in teaching, recognition through rewards and promotion (as in research), and support to foster good practice throughout the institution all need to become more widespread. At present, incentives for research and advanced study, consultancies and industrial partnerships (e.g. technology transfer) generally outweigh those for first years teaching and this balance needs redressing. Of particular importance is the use to be made of findings and methods of research, scholarship and consultancy in first years teaching. There is much uncertainty and there are conflicting claims which call for further policy consideration. Policies designed to divide or separate research and teaching functions, for example, are difficult to sustain; also the meaning and implications of research-based teaching are frequently unclear. A research culture for teaching, for example, need not mean that all teachers are or should be currently active researchers.

Decision-making in the new environment has become more complex and demanding. Tertiary education is no longer an enclave; governments and institutions benefit from increased community, professional and business participation in decision-making. Several countries have taken big steps in this direction in recent years. Buffer bodies and formal advisory structures exist in many countries and are useful for this purpose. But they are not the only, or always the best, means for this. The partnership movement at the regional and local levels is valuable; much effective work occurs at these levels through links made by individual study programmes and groups of teachers. Such partnerships can be used as a way of enhancing and invigorating teaching.

The lifelong learning orientation recommended by Ministers is well developed in some quarters, in others scarcely at all. There is little evidence, as yet, that strategic planning for the first years of tertiary education has incorporated the values and goals or drawn upon experience of lifelong learning. Much more system-wide effort will be required in order to reshape tertiary educational procedures as if they were part of universal lifelong learning. The lifelong learning issue, on the evidence of the review, is still poorly articulated. Weakness or unevenness in the continuity between secondary and tertiary education, in links between institution-based and community-based (including workplace) study, in fostering a breadth of pathways and options to meet wide-ranging needs and in provision of continuing education opportunities beyond completion of the first degree – all point towards a lack of overall policy coherence. Administratively, financially, culturally and in its social relations, tertiary education has in the past been somewhat apart and fragmented within itself. This is changing and may be expected to change much further as increased participation stimulates – and requires – greater integration not only of the administratively separate sector but of the various elements that condition continued learning. Such integration is not a matter of prescriptive government, but rather of a mutual recognition

by the stakeholders and the institutions that successful learning by students over the life cycle is a collaborative affair.

Expanded participation is leading to new and varied arrangements in order to secure the resources for the investment required. Continuing effort is needed to identify effective, relatively low-cost programmes and methods. Strategic financing has become more attractive to governments and institutions as a means to influence behaviour. One issue is the extent to which the institutions have the capacity, expertise and scope of action to respond to such financing. Questions which are being addressed concern: how much and what kind of financial and resource control and how much autonomy in management. A second issue is the extent to which the host of new incentives introduced with new criteria (formula funding or targeted funding) may come to work at cross-purposes. A third issue is how to balance competing financial interests, so that the public interest is not subverted.

Decentralisation and the recognition of market forces implies the need to give close attention to conditions under which such approaches can work. All parties – students and their families, employers and enterprises and third-party payers as well as institution managers and staff, system and government officials – require information and advice in order to make sound decisions. Institutions have become highly conscious of the need to market their wares, and students who are mobile and who are combining study programmes from different institutions require not only information but also clear pathways of study, well-articulated structures, transparent and flexible procedures for credit transfer and so on. For these and other purposes, system-wide steering and common principles to guide action have become of greater rather than lesser importance as devolution proceeds.

In some countries, a question can be raised about whether the costs to learners are too high or rising too quickly. Possible consequences are reduced access and success, particularly for those students and families least able to adapt to such costs, and poor choices among tertiary education options. A wide range of financing options merits close attention: from current income, targeted savings, types of debt finance, tax surcharges and various third-party arrangements. Students and their families are more likely to find solutions through choices from a menu of diverse family financing options. A related issue is the costs and financing options available for part-time and adult students, seen in terms of equity and in the broad framework of a lifelong approach to learning.

Two firm conclusions emerge from the attention given in the review to costs and finance. First there is an obligation on all parties to seek further economies as overall costs continue to rise. There are innovations in teaching and in institutional management that will result in greater efficiencies and this is an appropriate challenge for institutional management. Second, if different sources of finance across the community, including student contributions, are mobilised, the costs can be met. But there remains a major financial role for government and we have argued that as participation levels increase, the case for a strong contribution from the public budget is reinforced.

The agenda for reform and policy development in tertiary education is extensive and volatile. Priorities and needs are not uniform across countries; moreover, the contexts of action and opportunities vary quite substantially. There can be no suggestion, therefore, that all countries could or should pursue a closely defined set of common directions and in similar ways. This is not the nature of educational policy. Communication among as well as within national systems has greatly improved; there is good cross-border knowledge and many international programmes enable experience to be shared. There is a growing convergence of policy directions, but it embraces a wide range of experience. The following items stand out:

- Tertiary education in some form or other for the large majority if not all people is an appropriate policy target; it should be inclusive not, as in the past, exclusive; and it should form an integral part of lifelong learning with close links to secondary schooling for younger students and to the community for all students.

- Only through a great variety of inter-related, well-recognised and attested study opportunities and settings, programmes and institu-

tions, and methods of teaching and learning can the goals of high quality and relevance be achieved.

- The career of teaching for initial qualifications has often been undervalued and tertiary educators have often not been well prepared for or supported in their teaching role; the needs of students and of the society will be better met by more attention to the teaching functions and the role and status of teachers.

- The resources of the whole community need to be mobilised to make growing participation possible and effective; the benefits are no less social and shared than individual, and so will continue to warrant public as well as private investment; but costs are very unevenly distributed and all possible financial means and mechanisms should be explored.

- Leadership qualities of the highest order are required to steer, guide, and stimulate the extremely complex and powerful forces at work as tertiary education moves to meet the challenges posed by society, the economy and individuals.

- The scale and importance of tertiary education are not matched by the resources available for educational research, evaluation and experimentation. There are large information gaps relating to performance, results and effects over time which need to be filled through more systematic data and comparative analysis.

- The greatest challenge presented by the emergence of large-volume tertiary education is to provide a high quality of education for all at an affordable cost. As countries explore ways of achieving this, they will benefit from a continuing exchange of experience and the systematic, comparative evaluation of results.

If this review contributes to these endeavours, it will have served its purpose.

BIBLIOGRAPHY

The primary literature source for the report is:

TAYLOR, W.T. (1996), "The Early Years of Tertiary Education: A Selective Review of Recent and Current Literature", mimeo, OECD, Paris.

Items cited below are those directly referred to in the text:

BOYER, E. (1990), *Scholarship Reconsidered: Priorities of the Professoriate*, Carnegie Foundation for the Advancement of Teaching, Princeton.

CASPER, G. (1996), "Come the Millennium Where the University?", *Minerva*, Vol. 34, pp. 69-83.

CERI (CENTRE FOR EDUCATIONAL RESEARCH AND INNOVATION) (1996a), *Internationalisation of Higher Education*, OECD, Paris.

CERI (CENTRE FOR EDUCATIONAL RESEARCH AND INNOVATION) (1996b), *Learning Beyond Schooling: New Forms of Supply and New Demands*, OECD, Paris.

CERI (CENTRE FOR EDUCATIONAL RESEARCH AND INNOVATION) (1997), *Post-compulsory Education for Disabled People*, OECD, Paris.

COUNCIL OF EUROPE (1996), *A Study of Dropout in European Higher Education*, Strasbourg.

GIBBONS, M., LIMOGES, C., NOWOTNY, H., SCHWARTZMAN, S., SCOTT, P. and TROW, M. (1994), *The New Production of Knowledge: The Dynamics of Science and Research in Contemporary Societies*, Sage Publishers, Newbury Park, CA.

HENKEL, M., KOGAN, M., BAUER, M., MARTON, S. (1994), "The Impacts of Reform of Higher Education: An Anglo-Swedish Comparative Study", mimeo prepared for the Annual Conference of the Consortium of Higher Education Researchers (CHER), Enschede, the Netherlands.

HOBSBAWM, E. (1994), *The Age of Extremes: The Short Twentieth Century, 1914-1991*, Michael Joseph, London.

KEEP, E. and MAYHEW, K. (1996), "Economic Demand for Higher Education – A Sound Foundation for Further Expansion?", *Higher Education Quarterly*, Vol. 50, pp. 89-109.

OECD (1974), *Towards Mass Higher Education*, Paris.

OECD (1985), *Universities Under Scrutiny*, Paris.

OECD (1990), *Financing Higher Education - Current Patterns*, Paris.

OECD (1991), *Alternatives to Universities*, Paris.

OECD (1994), *The OECD Jobs Study: Facts, Analysis, Strategies*, Paris.

OECD (1996a), *The OECD Jobs Strategy: Pushing Ahead with the Strategy*, Paris.

OECD (1996b), *Lifelong Learning for All*, Paris.

OECD (1997), *Education at a Glance – OECD Indicators*, Paris.

SCHUSTER, J. H. (1997), "The Faculty in Transition: Implications for a New Era in Higher Education", *The Academic Workplace*, Vol. 8, New England Resource Center for Higher Education.

TROW, M. (1996), "Comparative Reflections on Diversity in British Higher Education", *Higher Education in the 1990s – A Special Digest Report of the Quality Support Centre*, The Open University, Milton Keynes.

TUILIER, A. (1996), "Interview with Roni Amelon", *The Chronicle of Higher Education*, January 12, p. A39.

UNESCO (1996), *Higher Education in the 21st Century. A Student Perspective*, Paris.

WAGNER, A. (1996), "Financing Higher Education: New Approaches, New Issues", *Higher Education Management*, Vol. 8, OECD, Paris.

COUNTRY PROFILES

The organisation charts represent the institutional structure of education systems. They provide information on:

- the ISCED levels of education to which major types of education programmes and institutions have been assigned for the purpose of the OECD education indicators;
- typical student flows and recognised exit points in the education system;
- the degrees and qualifications awarded after the successful completion of major educational programmes;
- the theoretical duration of studies in the programme types as well as typical starting and ending ages.

Except where otherwise indicated, the size of the graphical elements provides no indication of the size of the enrolment in the corresponding educational institutions.

Institutional structures are pattern-coded by ISCED level of education (pattern codes are explained at the left hand side of each diagram). For some countries numbers on the arrows indicate the proportion of completers who take this route. Arabic numbers indicate typical starting and ending ages. Roman numbers indicate theoretical years of study in the corresponding programme.

AUSTRALIA

Australia, a country of 18 million spread over a continent roughly the size of the United States, has a diversified economy in which activity is shifting from goods-producing industries to services. The economy has been subject to increasing international competition; trade links in the Asia-Pacific region continue to expand and deepen. The country has experienced a sustained period of economic growth to the mid-1990s, which is expected to continue at about a 3 per cent annual rate to 1998. Unemployment has been falling since 1993, from a peak of 11 per cent to a projected 7.8 per cent for 1998. That performance masks relatively high youth unemployment and long-term unemployment. Overall government policies incorporate the education sector as a major factor in societal development and economic growth; hence, the national significance of a reform agenda launched in the late 1980s and the continuing efforts since then to strengthen the quality and performance of the system. Reform objectives include increased retention through year twelve (completion of upper secondary education), expansion of participation in colleges of Technical and Further Education (TAFE) and in tertiary education institutions and recognition within the common Australian Qualifications Framework of skills and knowledge acquired through schools, training or experience.

Tertiary education is provided mainly in 36 universities, now in a unitary system bringing together the former universities and colleges of advanced education. A process of consolidation accompanied the move to a unitary system; the mergers reduced by half the number of institutions, but increased their average size. Within the unitary system, diversity is being realised as institutions stake out their own "profiles" in terms of programmes, teaching and learning. At the same time, institutions exhibit internal diversity in programmes arising from the mergers and links between universities and with TAFE colleges. The first qualification is the bachelor's degree, of three or four years duration. Tertiary education is also provided in TAFE colleges and through distance learning, either through individual institutions or a separate distance education entity, Open Learning Australia.

Admission to tertiary education is usually through satisfactory completion of the final year of secondary education at school, although about half of those commencing bachelor's degree programmes present only this qualification (almost 30 per cent have undertaken TAFE or other tertiary-level studies). While overall there appear to be enough places to accommodate all who wish to commence studies, quotas are in place for most courses, with students selected on the basis of their marks in the final year of upper secondary education.

Tertiary-level enrolments grew by 63 per cent in the ten-year period to 1995. Participation rates have increased, more rapidly in post-graduate studies than in courses leading to the first qualification. Some 28 per cent of students are enrolled part-time, and another 12 per cent on distance education programmes. The expansion has brought increased participation from under-represented groups, and in the case of Aborigines and Torres Strait Islanders an increase of some 30 per cent per year into the mid-1990s. Relative differences in participation rates by family income and wealth, however, remain and are a matter of policy concern. Concern over quality in tertiary education, especially teaching and learning in the face of an expanded and more diverse student population, has led to government and institution-level activities and initiatives. A non-statutory body, the Committee for Quality Assurance in Higher Education, was established in the early 1990s to allocate additional funds to institutions according to an assessment of institutional achievements in both processes and quality outcomes. A second initiative, now the Committee for University Teaching and Staff Development, allocates funds on a competitive basis to foster the development of good teaching and to identify and provide good practice.

AUSTRALIA

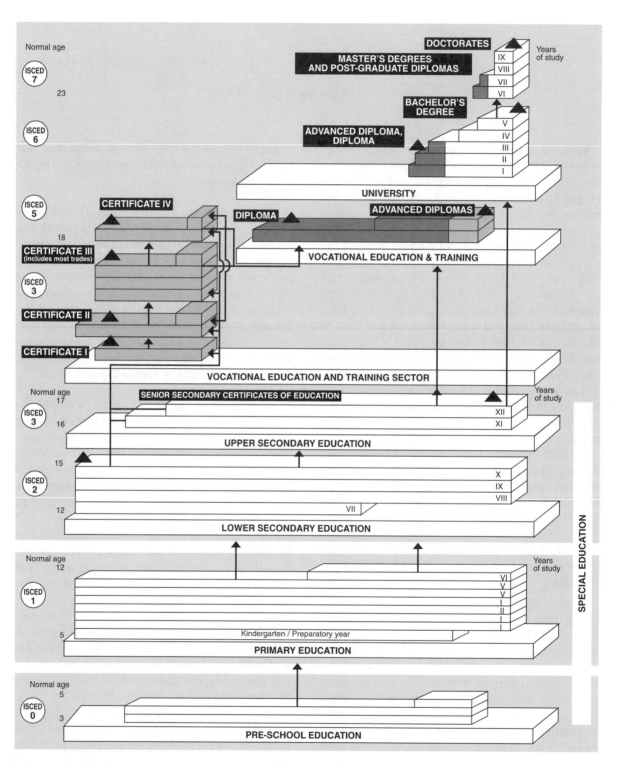

Programmes designed for part-time attendance.
Vocational education and training.
Recognised exit point of the education system.
Typical student flow. The size of the graphical elements provides no indication of the enrolment in the corresponding educational institutions.
Source: Education at a Glance – OECD Indicators (1996).

Most graduates find their way into employment within a reasonable period of time: six months after graduation only 6 per cent are seeking suitable employment. Into the mid-1990s, surveys of young people indicated a growing concern about unemployment. To be better positioned on the labour market and for new employment destinations and career paths, students appear to be choosing in greater numbers professional and vocational education provided in TAFE, double degrees (*e.g.* arts-law) and post-graduate studies.

Although constitutional authority for education is vested in the states and territories, the Commonwealth government is the principal policy-setting body and source of funding for the tertiary education sector. The Department of Employment, Education, Training and Youth Affairs has responsibility for oversight, policy advice and policy implementation, while the Australian Vice-Chancellors' Committee, unions of staff and students and other bodies are in a consultative relationship with the government. Within a framework of co-operative federalism, working relations on matters such as the distribution of additional student places are maintained with the states and territories. Within the broad policy framework and working to agreed institution "profiles", institutions have autonomy over the allocation of budget, staffing and curriculum matters. There is within institutions greater application of modern business-related practices to accompany the system-level changes in structures and funding and increasing levels of entrepreneurial activity.

Funding for tertiary education shifted in 1992 with the introduction of the Higher Education Contribution Scheme (HECS), through which students now contribute about 25 per cent of the costs of their studies. The HECS is repaid by automatic contribution through the income tax system, when the taxable income of the graduate equals or exceeds the equivalent of average weekly earnings payable for all Australians. Students can meet the obligation "up-front" by paying their contribution at a discount (now, at 25 per cent). The sums collected in "up-front", voluntary repayments and payments "on schedule" provided about 15 per cent of the overall revenue available to tertiary education in 1995. Institutions generate revenues through full-cost fees paid by overseas students and, on the proposal of the government, fees paid by domestic students for whom funded places are otherwise not available (additional enrolments, subject to certain limits). Public funding to institutions is the principal source of finance for teaching, allocated largely in line with student numbers. The operating grant is based on prior year funding, with adjustments for additional growth and changes in the distribution of students across fields. Funding is provided on a three-year rolling basis.

BELGIUM (FLEMISH COMMUNITY)

The Flemish Community of Belgium has a highly-developed and competitive economy, although there continues to be cause for concern with respect to high levels of long-term unemployment and the overall debt burden. The Flemish Community, as is characteristic for Belgium as a whole, has long, rich and active international relationships and well-developed international expertise both culturally and commercially. Membership in the European Union, with its headquarters in Brussels, figures prominently in the orientation of policy at the national and community levels and in the evolution of economic activity.

Tertiary education in the Flemish Community is provided mostly through institutions defined as higher education, principally universities and colleges of higher education (*hogescholen*). The latter constitute the "non-university" sector. Studies for the initial award or qualification are organised in cycles. In the universities, the first cycle of two years leads to the degree of candidate, which has no recognition on the labour market; the first university qualification so recognised is the license, which is obtained on the completion of a second cycle of usually three years. In the colleges of higher education, one-cycle vocationally-oriented programmes of two years lead to diplomas; two-cycle programmes requiring 4 to 5 years of study overall lead to the degree of license in professional and vocational fields. In fields such as economics and business, two-cycle programmes in the universities and the colleges of higher education are similar in coverage and overall quality. However, the scope for credit transfer is limited.

A principle of freedom of education is understood in the Flemish society to mean open access to education at all levels and, further, virtually guaranteed access to the type of programme (excepting engineering and medicine) and religious or philosophical orientation of institution. A high proportion of school-leavers enrol each year, estimated at over 40 per cent of 18-year-olds; about half of new entrants do not successfully complete course requirements of the first year. Of those who fail, some will retake and succeed in the end-of-year examinations, others will enter other programmes and institutions (usually moving from university to college of higher education) and still others leave the system without a tertiary-level qualification. The government is concerned about the failure rate, and introduced a policy obliging tertiary education institutions to develop and implement a "10-point programme" to improve rates of success.

In a marked shift in policy direction, the government introduced in 1995 a reform requiring consolidation of colleges of higher education. The result has been a reduction in the number of colleges from 160 to 29. The push for consolidation aimed at improving efficiency in the "non-university" sector, but it was also prompted by concerns about quality throughout tertiary education. At present, the universities are obliged to carry out internal self-evaluations and external discipline-based reviews. One-cycle non-university programmes are monitored by the Inspectorate through extensive data collection and analysis and a complementary process of site visits. Comprehensive reports for all programmes in a particular field are published; evaluations of institutional programmes are not.

The employment experience of new graduates in the Flemish Community has been strong, with one of the lowest rates of unemployment within the OECD area.

The Education Department of the Ministry of the Flemish Community has responsibility for tertiary education. Policy is advanced by decree, legislation and regulation, providing a framework in which freedom of education can be exercised (*liberté encadrée*). The Flemish Education Council (VLOR), a representative body covering all levels and sectors of education and comprised of the various internal education, community and economic interests, undertakes analyses and provides policy advice to government. Two separate councils, one operated

BELGIUM (Flemish Community)

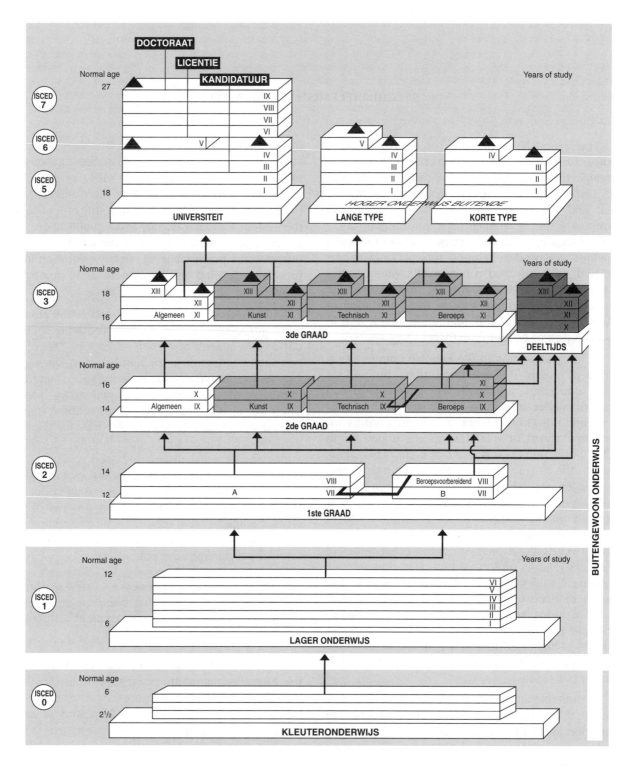

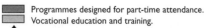
Programmes designed for part-time attendance.
Vocational education and training.
Recognised exit point of the education system.
Typical student flow. The size of the graphical elements provides no indication of the enrolment in the corresponding educational institutions.
Source: Education at a Glance – OECD Indicators (1996).

by the universities and the other by colleges of higher education, discuss and present views on issues and developments from their respective sector. Reforms in the early 1990s had among their key elements greater autonomy for institutional management and governance.

Public expenditure on tertiary education in the Flemish Community is somewhat below the OECD-wide average. Students pay no tuition fees, although all students pay a modest enrolment charge. Public funds are distributed on the basis of student numbers, which attract different funding rates according to broad field of study. Institutions must be of a minimum size to be eligible for funding, as do study programmes. Students receive bursaries and families benefit from tax breaks during the period when students are enrolled. These bursaries and tax breaks do not cover all costs of attendance.

DENMARK

Economic activity in Denmark is in a period of a realignment with the wider global economy, as the small and medium-sized enterprises that form the core of the Danish economy are establishing new links to larger multi-national firms throughout Europe and its larger enterprises are extending their activities into more distant markets in the Americas and the Asia-Pacific. Behind this new global reach is a public interest in building on the strengths of a highly literate population to develop a high performance, knowledge-based economy. Partly recognising both the importance of education in such a vision and the value in adopting a more strategic approach, sweeping education reforms were introduced in the 1990s for youth education and tertiary education. At the tertiary level, new policies reflect significant departures from prior orientations by expanding options for learners, increasing autonomy for both students and institutions and introducing new governance and financing arrangements, the latter involving innovative performance incentives. The reforms embody a Danish respect for liberty, and are based on consensual politics and communal values.

Tertiary education in Denmark consists of long-, medium- and short-cycle programmes. The university sector comprises five universities with a full-range of medium- and long-cycle programmes and seven specialised professional institutions. The Danish university operates on a 3-2-3 programme: completion of a three and a half years bachelor's degree is followed by two additional years for the well-established long-cycle master's degree. A further three years is normally required to complete the doctorate. At present, most students who follow university courses continue studies beyond the medium-cycle bachelor's degree as this qualification is not yet fully established on the labour market. A second group, consisting of 90 small colleges, offer specialised training in business, teaching, health and social service fields in medium-cycle programmes of three to four years. Short-cycle programmes of advanced technical and commercial

education are offered by vocational schools. These programmes require one to three years of study, are less theoretical, are highly responsive to labour market needs and enjoy a close relationship with enterprises.

Enrolment at the tertiary level has expanded rapidly; it is estimated that 45 per cent of an age cohort will participate at some point over their lifetime. The government sees growth and development of the medium-cycle bachelor's degree at the university and short-cycle programmes as the most appropriate response to increased participation in tertiary education. On present data, the projected breakdown in qualifications for an age cohort is: 29 per cent complete a long-cycle university programme; 54 per cent, a medium-cycle programme primarily at a college; and 17 per cent complete a short-cycle programme at a commercial or technical school. Another target for expansion is Open Education, a vocationally-oriented, part-time adult education aimed primarily at those already in regular employment. Open Education can be provided by any institution; participants in Open Education programmes pay 20-30 per cent of the costs.

Access to tertiary education is open and free to all who present entry qualifications, usually completion of youth education at about age 19. There are no formal *numerus clausus*, but some faculties and institutions may be unable to accommodate the "first choice" of all those who wish to enrol. One consequence is queuing, as students seek to build up entry qualifications to improve their chances for entry into high-demand fields or institutions in subsequent years. In general, demand has exceeded supply in teaching, health and business fields, while there are unfilled places in engineering, science, technical and commercial studies. Demand for places is generally lower for smaller, regional institutions and higher for places in Copenhagen (but even there, places in some fields are not filled). There remain differences by social and economic background in participation rates: those from lower social class backgrounds are less likely to enrol in tertiary

DENMARK

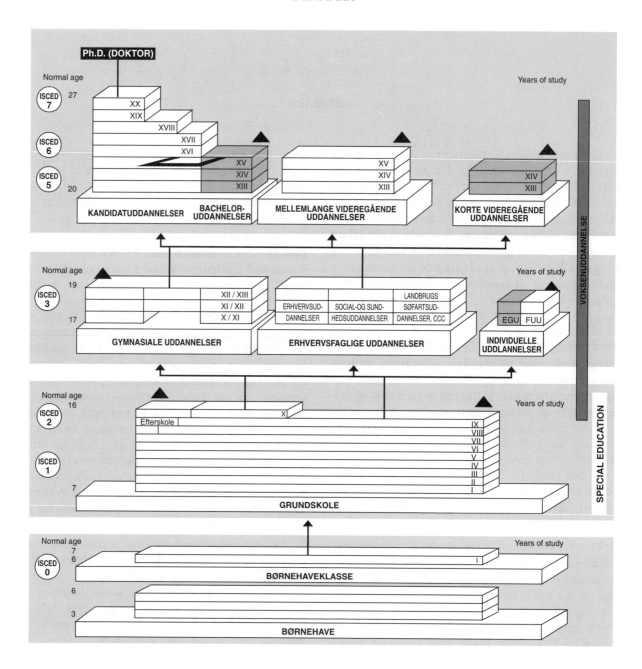

Programmes designed for part-time attendance.
Vocational education and training.
Recognised exit point of the education system.
Typical student flow. The size of the graphical elements provides no indication of the enrolment in the corresponding educational institutions.
Source: *Education at a Glance – OECD Indicators* (1996).

education, and particularly to enter long-cycle university courses.

Partly as a result of queuing and partly owing to comprehensive support for student maintenance, students commonly are 30 years of age or older when they complete long-cycle university programmes (among the highest average age at programme completion in the OECD area). A related concern is a relatively high rate of non-completion or drop-out: some 40 per cent fail to complete the programme in which they are enrolled, although the proportion who enter but fail to acquire a tertiary-level qualification is estimated to be 23 per cent. Both the long duration of studies and the high non-completion rate have been identified as particular targets for policy, on which there is some indication of improvements.

The position of graduates on the labour market is strong, with 4-6 per cent of 1994 graduates unemployed compared to an overall unemployment rate of 12.4 per cent. Medium- and short-cycle students (apart from bachelor's degree recipients) tend to fare the best, owing to programmes which are geared to specific, well-defined employment destinations. The position of bachelor's degrees on the labour market has been varied, with good experience in engineering and very weak experience in a range of other fields. The government "ice breaker" initiative to encourage the employment of graduates of medium-cycle programmes (including those with bachelor's degrees) through employment subsidies was generally successful, as the majority of those employed under the scheme were retained by their employers after the subsidy was withdrawn. A second initiative to improve the attractiveness of the bachelor's degree on the labour market is to augment the three-year bachelor's degree programme with a six-month vocational module.

Governance, planning and co-ordination take place within a centrally-defined framework. The University Act of 1993 enhanced the authority of the university rector and outlined a management structure that redefined responsibilities among deans, heads of departments and course supervisors. Institutions were given more autonomy over the allocation of their budgets and wide flexibility to secure external revenue. These reforms now apply, with some variation, in other types of tertiary education institutions. At the same time, the government strengthened monitoring and oversight through the creation of a quality assurance agency and national advisory boards. The Center for Quality Assurance

and Evaluation provides and supports a structure of quality assurance in tertiary education. The quality assurance effort is focused on teaching and learning within specific fields or disciplines across the country. Each institution prepares its own self-evaluation of the field under review, with follow-up by a review team comprised of students and academics from that field. External examiners are used to ensure expertise and provide legitimacy and comparability. The Centre's secretariat publishes reports for the system as a whole, but individual institutions are provided with the review team's conclusions and recommendations for their own programmes. The evaluations have no direct financial implications.

Each of the five national advisory boards is separately responsible for covering programmes in a particular field: technology, social sciences, natural sciences, humanities and health education. Each board monitors all long-, medium- and short-cycle programmes within the field, regardless of the institution in which the programmes are offered. A chairman's conference, comprised of the chairs of each of the advisory boards, undertakes transversal tasks, provides general advice to the Minister and ensures co-operation in the work of the boards across the respective fields. A separate Council for Further Technical Education (CFTE) was established to assess and propose reforms for the full-range of short-cycle technical programmes. The Education Minister retains full responsibility to approve courses and to take any actions deemed necessary, drawing on advice from the advisory boards and Ministry staff. The Ministries of Labour, Culture and Health also have oversight for tertiary-level professional education in their respective fields of responsibility.

Following a period of severe budget constraint, tertiary funding levels improved in the 1990s and were accompanied by significant changes in governance and funding criteria. There are no tuition fees and students receive grants to cover living costs. Retaining the principle of free provision, but with an interest in shortening the time to degree and reducing drop-out, both institutional funding and student grants have been put on a "taximeter" system. Institutions are funded according to "active students", by which is meant the number of passed exams (rates vary among study fields, with differentials reflecting presumed differences in costs). Students are eligible to receive grants for up to six years of study; these do not have to be consecutive years.

GERMANY

Political, economic and social developments in Germany have combined to pose new challenges and set new directions for its tertiary education system. The reunification in 1990 of the Federal Republic of Germany (FRG) and the former German Democratic Republic (DDR) has engaged the efforts and commitment of people and communities from all corners of the country; the reunification process continues to influence reflection and debate on the society, its values and future directions. Germany has played a key role in ensuring that all Central and Eastern European economies in transition have access to the wider European space; at the same time, economic and social developments in those countries have opened up possibilities for new cross-border arrangements and new markets with significant implications for Germany's domestic industry and employment. The steps taken towards closer economic and social integration within the European Union have not only guided domestic policies but also constrained the scope for policy action in a range of economic and social fields including education. All of these developments have come at a time when growing international competition in existing and emerging product and service markets has placed new pressures on German industry and on employment. Overall, unemployment remains stubbornly high, at rates exceeding 10 per cent. Germany has many strengths on which to draw in responding to these circumstances and developments, not least its highly-educated and skilled population.

At the tertiary level, the reunification brought two different orientations together. Programmes in the "new" Länder evolved from a centralised policy stressing political aims and the needs identified for the command economy. Programmes in the "old" Länder developed originally from a concept of a "modern" Humboldtian university which stressed the unity of research and teaching and overall autonomy. The current policy debate may be seen partly as a transition away from a narrow view of this concept, both to respond to wider aspirations and needs and to accommodate existing constraints.

The right for qualified students to attend tertiary education is enshrined in the Constitution. Those who pass the school-leaving exam, either the *Abitur* or the *Fachhochschulreife*, may continue onto academic or vocational tracks. Tertiary education options are available in universities which offer a full range of academic programmes in the disciplines generally leading to the *Diplom*, *Magister* or state examination after 6 years of study; *Fachhochschulen* which offer professional courses in public administration, engineering, applied arts, commerce and social professions also leading to the *Diplom* after 4 years of study; specialised institutions which offer programmes in music and the arts; and *Berufsakademia* which provide courses combining institution-based study with regular employment in an enterprise (not specifically covered under higher education legislation). A distance education university, based in Hagen, also offers tertiary education study options. Admission into the *Fachhochschulen* and specialised institutions is selective and competitive; demand exceeds the supply of places.

Presently, about 29 per cent of the cohort pursue studies in tertiary education institutions. These include increasing numbers of students who have followed the dual system of vocational training (some 40 per cent of those in the dual system eventually enter tertiary education), leading to a student population which is somewhat older and with more life and work experience. A specific policy aim is to expand the range of courses and the volume of enrolments in the *Fachhochschulen*, such that the proportion of tertiary education enrolments in this sector increases from 30 to 40 per cent. A related policy aim is to increase the co-operation between universities and *Fachhochschulen* through exchange of personnel, cross-enrolment in course modules and shared use of facilities. These new policy directions would correspond with and facilitate the varied, non-traditional choices young people already are making through and beyond secondary schooling.

GERMANY

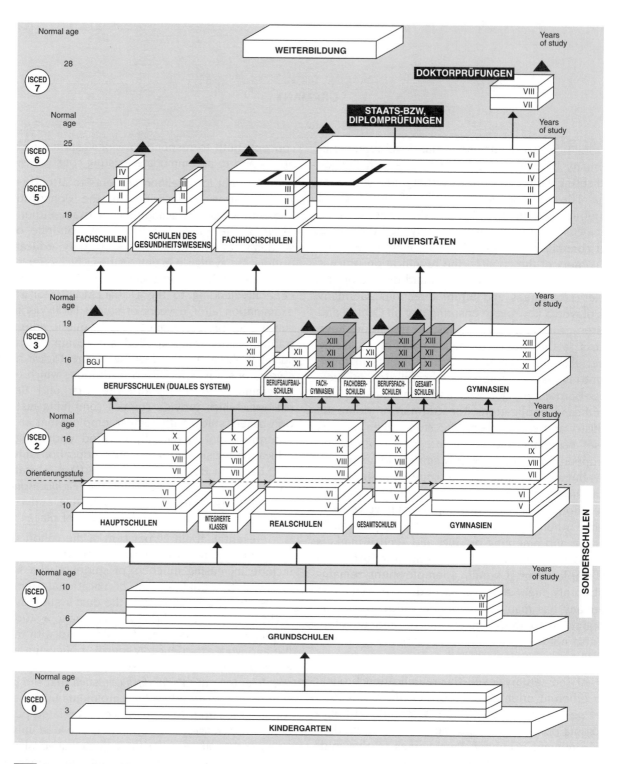

Programmes designed for part-time attendance.
Vocational education and training.
Recognised exit point of the education system.
Typical student flow. The size of the graphical elements reflects the gross enrolment rates in the corresponding institutions at the corresponding level of education. At ISCED 3, after completing a first programme, many students follow a second or further programme at the same level.

Source: Education at a Glance – OECD Indicators (1996).

Recent shifts in student interests, partly reflecting changes in the job market, have led to lower enrolment in computer science, mechanical and electrical engineering and increasing numbers of students entering architecture and civil engineering. While graduates of the *Fachhochschulen* receive lower salaries than do university graduates, university graduates are more likely to be unemployed. Generally, industry does not appear to discriminate between graduates from universities and the *Fachhochschulen*, but the public service does. Forecasts anticipate that the supply of graduates will exceed demand out to 2010; such a situation coupled with restructuring driven by wider global trends is expected to open the way for more significant changes in work organisation leading to new employment destinations and new job assignments for graduates.

Tertiary education operates under the Federal Framework Law for Higher Education which sets down general principles regarding study, teaching, research, staffing, organisation and administration of tertiary education institutions. This federal steering guarantees some element of homogeneity throughout the system, while allowing each *Land* to regulate the details of tertiary education programmes within its borders. Courses and curricula are developed and monitored by the institutions, except for those in health sciences, medicine, law and teacher education which are subject to central regulations. However, policy directions and implementation result from the active engagement of a number of actors at the central, regional and local levels. The Bund *Länder* Commission for Educational Planning and Research Promotion (BLK) decides on the promotion of research for the whole tertiary education system and recommends policies to governments. The main policy advisory council is the *Wissenschaftsrat*, the Science Council, which advises the BLK on research policy, investment in buildings, land and equipment, and conducts evaluations of the tertiary education system. The Conference of Rectors, consisting of 240 heads of universities and *Fachhochschulen*, acts as an interface between the various ministries and the higher education system. The Standing Conference of Ministers for Education and Cultural Affairs (KMK) is the co-ordinating body of the *Länder* concerned with education matters. This Bund/*Länder* system is complex, but it serves to bring together the wide array of interests within and outside governments at all levels.

Academic staff have autonomy and personal freedom, and security of employment as civil servants. Evaluation at programme and institution levels is undertaken within the ongoing programme of Association of European Universities (CRE), through self-evaluations and peer group visits. In addition, there are a wide variety of institution-level evaluation activities ranging from reviews by external experts to reports on teaching.

In 1993, Bund *Länder* working party presented a key issues paper which outlined joint reform measures for consideration by authorities at both levels. Among others, the paper proposed reforms in course structures which would permit and encourage university students to graduate in four or five years instead of seven or more years. The longer duration of university studies was believed to be associated with drop-out rates of 29-31 per cent; for *Fachhochschule* studies, completed on average in 4.2 years, the drop-out rate is an estimated 18-20 per cent. Assessment and exams were also to be revised, to include intermediate exams and mandatory proofs of study programmes. A reform of the Framework Law is being introduced, with the specific aim of reducing the complex of existing laws and giving more flexibility to the *Länder* and to institutions. With regard to the latter, it is expected that institutions will be given greater scope for the management of their own resources and possibilities for staff recruitment into new career profiles. Further, staff will be expected to engage in a wider variety of teaching and teaching support activities such as advising and mentoring, home and international student orientation and self-evaluation. Institutions would be subject to increased comparative evaluation based on performance indicators.

Presently, the great majority of funding for tertiary education and student maintenance is provided from public sources. Students pay no tuition fees. Costs for capital works, large equipment and land is split evenly between the Bund and the *Länder*, on the basis of recommendations of the Science Council. Salaries, material and operating costs are paid by the *Länder*. The federal financial assistance programme, BafoG, provided support in 1994 for 28 per cent of students in the "old" *Länder* and 43 per cent of those in the "new" *Länder*. Assistance is split evenly into grant and repayable loan components; students are eligible for such assistance for a period of 6 years, after which they receive support only in the form of loans. While institutions now receive very little income from the private sector, an increasing amount of revenue is being generated through activities funded through competitive research grants and contracts, and project funding. Support for these activities comes from the federal government and third parties such as charitable and international organisations, industry and special interest committees.

JAPAN

After dramatic economic growth and social advances in the post-war era, Japan has entered a period of uncertainty and change. Increasing international competition, from the Asia-Pacific region as well as the Americas and Europe, have required shifts in production and employment in traditional manufacturing, while products and services in technology and finance sectors have lagged. A prolonged period of slow growth, rising un- and under-employment and uncertain economic prospects have been reflected in political uncertainty as well, with shifting alliances in the Diet and challenges on the part of prefectural authorities and private entities to the leadership and authority of national Ministries. There is a sense that change is needed, to build on embedded Japanese values of social cohesion, collective methods, and dedication to high quality and on the evident strengths of its highly-educated population and productive and innovative capacity, but to go beyond these in ways which will better equip individuals, the society and economy to advance.

Education is seen to play a crucial role in bringing about and supporting change, and there is a commitment to reform at the secondary and tertiary levels. Those reforms aim to develop within individuals greater enterprise and critical thinking skills and to encourage flexibility. The reforms seek to open up curricula and to encourage diversity, responsiveness, quality and efficiency in programmes, teaching and learning. These reforms need to be seen against existing education practices which reflect a strong and shared belief in equality. Thus, access to individual secondary and tertiary institutions is based on objective, competitive examinations, and students devote considerable time and effort to mastering the content needed to do well on the examinations. A variety of initiatives have aimed to widen evaluation and assessment criteria on the one hand, and to diversify curricula on the other. The newly introduced "integrated course", in which secondary education students may choose from clusters of modules to pursue a particular vocational interest within the framework of a broad general education, is one example of the latter.

At present, over 95 per cent of an age group completes secondary education; some 62 per cent proceed on to some form of tertiary education (one of the highest participation rates in the OECD area). Owing to already high participation rates and demographic trends, overall enrolment at the tertiary level is expected to decline from 2 million in 1992 to a projected 1.2 million in 2010. Students may enter study programmes in national universities, which cover all fields and disciplines; private universities, which tend to offer courses in the social sciences and professional fields other than the sciences and engineering; junior colleges, mostly private, which now offer short technical and professional courses leading to associate's degrees, but also "post"-degree courses fulfilling most requirements for bachelor's degrees; and special training schools, providing a wide range of short occupational, technical and vocational courses at the secondary and tertiary levels leading to certificates or diplomas. The University of the Air offers possibilities for distance learning at the tertiary level. Students may acquire full degrees through this free-standing institution. A separate institution, the National Institute for Academic Degrees, evaluates qualifications from a range of foreign and domestic programmes, awarding credit or degrees based on the assessments.

Entrance is competitive; students ranking the highest on examinations are most likely to enter a national university or one of the elite private universities, while students of average ability will most likely pursue studies at a private university. Until recently, junior colleges were the primary destination for women, although they now are entering universities in increasing numbers. Special training schools cater for vocationally-oriented students; while they vary in the breadth, depth and quality of programmes, some of the more advanced are now beginning to offer combined degree programmes with private universities. While there are differences

JAPAN

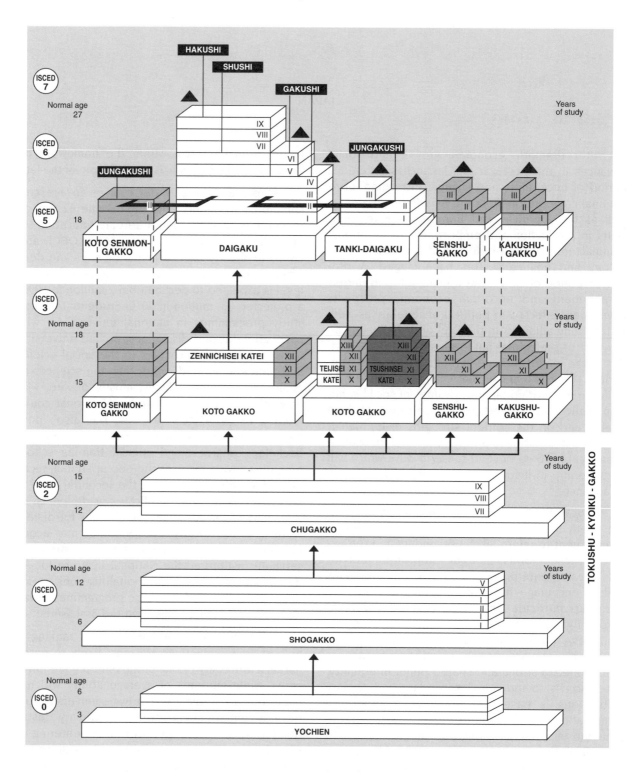

Programmes designed for part-time attendance.
Vocational education and training.
Recognised exit point of the education system.
Typical student flow. The size of the graphical elements provides no indication of the enrolment in the corresponding educational institutions.

Source: Education at a Glance – OECD Indicators (1996).

in participation rates by income group, these are not large.

The employment rate of graduates is generally good, although overall unemployment rates for young people have risen in the current economic slowdown. Recruitment by large firms and into the public sector is largely on the basis of established links with the prestigious universities rather than in line with particular fields of study. Graduates entering these enterprises and agencies are expected to develop skills in the course of working in a number of areas, and the employer assumes the responsibility for specific training required over the course of lifelong employment. Graduates from other tertiary education institutions are destined mainly for a variety of small and medium-sized enterprises. The previous patterns are weakening, however. Some employers now recruit from a wider range of programmes and institutions than in the past. As recruitment needs have declined, the destinations of graduates of these institutions have widened in recent years. For their part, young graduates appear more inclined to consider different destinations for the opportunities they provide to advance rapidly in new fields.

Tertiary education is primarily the responsibility of the Ministry of Education, Science and Culture (Monbusho), which charters tertiary education institutions (except special training schools), sets down regulations covering curricula and qualifications and (with the Ministry of Finance) allocates funds to institutions and students and oversees their use along with funds derived from third-party research grants and grants and contracts from private businesses. Institutions have autonomy on academic matters, with the responsibility for the improvement of curricula and teaching vested in the institutions, academic departments and individual teachers. Funding levels and overall policies guiding the system are matters for national and regional authorities and the governing bodies and trustees of private institutions.

The Ministry utilises a central apparatus of councils for advice and to foster and support change. The University Council was established in 1987 to advise Monbusho on needed reforms. The Council has drawn attention to weakening levels of student interest in science and technology fields, as students turn to other fields offering better and more varied prospects for initial employment and careers. The Council has also recommended possible reforms in the admissions process and greater attention to the quality and effectiveness of programmes, teaching and learning of individual students. In response, Monbusho has reduced its control over specific elements of the curriculum and encouraged universities to develop new approaches which combine more specific professional studies previously offered only in the last two years of a bachelor's degree programme with the general studies which have traditionally been reserved for the first two years. Further, tertiary education institutions are being asked to prepare mission statements, a set of objectives and a programme of implementation as part of a broader process of self-evaluation intended to identify weaknesses to address and strengths on which to build. These steps are seen as a means to promote institution-wide involvement in and approaches to teaching and learning. Policy attention is also being directed at the research profile of universities, where substantial new funding is intended to raise the volume and quality of research in science and technology. A further policy priority is to advance a concept of lifelong learning in tertiary education, for which special entry arrangements for adults and more non-degree programmes are to be implemented.

Funding for tertiary education comes largely from public appropriations and tuition fees. National public institutional funding is destined primarily for national universities which enrol about 20 per cent of all tertiary education students. Public institutional funding from local sources is provided to a small number of universities and colleges. More than three-fourths of university, junior college and special training school enrolments are in programmes and institutions funded primarily by tuition fees. However, even students in the national universities pay tuition fees amounting to about 30 per cent of the costs. Since 1970, private universities and junior colleges have received a "current costs subsidy", administered by the Japan Private Promotion Foundation, based on a formula which takes into account student enrolment and costs per student. Per-student funding is higher in fields which prepare graduates considered to be of high public value. In the present constrained economic environment and in the light of a stagnant volume of enrolments, there is a concern that private institutions will be unable to maintain quality and respond to new demands and expectations. Consideration is being given to new forms of targeted financing in support of government reforms. While there is limited generation of income from the sales of services in any of the sectors, government reforms in this area are intended to make it easier and more attractive for institutions and programmes to do so.

NEW ZEALAND

Prompted by an economic crisis in the mid-1980s and mounting pressures from an increasingly competitive and interdependent global economy, New Zealand undertook dramatic reforms addressed to all spheres of economic, social and political life. The adoption of the 1989 Public Finance Act marked a move from a centrally-administered society to a more open and devolved one, aimed at fostering a self-managing enterprise culture. The reforms brought about substantial change in education provision, governance and finance. Responsibility for operational decisions was shifted to providers at all levels, schools, tertiary education institutions and employers among them. The government set goals and established the means to develop and assess standards and results. An over-arching vision in the education reform is "seamlessness", i.e. provision which permits fluid, transparent and flexible movement within and among a wide range of learning options. A green paper issued in the last half of 1997 signals a reinforcement of the directions.

The shift in orientation also led to an opening up of educational options and a commitment to expansion at the tertiary level. By 1993, 45 per cent of school-leavers continued into some form of tertiary education, a doubling in size compared to 1985. Students may choose among programmes provided in five types or institutions or settings: universities, polytechnics, colleges of education, Wananga (relatively new Maori institutions) and Private Training Establishments (PTEs). Currently, universities and polytechnics enrol about 90 per cent of new entrants, evenly divided between these two sectors. Most of the programmes of the seven universities are campus-based and are aimed at full-time students. Massey University has an extensive distance education programme, with links to regional polytechnics. With high demand for universities and some competition from the PTEs, some polytechnics are seeking to position themselves closer to universities. Some polytechnics have sought university status; others have proposed the establishment of a sector-wide entity, the New Zealand University of Technology, which would permit co-operating polytechnics to offer degrees through an approval process within the tertiary sector itself.

Entrants to university qualify for admission through a national entrance examination. For polytechnics and colleges of education, there are no nationally-prescribed entrance qualifications, and transfer is possible. Regardless of previous qualification, mature students receive provisional entry to university for a first degree. Some 30-40 per cent of entrants are 25 years of age or older (one of the highest proportions in the OECD area). Provision is demand-led, and student interest continues to peak in commercial and business studies, though national priority fields are science and technology.

About 30 per cent of students continue on for specialised degrees after their first academic or general degree, others complete complementary studies of technical or vocational nature. Those with professional degrees typically enter the workforce directly. Generally, the chances of tertiary education graduates for employment are lower than those faced by their predecessors, but are still relatively good: unemployment rates for those with degrees were 1.25 per cent in 1986 and 3.2 per cent in 1994; unemployment rates for those with other tertiary qualifications were 1.86 in 1986 and 6.90 per cent in 1994. Enrolments of women and of previously under-represented groups including the Maori have increased through the mid-1990s, as has participation in industry training. The latter is offered through a range of providers, including polytechnics, following specifications set down by Industry Training Organisations (ITOs) which are funded jointly by the government and industry.

Decision-making takes place within a policy structure set down by the government. The Ministry of Education has overall responsibility for tertiary education. It requires institutions to submit output objectives, reports on actual performance in relation to these objectives and annual financial statements

NEW ZEALAND

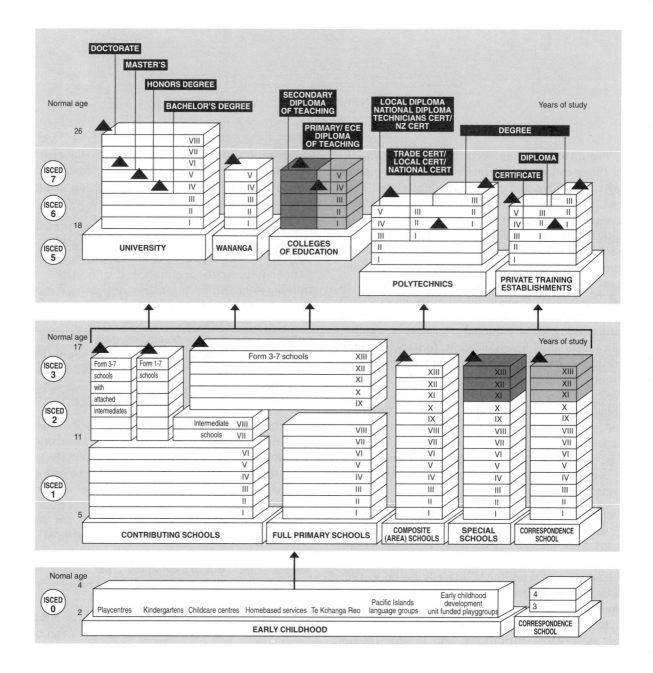

 Programmes designed for part-time attendance.
Vocational education and training.
Recognised exit point of the education system.
Typical student flow. The size of the graphical elements provides no indication of the enrolment in the corresponding educational institutions.

Source: Education at a Glance – OECD Indicators (1996).

as part of the state-legislated monitoring process. Each institution operates under a common governance structure and an appointed Vice-Chancellor, although governing boards broadly comprised of members of stakeholder groups oversee general directions and overall functioning of the institution. The government is exploring a possible redefinition of the responsibility of the governing board, towards a more specific oversight of management and resource use.

Separate agencies carry out a number of auditing, assessment, evaluation and funding functions. The New Zealand Qualifications Authority (NZQA) oversees the operation of the Qualifications Framework (QF), through which all qualifications are authorised and recognised. Based on an 8-level scale, all qualifications are registered in terms of "unit standards" which are intended to define the specific outcomes realised or competences developed through the course module. By design, the QF encourages diversity and competition in provision, curbs overlap of functions, facilitates the acquisition and transfer of qualifications and promotes "seamlessness". Although universities, through the New Zealand Vice-Chancellors' Committee (NZVCC), retain the authority to approve new degree programmes, a continuing issue is how such degrees should be entered on the QF. Quality assurance is carried out by the Ministry in its review of plans submitted by institutions, the NZQA in its oversight of standards and the NZVCC through its sub-committees and Academic Audit Unit. Most institutions now have in place procedures to monitor quality and outcomes.

Funding for first years programmes is provided through lump-sum grants out of the public budget to institutions and tuition fees. The public appropriation to each institution is based on the Equivalent Full-Time Student (EFTS) scheme, in which funding is based on student enrolment. Funding per student varies according to "base rates" which broadly reflect the costs of different study programmes. The eleven categories contain three broad groupings of academic fields, with separate categories for advanced degrees, health and teaching and Private Training Establishments (PTEs). Each institution submits a proposal for enrolment (by field and level), and therefore for funding. If the Ministry accepts the proposal, the institution is obliged to meet the enrolment target or return funds for any shortfall (no additional funding is provided for enrolment exceeding the agreed target). An absolute number of study places is established in the overall budget, which may lead the Ministry to reject some proposals. The government has agreed to increase the number of funded places by 2 per cent each year until the year 2000, though the level of subsidy per EFTS has decreased steadily during the 1990s. Through a "study right" scheme, students who are entering first degree programmes and are under age 22 draw 95 per cent of "base rate" funding; all others are funded at 75 per cent of the "base rate". The balance is made up through tuition fees, which are expected to increase to 20 per cent of costs by the year 2000.

Means-tested student grants are available partly to cover costs incurred by the student and his or her family. Also, students may borrow from the government to pay compulsory fees as well as living expenses. Borrowers repay their loans through the income tax system; repayments are income contingent and, in certain cases, interest or principal may be forgiven.

Additional funding is made available through the Education and Training Support Agency (ETSA). ETSA responds to labour market needs by providing funding for Industry Training Organisations (ITOs) to establish unit standards for industry training and the Training Opportunities Program (TOP) to provide technical and life skills training to early school-leavers and the long-term unemployed. Providers include tertiary education institutions (mostly polytechnics, but also some secondary schools), and some of the programmes are at the tertiary level.

NORWAY

With a population of four million spread among a few cities and widely across its length, Norway has a strong orientation towards regional development in its policies, which are built on traditions of self-empowering direct and local democracy as well as a commitment to social equality. The Nordic approach, as reflected in Norway, relies on informal contacts and networks which facilitate consensus and shared purposes. Over the past ten years, revenues generated through its oil industry have fuelled rapid economic growth. The present period is characterised by growth at a slower and more sustainable rate, with relatively low unemployment. Norwegians enjoy a high standard of living, and a relatively equal income distribution.

Norway's tertiary education system has experienced considerable change in first half of the 1990s. Owing to high levels of participation in upper secondary schools, new aspirations of previously low participating groups and significant structural changes in the system itself, enrolment increased from 110 000 in 1988 to 175 000 in 1993. A major concern is overcrowding and its implications for the quality of programmes, teaching and learning in tertiary education.

Tertiary education is provided in universities and the non-university sector, the latter comprised of the regional colleges. Students may follow studies in private institutions (accounting for about 10 per cent of the total student population), as well as the mainstream public institutions; and there are opportunities for following studies at a distance. Intake is centrally determined, but the distribution of students among fields is determined by demand. Admission to humanities, social science and natural science programmes has generally been open to those who have finished a three-year course of secondary general or vocational education. However, a cap on study places was effected in 1990 as a temporary measure in response to strong demand. Applicants to professional programmes in the universities and regional colleges have generally exceeded the number of available places, and admission based on the strength of entrance qualifications. Beyond these selection processes, no other mechanisms to steer demand have been introduced. Students may, and do, accept an offered place in a second choice field to build up qualifications for a subsequent application to their first-choice programme. The result is "queuing", thus prolonging the duration of studies.

Tertiary education programmes consist of professional and academic tracks in universities, plus theology, medicine, music and other specialised fields offered in university-level colleges. Pre-professional students earn a full degree in medicine, law, technology and veterinary studies after five to six years. The academic track includes programmes of 3½ years in the social and natural sciences and humanities, leading to a first degree (cand.mag.) that qualifies the holder for advanced studies or for entry into employment. Students with this degree are less likely to find employment, and many apply studies at this level towards higher academic degrees or combine them with professional studies (*e.g.* teacher training). Higher academic degrees require an additional two to three years of study.

The non-university sector comprises 26 regional colleges, offering programmes of 2 to 4 years duration in vocational and technical fields plus some courses comparable to lower degree studies in the universities. A diploma from one of the regional colleges permits students to enter the labour market or transfer to a university. Regional colleges have been particularly attractive to those of mature age who prefer to follow tertiary education studies in their local communities, owing to family responsibilities and/or employment. To ensure that younger students have access to programmes in regional colleges, 30 per cent of places are reserved for those 21 years of age or less.

New graduates appear to be less likely to find stable employment directly related to their field of study: the percentage of new graduates without such employment six months after graduation rose from

NORWAY

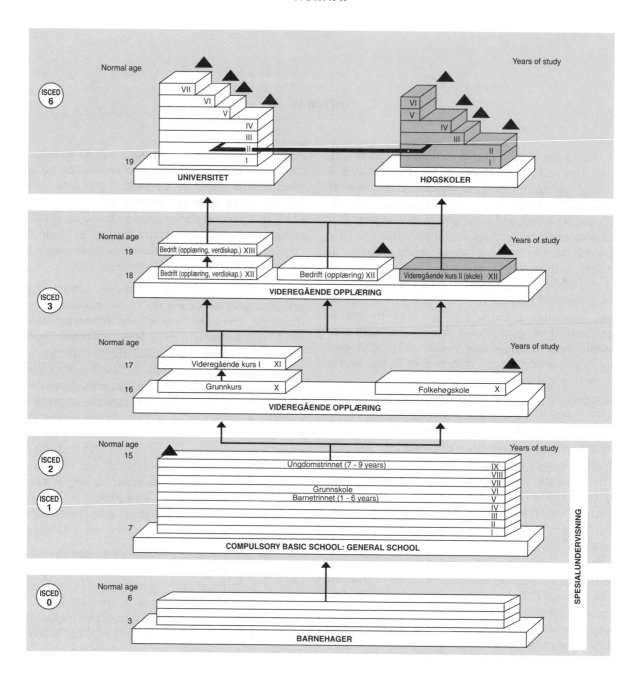

Programmes designed for part-time attendance.
Vocational education and training.
Recognised exit point of the education system.
Typical student flow. The size of the graphical elements provides no indication of the enrolment in the corresponding educational institutions.
Source: Education at a Glance – OECD Indicators (1996).

3 per cent in 1987 to 11 per cent in 1993. Experience varies by field, in both the university and non-university sectors. An emerging concern is a possible mismatch between labour market demand and the supply of tertiary education graduates with regard to particular fields of study.

The regional colleges have been a particular target for government policy, with the aims of promoting the development and supporting the distinctiveness of regions, but also to extend educational opportunities broadly across the country and strengthen the scientific and technical basis for traditionally craft-based industries. In 1994, the government undertook to consolidate 98 small, state-owned institutions into the present 26 regional colleges. The consolidation is still settling as the institutional partners in the mergers develop a new, distinct identity. An element of the 1994 reform is the proposed Network Norway, a vision of concentrated regional development which draws on and evolves within the national unitary tertiary education system.

Governance in tertiary education has shifted from regulatory mechanisms to an approach emphasising strategic goal-setting, monitoring at the central level and increased institutional autonomy in teaching and research. Recent legislation provides for streamlined governance arrangements, wider participation from external stakeholders on smaller governing bodies in the institutions and enhanced decision-making powers at the institution level. Permanent administrative posts exist for Director, Registrar , etc.; academic leadership up to and including the Rector is elected for limited terms. The government has proposed to the national assembly a Network Norway Council to act as a general advisory body to the Ministry, produce strategies for quality monitoring and replace existing specialised bodies and councils. System-wide evaluation and quality assurance processes are still evolving, with experience being gained through pilot projects and institutional initiatives.

Funding is provided almost entirely from the public budget; the amounts provided increased by 50 per cent from 1993 to 1995. There are no tuition fees in the public institutions. Funding to institutions is based on the previous year's budget, with adjustments taking into account inflation and increased enrolments, and incremental funding for the latter varying according to the number and level of the new study places. About 4 per cent of the university funds are now allocated on the basis of results in terms of student credits earned and higher-level degrees awarded (with the funding for female candidates set at a higher level than funding for male candidates). Institutions are free to generate external funding, which the government expects will amount to at least 10 per cent of institutional budgets. Financial assistance to support student living costs is provided in the form of interest-free loans.

SWEDEN

Sweden is an industrialised, multilingual, increasingly multi-ethnic nation of about 9 million people. It has a diverse economy, anchored in the region but with well-established and broadening international ties in trade and investment which have been reinforced with its 1995 entry into the European Union. The country is emerging from a period of no or slow growth and high unemployment. Successive governments have sought to tackle the challenges of high (and rising) levels of public spending, growing international competitiveness and the need for greater efficiency. Its democratic culture, characterised by strong social welfare and egalitarian traditions, however, leads to the search for a "Swedish Way" to respond. A key element is the re-balancing of the relationship between the government and citizen, including enhanced autonomy and choice and incentives on the one hand, but also retaining a strong, strategic public role in fostering economic growth and the development of a knowledge-based economy and society. Education, long accorded high value in Swedish society, has been affected by both these changes.

In 1994/95, about 270 000 students enrolled in first-degree programmes, and existing data suggest that about 40 to 50 per cent of an age group will participate in tertiary-level studies over their lifetime. This level of participation results from continuous expansion since the late 1970s, and the government aims for further growth. Although improving with expansion, supply continues to lag demand: an estimated one-third of applicants are denied admission in a given term. Admission to tertiary education is competitive, determined by the individual tertiary education institution (in nationally regulated fields, following set criteria) and is usually based on school marks, but may include other criteria such as results in the university aptitude test (voluntary), special tests (interviews), previous education or work experience. There is concern that the procedures and criteria are unduly complicated, and the government through its National Agency for Schools and National Agency for Higher Education has moved to put in place a number of standard entry qualification requirements.

Tertiary education is provided through 7 universities, 16 university colleges and 5 specialised institutions of health sciences or arts, within a unitary system established in 1977. Study in the first years leads to a diploma (on the completion of a two-year course), bachelor's degree (on the completion of three years) and master's (on the completion of four years). Professional first degrees are awarded in health fields, teacher training, engineering, design, etc. Study options and patterns are varied. About one-third of all new entrants are over age 25 and enrol part-time, frequently in evening classes. Ten per cent of the total are following courses at a distance. There is a strong regional element to tertiary education provision, through the university colleges; recently, with the establishment of new universities; and with various forms of co-operation between universities and the regional university colleges.

Following 1993 legislation which provided for more institutional autonomy, curriculum development in tertiary education institutions is highly decentralised. While a Degree Ordinance identifies different general and vocational national degrees and the normal length of studies for them, institutions develop the content of programmes and courses. The variation in study programmes has raised concerns about quality and transparency for potential students and the employers of graduates. The quality audits and other activities of the National Agency for Higher Education, based on institutional self-assessments of individual disciplines over a three-year cycle, help to provide needed information and allow for a sharing of experience in support of individual programmes.

The unemployment rate of new tertiary education graduates was about 6 per cent in 1994, roughly half the rate for new graduates from upper secondary education. However, concern about a possible deficiency in middle-level skills in the labour force

SWEDEN

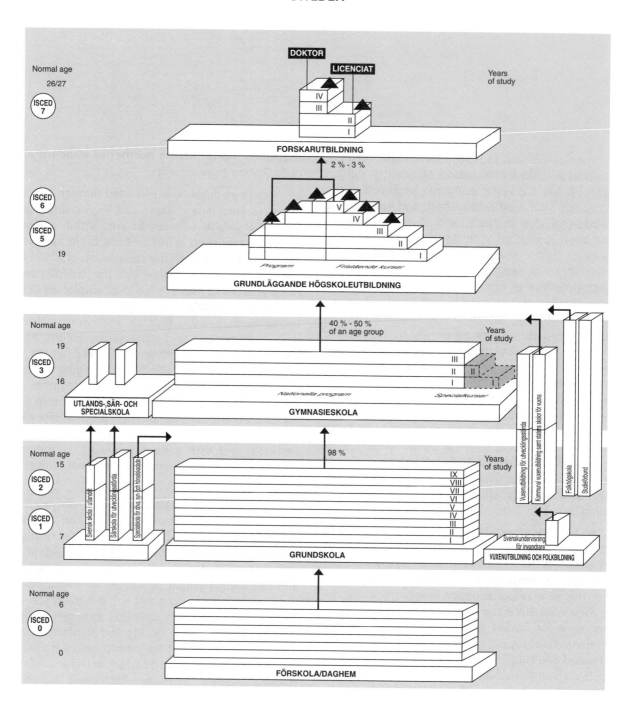

Programmes designed for part-time attendance.
Vocational education and training.
Recognised exit point of the education system.
Typical student flow. The size of the graphical elements provides no indication of the enrolment in the corresponding educational institutions.
Source: *Education at a Glance – OECD Indicators* (1996).

and a lack of further education possibilities for young people who have followed vocationally-oriented upper secondary programmes has led the government to set up a national committee to implement, on an experimental basis, new vocationally-oriented programmes at the tertiary level.

Responsibility for the structure, organisation and funding of tertiary education rests with the Ministry of Education and Science. In 1993, the enactment of the Higher Education Act ushered in a dramatic deregulation and decentralisation of tertiary education, in which individual institutions are afforded considerable autonomy over their affairs. The Act eventually led to the formation of the National Agency for Higher Education, which is not superior to the institutions; the latter receive their broadly-framed assignments directly from the government. The Act regulates the rights of professors and other teachers, and establishes their competence and obligations. At the institution level, a board carries responsibility for oversight of institutional matters. The Rector, elected in an internal process but appointed by the government on recommendation of the board, is responsible for educational and administrative matters for the board.

Funding for tertiary education teaching is provided primarily from national and regional authority grants. In 1993, the funding basis for national grants shifted to a goals-oriented approach based on credits accumulated by students in different fields (a performance component, accounting for about 60 per cent of the grant) and the number of students (40 per cent of the grant). Each institution reaches agreement with the government for the enrolment "targets", but is otherwise unconstrained in its use of funds. A quality component was considered, but not implemented. Special projects are separately funded, as is research. Students pay no tuition fees, and are eligible for up to six years of financial assistance, in the form of grants and loans, to meet living costs and other expenses. The grant accounts for 28 per cent of the assistance provided; a government commission has proposed increasing the grant share to 40 per cent.

UNITED KINGDOM

The United Kingdom has experienced strong economic and employment performance into the mid-1990s, as there have been improvements in efficiency, effectiveness and competitiveness. At the same time, the composition of economic activity continues to evolve as high tech, finance, distribution and service sectors grow in relative and absolute terms. A key factor in growth and restructuring is seen to be international competitiveness, enhanced in part through high levels of education and skills distributed broadly in the population and workforce. Tertiary education plays an increasingly central role, both by accommodating larger numbers of students and preparing those students for employment in the dynamic economic environment now found in the United Kingdom. The drive for competitiveness, responsiveness and a "client" orientation extends to domestic public sector activities, including tertiary education. Public services have been privatised, unit costs have been driven down in a number of them and "clients" have been given a larger role in determining the level and nature of the services to be provided, either by a shift to fund on the basis of demand and performance or by having "clients" pay directly all or part of the costs of the service. The new Labour government, while giving particular emphasis to social, equity and access issues, subscribes to the competitiveness imperative and pursues the general policy orientations of decentralisation and a "client" focus.

Tertiary education expanded rapidly from the late 1980s: full-time student numbers increased by almost 70 per cent from 1989 to 1995, and the participation rate of young people has doubled to 32 per cent. Full-time enrolment (eligible for full public funding) has been capped since 1994. A Committee of Inquiry reporting in July 1997 proposed further expansion. At present, those entering first-degree courses after a delay of three or more years are in the majority. It is estimated that, over a lifetime, more than 60 per cent of an age group will have participated in tertiary education. Part-time students account for about one-third of student enrol-

ments. Differences in participation rates by social class remain a matter of policy concern, to be addressed through improvements in success rates through secondary education, adaptations in teaching and learning in tertiary education and targeted financing as proposed by the new government.

Tertiary education is provided in a unitary system, encompassing "old" universities; "new" universities, formerly the polytechnics; and colleges of higher education. The most common "first qualification" is a bachelor's degree, usually requiring three years of full-time study (four years in Scotland). Students may also receive a sub-degree, higher national diploma, on completion of a two-year course in a college of higher education. The Committee of Inquiry recommended that further expansion should be concentrated in such courses. Admission to tertiary education is selective; for each course, institutions choose those with the best entry qualifications from the applicants for the course. Results on A-Level examinations, sat at the end of upper secondary schooling at age 18 or 19, provide the basis for selection, although a recent trend accompanying expansion has been an increase in the use of alternative qualifications such as the General National Vocational Qualifications (GNVQs) and admissions or course credits based on work experience. Institutions and courses vary in admission rates, but there appear to be enough places to accommodate somewhere everyone who seeks to undertake tertiary education.

The elimination of the formal distinction between sectors in 1992 was not intended to reduce the diversity of programmes, teaching and learning available within the system as a whole. Thus, students continue to choose among academic studies in the disciplines (more characteristic of the "old" universities), courses with a stronger, more specific emphasis on relevance to work (more characteristic of the former polytechnics) and courses with more intensive, structured teaching (more characteristic of the colleges of higher education). In fact, these features and orientations no longer distinguish particu-

UNITED KINGDOM (England and Wales)

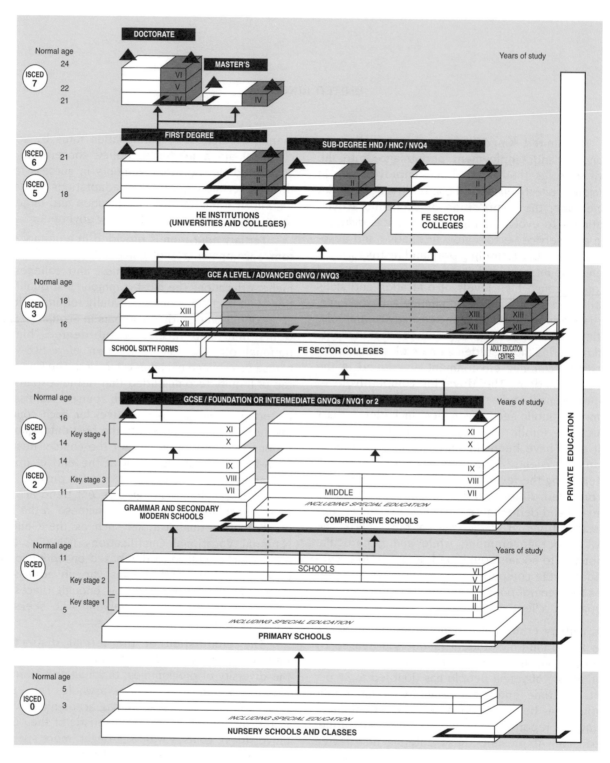

Programmes designed for part-time attendance.
Vocational education and training.
Recognised exit point of the education system.
Typical student flow. The size of the graphical elements provides no indication of the enrolment in the corresponding educational institutions.
Source: Education at a Glance – OECD Indicators (1996).

lar institutional settings, nor are they mutually exclusive. The Open University continues to provide courses at a distance, domestically and internationally. In addition, students may pursue tertiary-level studies in further education colleges and through various public and private training options, some offered by employers, for which credit towards a degree may be given.

Expansion accompanied by new demands and expectations from students and the economy and society has challenged the traditions of a formerly highly-selective system. While completion rates continue to be high in absolute terms and in comparison with other OECD countries, there is some indication of an increase in non-completion. In the face of the pressure of numbers, a declining per-unit resource and shifts in demand, institutions are undertaking a range of adaptations in programmes, teaching and learning.

Graduates fare better than non-graduates when seeking employment, and the restructuring still in process in the United Kingdom is leading to a widening of career options and paths for graduates. Surveys of employers and research studies suggest an increased demand for graduates, or different roles and requiring generic and vocationally-relevant skills as well as the breadth and understanding acquired through discipline- or field-based knowledge. Students increasingly combine study options in ways which permit them to develop this mix, including through combinations of work and tertiary-level studies, either concurrently or through entry or re-entry into tertiary education at older ages.

In tertiary education, responsibility, decision-making and advice are not concentrated in any single agency. Within the overall framework of government policy, decision-making is shared with different kinds of steering and responsibility exercised by a range of public, quasi public and independent agencies: the education departments or offices of England and Wales, Scotland and Northern Ireland; separate higher and further education funding bodies or offices; the Committee of Vice Chancellors and Principals, including its Higher Education Quality Council (now incorporated into the Quality Assurance Agency for Higher Education); and a number of peak bodies or research and advisory councils such as the Council for Industry and Higher Education, the Confederation of British Industry, and others. Tertiary education institutions have autonomy in their control of funds and are free to generate external funding. For the public funds they receive, there are clear procedures of accountability and, during the last five years, national assessments of research and teaching have become detailed and highly demanding.

Funding for tertiary education is provided to institutions from grants allocated by the funding councils and tuition fees. The institutional grants have a relatively fixed base, calculated according to student numbers by field, and a supplementary component to cover enrolment increases and special teaching initiatives. At present, tuition fees for full-time students are paid by the government and vary by field. For tertiary education as whole, funds derived from institution grants are 30 per cent more than tuition fees. In the six-year period to 1995, public funding per student declined by about 25 per cent. Students also receive means-tested maintenance grants and may take out loans to meet living expenses not financed from other sources. In response to new funding recommendations of a Committee of Inquiry, the government has proposed the introduction of a tuition fee of £ 1 000 to be paid by students. The tuition fee is to be means-tested. All maintenance costs would be financed by the student (or student's family) or by income-contingent loans.

UNITED STATES
(COMMONWEALTH OF VIRGINIA)

Following a recession in the early 1990s, the Commonwealth of Virginia, a south-eastern state on the Atlantic coast with a population of 6.5 million and a labour force of 3.5 million, is undergoing economic restructuring and experiencing vigorous economic growth. Due to a lower cost of living and a high accessibility to markets and population centres, Virginia has become a choice site for the relocation and construction of new businesses in services, distribution and high-tech manufacturing. A pro-active and responsive political leadership has supported this development by seeking to provide the improved education and training, physical and technical infrastructure that the new businesses require. In this regard, state policy also focuses on development needs in those regions of the state with declining industries and high unemployment. At the same time, policy continues to seek to overcome the effects of historical discrimination against African-Americans, in part through state support of historically black institutions, recruiting programmes and targeted scholarships and grants. This long-standing policy commitment can be seen against a widening mix of cultural backgrounds in the state, posing a considerable challenge to traditional methods of teaching and assessment. A prominent issue in the current policy debate is uneven levels of achievement at lower levels of schooling and remediation for young adults who have not acquired knowledge, disposition and skills expected of those completing secondary education.

In common with most US states, tertiary education in Virginia is provided through a diverse and decentralised system which allows many individual and institutional choices: public four-year universities and colleges which award the bachelor's degree, some awarding advanced degrees through the doctorate; private four-year colleges and universities, which offer mostly bachelor's degree programmes and account for 15 per cent of enrolment in the state; a state-wide system of 23 public community colleges which offer a two-year associate's degree (or credits for component course modules) accepted for advanced placement in a bachelor's degree programme at a public or private university or college, or certificate or diploma courses of an advanced vocational or technical nature; and private, profit-making career schools which offer vocational or technical certificate or diploma programmes in fields such as medical technology, cosmetology and mechanics. The standard admission requirement is a high school diploma, typically received at age 18. Individual learners may choose to study full- or part-time, at a distance or combine studies at different institutions or in different modes through a wide range of credit transfer arrangements (now being encouraged within a state policy framework). Such breadth implies responsiveness and inclusiveness: most who wish to pursue tertiary education can find a programme to meet their educational needs and individual circumstances. Participation is high: some 70 per cent of high school graduates plan to attend 2- or 4-year institutions to further their studies. Not all chose to do so immediately after graduation: one-third of undergraduate students are 25 years of age or older.

In recent years, overall employment prospects for graduates have been good, with graduates in science and technology fields faring somewhat better than those in humanities. The overall employment situation for tertiary graduates reflects in part a strong national, regional and state economy, but also with regard to humanities graduates, and in part the varied and extensive links between tertiary education, its students and employers. The employer/tertiary education links include co-op arrangements with in- and out-of-state enterprises, but also extend to less formal and structured adaptations for students already in employment who seek to update and build on prior education and work experience.

UNITED STATES

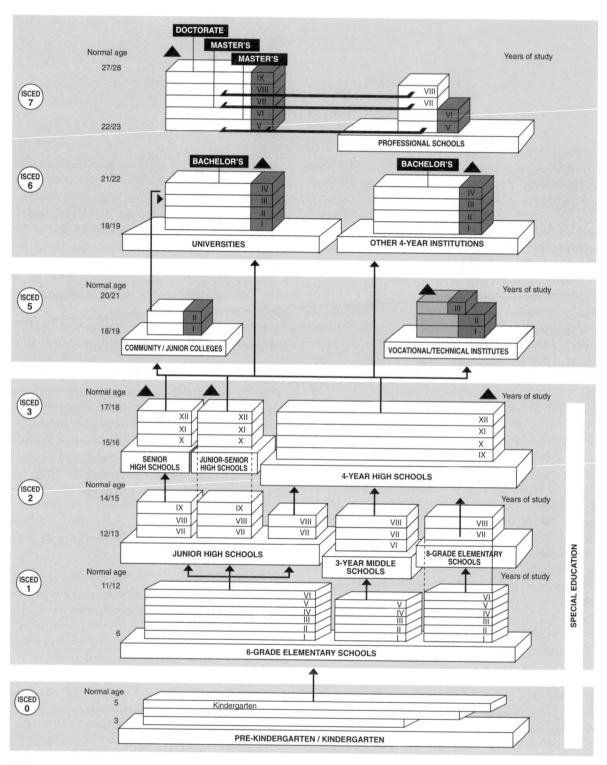

Programmes designed for part-time attendance.
Vocational education and training.
Recognised exit point of the education system.
Typical student flow. The size of the graphical elements provides no indication of the enrolment in the corresponding educational institutions.

Source: Education at a Glance – OECD Indicators (1996).

Tertiary education in the United States is primarily a responsibility of the individual states. The Commonwealth of Virginia has established a broad regulatory framework in which all tertiary education programmes and institutions operate. Each public bachelor's degree-granting institution is a separate legal entity; the twenty-three community colleges have been established as a single system. Private, non-profit institutions operate under a broad regulatory framework; while they receive no direct state funding, most benefit indirectly through state provided assistance for students from low income families, tax breaks concerning property, donations and operations as well as access to lending for capital projects and to telecommunications infrastructure at low cost. Profit-making career schools offering degrees come under the state's regulatory framework for higher education; other courses offered by career schools must conform to regulations covering professional fields and protecting consumers. Career schools receive no support from the state.

Each institution thus has substantial, but not unrestricted autonomy. Within the overall regulatory framework, each institution establishes admissions criteria, curricula and graduation requirements. It also has considerable discretion in the allocation of resources, to include recruitment and promotion of staff, securing funding through a range of means and setting tuition and other fees (the latter, to a lesser extent in the public institutions). State oversight of public institutions has increased in recent years through the use of institutional plans and the continuing development of indicators of conditions and performance. It is the governor and legislature which set policy and new directions through funding levels and allocations, both directly to institutions and increasingly for system-wide objectives such as student financial aid, technology and capital projects, economic development and public/private innovation and technology transfer initiatives. The State Council of Higher Education oversees the programmes of the colleges and universities, public and private. It serves as the contact point between state agencies and the legislature on the one hand, the institutions on the other; its co-ordinating and oversight work serves to increase transparency, influence the setting of directions and help to estab-

lish a climate of opinion for tertiary education as a whole.

The federal (national) interests are specific and advanced through indirect means, both financial (student financial assistance for students; competitive research funding; tax abatements) and regulatory (health, safety and non-discrimination regulations). Third parties such as accreditation boards monitor programme quality, performance and requirements, while professional bodies set down specific requirements in fields such as law and medicine. Enterprises also have an influencing role through the funding of contract research and teaching, among other activities.

Overall, the first years of tertiary education are financed primarily by tuition fees and state appropriations to institutions. In comparison with other US states, Virginia has relatively high tuition fees in its public institutions, covering about 30 per cent of costs in bachelor's degree-granting institutions and 20 per cent of costs in the community colleges. In private colleges and universities, tuition fees provide 75 to 80 per cent of the revenues. Owing to access to financial assistance for study, a wide range of study options and a strong demand for tertiary-level graduates, participation rates appear to be above the US mean. The volume of financial student assistance, most of which is means-tested, is available in the form of grants, subsidised loans or subsidised work-study. The recent trend towards a growing reliance on student loans is likely to be moderated by an increase in funding for student grants both in Virginia and at the federal (national) level and pathbreaking federal legislation which introduces substantial and new tax breaks for students and their families. Although eligibility criteria for the different sources and forms of assistance vary, all students regardless of the types of institutions and programmes in which they enrol have access to some financial assistance. Students and families lacking finances may choose, as was the case of the early 1990s recession, to opt for a first year or an associate's degree in a local low-tuition fee community college followed by a transfer to a four-year college or university to complete the bachelor's degree.

Annex 2

GUIDELINES AND LIST OF QUESTIONS

PURPOSE AND SCOPE

The developments giving rise to new expectations for the first years of tertiary education are common to most OECD Member countries: expanding or mass participation at the tertiary level, competing demands on scarce public resources and growing concerns about the contribution of tertiary education to the well-being of the population as a whole – not least in relation to economic development and employment.

Mass participation in some form of education at the tertiary level is becoming the norm. This may reflect cultural aspirations or the perceived emergence of a knowledge-based society in which prolonged education becomes a social norm. Mass participation also appears to be encouraged by the economic climate. There are high levels of unemployment, particularly among young people. A major concern for young people as well as adults is access to stable and qualified employment. At the same time, employers continually raise their requirements, in line with changes in technology, management methods and work organisation. Over time and in most countries, the number of low- skill jobs has stagnated or declined, while the content of other jobs (including those in areas experiencing rapid growth) is being enriched, thereby requiring higher levels of skills, including social skills.

These developments signal the nature of demand for participation in education at the tertiary level. In some countries, the expansion of demand may mean transition to mass participation. In all countries (including those with already high participation rates), the developments mean a search for higher quality, greater relevance and an appropriate sharing of responsibilities among the various authorities.

It is true that, in most countries over the past thirty years, there have been efforts to diversify and differentiate provision by introducing courses which offer studies with a more practical orientation and an emphasis on preparation for employment. In some countries, new institutions have been established; other countries have raised to tertiary status courses which previously were organised at the upper secondary level.

In recent years, however, participation in education at the upper post-compulsory level has become near universal; in addition, there has been a relative shift in enrolment at this level to more general courses in comparison to vocational and technical courses. As a result, many more students seek higher qualifications at the tertiary level. At the same time, more young people and adults continue their studies beyond the first tertiary-level degree.

It may be that educational provision at the tertiary level already shows signs of lagging in its responses to the new and diverse expectations in a context of mass participation. For example, despite public and private efforts to provide new education and training opportunities at the tertiary level, the increases or evolution in demand have been such that some traditional degree courses are absorbing the bulk of the flows; many courses and institutions at the post-compulsory and post-secondary levels are now being expected to serve purposes different from those for which they were designed. The growth of participation in the so-called "third sector" may be interpreted as a response to demands that have not been met in the formal sectors.

The increased pressure of the new demands, at a time when public budgets will continue to be constrained, means that country authorities in the OECD area will need to look carefully into existing programmes and courses at this level and to develop policies to: encourage changes in teaching and learning systems which adapt programmes to student interests and capacities; achieve greater coherence and better efficiency in tertiary provision; provide an appropriate balance between state responsibility and institutional autonomy, to include the role to be played by the "market"; develop effective and appropriate financing arrangements; and implement effective forms of quality assurance across the range of tertiary provision.

Within this broad concern about adapting teaching and learning to the specific needs of students, close attention also needs to be paid to changes which adapt programmes to major social and economic needs. This point has been stressed in the OECD *Jobs Study* (OECD, 1994). Flexibility and responsiveness to social and economic needs would certainly be a major contribution to improving the employment situation. Tertiary education in all its forms has an increasingly crucial role in this respect.

The thematic review of first years of tertiary education has two main purposes: *i)* an examination of the extent to which programmes, teaching and learning at this level are evolving to meet the expectations and capabilities of students and the needs of the economy and the society (including the need for flexibility and responsiveness); and *ii)* an analysis of how policies might best promote needed change. One expected outcome of the review will be to show the variety of policy options adopted and/or considered in countries as responses to the common concerns and issues.

Focus and definition of terms

Emphasis in the thematic review is placed on first years of tertiary education where the impact of participation trends and new expectations is more directly and immediately felt. With its accumulation of roles and functions and as affected by the developments in programmes and participation at the secondary level of education, the level of first years of tertiary education is where key policy and strategic issues now are emerging. *Attention is given to the student experience and, particularly, the extent to which the existing set of institutions, programmes and courses at the level of the first years of tertiary education adequately meets the expectations and capabilities of students and the needs of the economy and society.*

Tertiary" is intended to indicate a level of studies beyond secondary schooling, and thus is interpreted to be broader than higher education (as that term is normally defined in English with reference to universities). This definition is left intentionally broad, to permit each country to identify sectors, establishments and providers that are relevant to this level of studies. It is understood that terms such as "higher" or "post-secondary" education may be preferred in particular countries. In order to ensure

mutual understanding, the coverage will be discussed in each country, owing to differences in educational structures and systems, in such a way as to ensure strong, appropriate comparability (taking into account distinctive as well as common features).

To define "first years", several considerations may apply. Some have envisaged a reference to a certain number of years, *e.g.* two or three years. Others have referred to the first tertiary-level qualification which is recognised on the labour market. Still others wished to refer to a level in the ISCED classification, *e.g.* ISCED 5. It is recognised that all these considerations are relevant, but that no one consideration may suit all countries or even apply to all types of provision within one country. The main focus is on issues or issue areas of mass participation which manifest themselves at the tertiary level. The precise scope of the review will also be discussed prior to and during the visits to individual countries.

Quite apart from how the precise target is defined in each country in relation to the common concept of "first years" of "tertiary education", it is understood that the thematic review effort necessarily will entail the collection of information at the level of secondary education and in fields other than higher education, as well as on the interfaces between the "first years of tertiary education" and other types of provision, so that developments can be situated against the particular context and structures in individual countries and so that country differences as well as similarities in these respects can be drawn out more fully and clearly.

LIST OF QUESTIONS

The questions which follow have been developed with the aim of collecting relevant background information for the thematic review of first years of tertiary education and, further, as a part of the preparation for the intensive study visits by the teams of examiners. The questions have been revised on the basis of advice and comments provided at the meeting of country representatives, 27-28 October 1994.

Authorities in participating countries are invited to provide responses to these questions. It is recognised that the countries taking part in the thematic review differ in terms of economic, social and educational traditions, structures and circumstances. As a result, some questions may correspond to central concerns in some countries, whereas in others they may be less relevant, or may be perceived in other ways or at other levels. These nuances or differences in emphasis will be one of the main interests of the review, but clearly the exercise has to be based on a common and fixed list of questions.

The questions can be addressed in different ways. Of most value would be direct answers in the form of data compiled and analysed for the purpose. Countries also contributing to the Education Committee's activities on *mass tertiary education* (in particular the work on "individual demand for access and participation" and on *the changing role for vocational and technical education* (as preparation for the recent conference on "vocational education and training for the 21st century") may wish to respond to specific questions by making reference to sections or data displays in their contributions. Similarly, countries recently the subject of an education policy review may wish to refer to the relevant parts of background reports, examiners' report or other relevant materials. For some questions, brief answers may seem appropriate initially, to be followed by more extensive and detailed responses at the time of or immediately following the examiners' visit.

For most questions, there will be relevant existing reports and data tables. Suitably marked up or annotated, these would be of great value to the examiners and the Secretariat. In preparing answers to the questions, country authorities may wish to combine different questions or to rephrase and expand the questions in light of the specificities of country circumstances. The Secretariat may follow up with requests for clarification of responses. In all cases, authorities in the countries concerned will be able, at the time of the examiners' visit and subsequently, to augment the material provided in response to the questions.

It is recognised that, in covering aspects of context as well as targeted areas of concern, the questions range across a wide field. Such a reach is considered necessary in order to develop more fully the underlying concerns as well as to provide a firmer basis for diagnosis and comparison. Nonetheless, it is understood that each country will interpret the questions in the light of its own situation and, taking into account the intention of the question, may formulate questions a little differently or combine them in particular ways. Thus, there will be a certain focusing on individual country concerns, in the attention given to particular questions and distinctive features of national settings. Further focusing for the exercise as a whole will be achieved by the examiners, who will address problems very much with an eye to the homogeneity of the final report.

I.   THE NATIONAL CONTEXT

Background

Following a brief outline of the national/state education system in its social, cultural and economic setting, information is sought on two major dimensions of national contexts: i) the general nature and the factors of demand for access and participation, and ii) trends in employment. With respect to demand, work carried out by countries participating in the activities on *mass tertiary education* and VOTEC (Vocational and Technical) activities will be particularly relevant.

– Where are young people at 17-18? In which education and training courses? Is there a trend in enrolment towards more general, rather than vocational education, at this age? Is the trend likely to accelerate? What are the trends in terms of entry to some form of tertiary education among those who complete post-compulsory courses and those who complete general upper secondary courses? What are their destinations?

– How can the interests and aspirations of potential students, of whatever age, be described? Are there increased concerns about access to employment and marketable skills and qualifications, are there changes in motivation, values and attitudes among youth?

– Which are the open or hidden selection mechanisms that affect access opportunities to tertiary education and training and the distribution of the flows of students between such opportunities? Are particular sectors more open than others?

The information on employment trends which is required for the thematic review goes beyond what can be presented in statistical or analytical form, which in any event are developed through the OECD's work programme (most recently, in the *Jobs Study*) and will be drawn upon by the Secretariat for this thematic review. The first two questions below thus aim at generating descriptive background information, the third question is an attempt to draw out a broader discussion, also descriptive, of the many aspects to be considered.

- What is the current *employment/unemployment* situation in your country? What are the categories most severely hit by unemployment, in terms of age, sex and skill levels? Can youth unemployment be discussed in some detail? Is there a serious under-employment problem for particular categories? What can be said about employment/unemployment of adults?

- What are the outcomes in terms of *access to stable and "appropriate" employment* of the various types and levels of education and training programmes (the whole range of skills, from non-skilled to highly-qualified). In particular, what is the relative position of secondary v. tertiary graduates? Can the entry, or re-entry, into working life of graduates (and non-graduates) from tertiary education be discussed in detail?

- What are the main elements in *overall employment trends* that are felt relevant to a diagnosis of the current adaptability of the tertiary system to the needs of the economy and/or in designing a strategy for the future? Or is there simply a view that there are too many graduates at this level? Or too many graduates of the "wrong kind"?

The institutional landscape

The purpose of this section is to obtain information which will situate "tertiary education" and "first years" in the country. In this regard, the thematic review is concerned with the overall experience of students – conceived as a relationship between the existing provision of courses or programmes and the interests, aspirations and needs of actual and potential students. This relationship is set firmly within a context of changing social and economic realities.

From this perspective, programmes, courses or institutions not usually considered, because they fall within the competence of other ministries or authorities or are a result of private or local initiatives, are to be included. It is also recognised that a clear distinction between the secondary and tertiary levels is, to some extent, arbitrary, particularly as the more acute educational issues may be found at the interface between these levels. To obtain a better understanding of the links and relationships, it

will be useful to have an overview of both levels (*e.g.* a flow diagram).

- Where are *young people* at 20-21? What are the components of tertiary provision for *young people* or *adults* preparing for the first level of tertiary qualifications? Under which authority/authorities are they operating – in terms like national, regional or local levels, private or public sector, and the responsible administration – higher education, secondary education, VOTEC, labour administration, other ministries, etc.?

- In these different types of programmes, courses and institutions, what is the *first level of recognised qualification*? Are these qualifications also recognised in employment, either in whole or in part; do they correspond to marketable skills? Are there equivalencies between these qualifications in terms of possible transfers from one course or study programme to another?

- Can the *flows* entering these various lines be indicated, *e.g.* in terms of proportion of a generation? What are the salient trends and developments? Do these represent an extension of, or a departure from previous patterns? Is there a substantial increase in the proportion of adults in the student body?

II. THE SYSTEM AND ITS RESPONSES

Questions in this section seek information on major issues and concerns with the current state of the system, the ways in which it responds to the interests of the students and the needs of employment and society more generally.

- Is there firm evidence to support the claims that the *quality* of teaching, course content and study conditions is suffering as a result of the need to accommodate increased student numbers or to adapt to the diversity of capacities and interests characteristic of mass participation? Which parts of the system are most affected? How and by whom is quality ensured, defined, monitored, maintained and, where necessary, raised?

- What is the proportion of *drop-outs, repeaters or changes of orientation* in the first years of tertiary education? Is there a significant proportion of qualified candidates who are not given access to tertiary opportunities or who have to delay their entry, perhaps for several years? How is this explained and interpreted? Within institutions, what is done to facilitate successful participation by all students, including mature-age students? What are the respective responsibilities of tertiary and secondary (or VOTEC) authorities?

– Are there concerns about the *distribution* of students between the various parts of the system (particularly between the university and the non-university sectors)? What is the basis for such concerns (preparedness, employment relevance, cost, other)? What is the role of selection mechanisms in this situation? What incentives/disincentives are in place or envisaged to encourage students to follow particular programmes or courses of study in particular kinds of institutions?

– Taking into account the above question about student distribution, are there, in addition, concerns about the *relevance* of individual courses to employment? Are these explained mainly in terms of enrolment growth, or also in terms of changes in employers' expectations, or lack of appropriate contacts with the world of work? Are working periods in enterprises included in the curriculum? More generally, what are the contacts between institutions and enterprises, what is the nature of exchanges between them?

– In a mass system, many students have backgrounds that differ from the student profile of the past. What *continuities and support* are available to ensure both access and success in tertiary education? In some countries, particular attention will be paid to students coming from VOTEC courses and the opportunities open to them. Attention should also be given, in answering this question, to the profiles of mature-age students.

– Are there clear *relationships and complementarities* between the various education and training providers on the tertiary scene? Can the programmes, courses or institutions establish and maintain their identity or are there concerns about an "academic drift", for example, in some of the non-university institutions? Are there in place means or is there an intention to facilitate (or limit) transfers between institutions, programmes and lines of study? If transfers are frequent, are they a threat to the "value" on the labour market of particular courses and institutions? What are the proce-

dures for recognition of courses or qualifications for purposes of transfer (cross-crediting)? What is expected from the intermediate certificates, in countries where it is envisaged to introduce them?

– What is the origin and experience of *teachers*? In addition to those with the university, secondary or VOTEC status, are other categories of teachers involved, in particular those with an experience of work in enterprises? Is there a clear distinction between the various teacher bodies, or various mixes according to the nature of the course or institution? How is their competence (technical, but also pedagogical) ensured? What form of preparation and training do tertiary teachers receive and what are the judgements about its appropriateness and efficacy?

III. POLICIES/STRATEGIES AND THEIR EFFECTS

Country strategies: the core questions

In this section, the questions are intended to draw out the nature and importance of broader issues and policy orientations related to first years of tertiary education.

– What is the current policy position of public authorities regarding *future size, structure and evolution* in tertiary education? Are these objectives formulated in terms of a given percentage of each generation having access to tertiary education? Are they further divided in terms of access to "university/higher education" or to "non-university/non-higher education"? Or are public concerns mainly focused on quality and relevance and if so, on what aspects in particular?

– What are the main features of country strategies in the *management of growth or reform*? Is the emphasis on the regulation of demand through admission control or fees, or is there more emphasis on new forms of provision, new modes of teaching? Are the financial constraints leading to the promotion of new types of courses, or to set priorities for future evolution and growth? Or are public concerns mainly focused on quality and relevance?

– How is current policy articulated with *changes in employment*, particularly in relation to the current unemployment situation and especially as it affects graduates? Is a strategy being shaped? How is it formulated, in terms of balance between, or priorities for, existing types and levels of provision, or the need for a reconsideration of existing patterns? Is there, in particular, a priority for middle-level qualifications, for science and technology, for a reform of existing courses?

Strategy implementation

The questions in this section seek information on strategies, policies and their effects. A key issue in the implementation of governmental and other public sector strategies is the availability of financial resources and the influence of public policy over the dynamics of the system and individual institutions. These are very broad issues which cut across the questions which follow. Authorities may choose to address the broad issue separately, or to take up in responses to individual questions the ways in which these broader developments and circumstances affect the choices, importance or influence of the policies identified.

– The accumulation of roles and functions at tertiary level and the presence on the scene of many different actors, public and private, often are seen to call for *system-wide monitoring* in order to permit authorities to follow developments and innovations, to co-ordinate them and to ensure complementarities rather than competition. How, where it exists, is such monitoring organised? To what extent, and how, are traditional administrative boundaries and fields of competence crossed? How do established bodies, including professional associations, concur with, or hinder, this effort?

– How is development in tertiary education influenced by *governance arrangements*, in terms of state control, the role of buffer bodies, institutional autonomy, the role left to market forces? Several of these arrangements are likely to coexist: is there a rationale? What are the current or planned reforms in this area? What are the political difficulties raised? What is the role of the social partners, local communities and enterprises in policy development and implementation?

– What *policy instruments* (*e.g.* financial arrangements, admission procedures, quality initiatives) are being used to encourage programmes and institutions of tertiary education to be adaptable, responsive and flexible with regard to the needs of society, the economy and the interests and aspirations of the students? To what extent is funding on the basis of institutional performance? To what extent are innovations in education delivery being used to enhance accessibility and cost effectiveness? What are the main barriers to flexibility and responsiveness?

– There is a growing interest in many countries in new forms of *curriculum delivery*. These are offered by single purpose distance universities, bi-modal institutions and a variety of practices whereby students undertake part of their study off campus. What are the existing arrangements? How is this viewed and which proposals are there for further developments?

– An issue common to a number of countries is how provision for the first years of tertiary education can be organised to address *regional development* concerns and the availability of educational opportunities. What are the views of the different authorities, business and community interests and students? What is the current policy thinking and practice in this area? Is there a trade-off between national interests to seek economies of scale and scope and the concentration of means, on the one hand, and regional or local development? Is there evidence on the magnitude and nature of the trade-off? For which types of courses or institutions?

In addition to the material provided in answer to the above questions, please make any additional comments on the subject of the review that you believe will assist in understanding the specific conditions, trends and policy issues in your country.

Annex 3

REVIEW TEAMS

AUSTRALIA

Dr. Elaine El-Khawas
Vice President for Policy Analysis and Research
American Council on Education
United States

Professor Michel Hoffert
Université Louis Pasteur, Strasbourg I
France

Mr. Malcolm Skilbeck, OECD Secretariat

Mr. Alan Wagner, OECD Secretariat

BELGIUM (FLEMISH COMMUNITY)

Mr. Knud Overoe
Former Managing Director, Ferrosan
Denmark

Mr. Malcolm Skilbeck, OECD Secretariat

Professor Morikazu Ushiogi
Nagoya University
Japan

Mr. Alan Wagner, OECD Secretariat

DENMARK

Professor Don Anderson
The Australian National University
Australia

Dr. Agneta Bladh
Director General
National Agency for Higher Education
Sweden

Mr. Malcolm Skilbeck, OECD Secretariat

Mr. Alan Wagner, OECD Secretariat

GERMANY

Mr. Eric Esnault, OECD Secretariat

Professor Ingrid Moses
Deputy Vice-Chancellor
University of Canberra
Australia

Mr. Erland Ringborg
Counsellor, Education and Science
Embassy of Sweden (Paris)

Mr. Malcolm Skilbeck, OECD Secretariat

JAPAN

Professor William Cummings
State University of New York at Buffalo
United States

Mr. Eric Esnault, OECD Secretariat

Dr. Gerhard Konow
Former Secretary of State
Ministry of Science and Research
(North Rhine-Westphalia)
Germany

Mr. Malcolm Skilbeck, OECD Secretariat

NEW ZEALAND

Dr. Elaine El-Khawas
Vice President for Policy Analysis and Research
American Council on Education
United States

Professor Michel Hoffert
Université Louis Pasteur, Strasbourg I
France

Mr. Malcolm Skilbeck, OECD Secretariat

Mr. Alan Wagner, OECD Secretariat

NORWAY

Professor Denise Bradley
Vice-Chancellor
University of South Australia
Australia

Mr. Eric Esnault, OECD Secretariat

Mr. Erland Ringborg
Counsellor, Education and Science
Embassy of Sweden (Paris)

Mr. Malcolm Skilbeck, OECD Secretariat

SWEDEN

Mr. Abrar Hasan, OECD Secretariat

Ms. Toril Johansson
University of Oslo
Norway

Mr. Malcolm Skilbeck, OECD Secretariat

Professor Peter Nicholas Tarling
University of Auckland
New Zealand

UNITED KINGDOM

Professor Ian Chubb
Vice-Chancellor
The Flinders University of South Australia
Australia

Professor Georges Monard
Secretary-General
Ministry of Education, Flemish Community
Belgium

Mr. Malcolm Skilbeck, OECD Secretariat

Mr. Alan Wagner, OECD Secretariat

VIRGINIA (UNITED STATES)

Mr. Kunio Sato
Executive Director
Japan Society for the Promotion of Science
Japan

Mr. Malcolm Skilbeck, OECD Secretariat

Dr. Hilary Steedman
London School of Economics and Political Science
United Kingdom

Mr. Alan Wagner, OECD Secretariat

Annex 4

ADVISORY GROUPS OF COUNTRY REPRESENTATIVES

AUSTRALIA

Mr. Tom Karmel
Assistant Secretary, Coordination Branch
Department for Employment, Education, Training
and Youth Affairs

Ms. Shelagh Whittleston
Counsellor, Labour, Education and Social Affairs
Permanent Delegation of Australia to the OECD

BELGIUM (FLEMISH COMMUNITY)

Mr. Gaby Hostens
Director General for Secondary Education
Education Department of the Flemish Community

Mrs. Micheline Scheys
Division Head, Policy-directed Co-ordination
Division
Education Department of the Flemish Community

Mr. Jef Verhoeven
Professor, Department of Sociology
Catholic University of Leuven

DENMARK

Mr. Torben K. Rasmussen
Director General, Department of Higher Education
Ministry of Education

Mr. Erik Nexelmann
Head of Division, Department of Vocational
Education and Training
Ministry of Education

Ms. Ella Højbjerg Madsen
Department of Higher Education
Ministry of Education

Ms. Christine Hostbø
Department of Vocational Education and Training
Ministry of Education

FRANCE

Mme Suzy Halimi
Responsible for Higher Education
Délégation aux Affaires internationales
et à la Coopération (DRIC)
Ministère de l'Éducation nationale, de
l'Enseignement supérieur et de la Recherche

Professor Michel Hoffert
Université Louis-Pasteur, Strasbourg I

Mme. Agnès Konstantinov
Chargé de Mission
Délégation aux Affaires internationales
et à la Coopération
Ministère de l'Éducation nationale, de
l'Enseignement supérieur et de la Recherche

Mme Françoise Bonniot-Guillaumin
Former Chargé de Mission
Délégation aux Affaires internationales et à la
Coopération
Ministère de l'Éducation nationale, de
l'Enseignement supérieur et de la Recherche

GERMANY

Dr. Ingeborg Berggreen-Merkel
Bavarian State Ministry of Education, Science
and Religious Affairs

Dr. Wolfgang Moenikes
Head of Division
Federal Ministry of Education, Science, Research
and Technology

JAPAN

Mr. Naoki Murata
Director, Office for University Reform
University Division, Higher Education Bureau
Ministry of Education, Science, Sports and Culture

Mr. Masashi Akiba
First Secretary, Education
Permanent Delegation of Japan to the OECD

NEW ZEALAND

Mr. George Preddey
Chief Advisor Tertiary
Ministry of Education

Mr. Mark Blackmore
Permanent Delegation of New Zealand
to the OECD

NORWAY

Mr. Hans Gjertsen
Deputy Director General
Ministry of Church, Education and Research

Mr. Per Olaf Aamodt
Director of Research
Norwegian Institute for Studies in Research and
Higher Education (NIFU)

PORTUGAL

Mr. Pedro Lourtie
Director General, Department of Higher Education
Ministry of Education

M. Manuel Patricio
Former Director General, Department of Higher
Education
Ministry of Education

SWEDEN

Mr. Erland Ringborg
Counsellor, Education and Science
Swedish Embassy (Paris)

UNITED KINGDOM

Mr. Tony (C.A.) Clark
Director, Higher Education
Department for Education and Employment

Mr. Robert Gibson
First Secretary
Permanent Delegation of the United Kingdom
to the OECD

UNITED STATES

Ms. Maureen McLaughlin
Office of the Assistant Secretary for Postsecondary
Education
US Department of Education

Mr. Gordon Davies
Former Director
State Council of Higher Education for Virginia

Mr. Aims McGuinness
National Center for Higher Education Management
Systems

EXPERTS

Mr. Arvo Jäppinen
Department of Higher Education and Research
Ministry of Education
Finland

Mr. Claude Pair
Former Director
Institut universitaire de formation des maîtres
(IUFM), Nancy
France

Sir William Taylor
Former Vice-Chancellor and Principal
The University of Huddersfield
United Kingdom

OECD PUBLICATIONS, 2, rue André-Pascal, 75775 PARIS CEDEX 16
PRINTED IN FRANCE
(91 98 02 1 P) ISBN 92-64-16055-8 – No. 50015 1998